PEACE BETRAYED?

MICHAEL CROMARTIE is a research associate for Protestant studies at the Ethics and Public Policy Center. He received a B.A. from Covenant College and an M.A. from American University in Washington, D.C. He is the editor of *Gaining Ground: New Approaches to Poverty and Dependency* (1985), *Piety and Politics: Evangelicals and Fundamentalists Confront the World* (1987), and *Evangelicals and Foreign Policy* (1989).

ROBERT PICKUS is the founder and president of the World Without War Council in Berkeley, California, and chairman of the James Madison Foundation, Washington, D.C. He was a member of the American Friends Service Committee working group that wrote *Speak Truth to Power* (1955) and an author of *To End War* (1976). He recently contributed "New Approaches" to the forthcoming *Conceptual Approaches to Peace,* to be published by the United States Institute of Peace in 1990.

PEACE BETRAYED?

Essays on Pacifism and Politics

Fifteen Responses to
Peace and Revolution
by Guenter Lewy

Edited by
Michael Cromartie

Foreword by
Robert Pickus

ETHICS AND PUBLIC POLICY CENTER

Library of Congress Cataloging-in-Publication Data

Peace betrayed? : essays on pacifism and politics / edited by Michael Cromartie ; foreword by Robert Pickus.
p.   cm.
"Fifteen responses to Peace and revolution by Guenter Lewy."
Some papers originally presented at a colloquium held 9/88 in Washington, D.C. and sponsored by the Ethics and Public Policy Center.
Includes bibliographical references.
1. Pacifism.   2. Peace.   3. Peace movements—United States.
I. Cromartie, Michael.   II. Lewy, Guenter, 1923–   . Peace & revolution.   III. Ethics and Public Policy Center (Washington, D.C.)
JX1952.P332   1989   327.1'72'0973—dc20   89–23545 CIP

ISBN 0–89633–143–1 (alk. paper)
ISBN 0–89633–144–X (pbk. : alk. paper)

JX
1952
.P332
1989

Distributed by arrangement with:

University Press of America, Inc.
4720 Boston Way
Lanham, MD 20706

3 Henrietta Street
London WC2E 8LU England

Ethics and Public Policy Center
1030 Fifteenth Street N.W.
Washington, D.C. 20005
(202) 682–1200

Contents

Preface

The story bears repeating once again: A Quaker farmer owned a stubborn mule who continually refused to obey his commands. Finally the farmer leaned over and whispered in the animal's ear: "Thou knowest I cannot beat thee, but I can always sell thee to a Presbyterian."

No mules were bought or sold, but a great variety of opinions were exchanged when Quakers and Presbyterians, along with other Protestants both evangelical and mainline, Roman Catholics, Mennonites, and a Jewish pacifist, assembled in Washington in September 1988 at the invitation of the Ethics and Public Policy Center. Their purpose was to discuss a provocative new book by Guenter Lewy, *Peace and Revolution: The Moral Crisis of American Pacifism* (Eerdmans, 1988). For a day and a half the twenty-five participants engaged in a lively, pointed, and sometimes very heated exchange.

The starting point was Lewy's central indictment of American pacifism: "While at one time pacifists were single-mindedly devoted to the principles of non-violence and reconciliation, today most pacifist groups defend the moral legitimacy of armed struggle and guerrilla warfare, and they praise and support the Communist regimes emerging from such conflicts." Lewy, professor emeritus of political science at the University of Massachusetts at Amherst, supports his charge with a meticulously researched account of the behavior of the four major pacifist organizations during and since the Vietnam war years.

In papers presented at the colloquium and in additional essays, the fifteen contributors to this book—some longtime pacifists, others interested observers—offer a wide spectrum of response. Their comments are preceded by an excerpt from Lewy's book that summarizes his argument. Then, after the fifteen respondents have had their say, Lewy has the last word.

I want to thank Robert Pickus, a forty-year veteran of these debates, for his superb service as "moderator-clarifier" of the Peace and Revolution colloquium and for his thoughtful introduction to this volume. A more principled and exemplary pacifist one may never meet. Steve Beard's assistance with details of the colloquium was indispensable. And a special thank you to Carol Griffith, the Center's senior editor, for turning a manuscript into a book with her usual consummate skill.

MICHAEL CROMARTIE
Research Associate for Protestant Studies

Ethics and Public Policy Center
Washington, D.C.
September 15, 1989

Foreword

Robert Pickus

Allow a literary beginning. To introduce this book's many faceted, long overdue reopening of the argument about pacifism and politics requires more than abstract analysis. Simone Weil, writing about the *Iliad* as the "poem of force," explores the "merciless necessity . . . the petrifactive quality of violence . . . as pitiless to those who use it as to those who endure it." For Weil this is the true subject of the *Iliad*. War, that most terrible expression of violence among men, stands at the center of human history. In war, violence, "that which turns a man into a thing, in the most literal sense: it makes a corpse out of him," reaches its fullest magnitude. The mass violence of war most starkly reveals the subjection of the human spirit to brute power that asserts its dominion over every other consideration of man's nature.

A very old tradition of opposition to war, known in this century as "pacifism," directly confronts that reality. Appearing in many guises amid different religions and civilizations, pacifist belief informed both the Emperor Asoka's construction of a politics of peace in ancient India and, 2,300 years later, e. e. cummings's tribute to *"Olaf, glad and big / whose warmest heart recoiled at war: / a conscientious object-or."*

Differing strands in the pacifist tradition emphasize the personal refusal to participate in war, opposition to all preparation for war, or the development of alternatives to war in the resolution of political conflict. Geoffrey Nuttall has traced five very different rationales for pacifism within the Christian tradition alone. Individual anti-war stances abound also: Simone Weil's brother Andre, for instance, explained that his conscientious objection to military service was rooted in his refusal to kill someone he did not know.

All of us, pacifist and non-pacifist alike, respond to the ancient truths that animate this congeries of traditions: that love endures and can overcome; that hatred destroys; that the duty of a human being is to diminish hatred and promote love; that man is one; that this implies unity with the enemy; that the spirit does inform human life and can prevail over the brutal in man.

When these ancient truths have led American pacifists to address problems of slavery, of prison reform, or of care for the mentally ill, a proud record of humane-over-violent patterns emerges. In child-rearing, in attitudes toward women, and in race relations, to name just three more frontiers, pacifists have taken the lead in enlarging the area in which the dignity of the individual is affirmed and violence rejected. By pioneering the socially organized withdrawal of consent within a perspective that affirms rather than denies community, some pacifists have demonstrated a creative lever for non-violent change in the social and political order.

In every decade we see fresh examples of the power and utility of this approach to defending values and forcing needed change. The deliberate choice of non-violent resistance in Tiananmen Square in Beijing in June 1989 thrilled us. That frail figure in shirt sleeves confronting a line of tanks symbolized a victory, though all too temporary, of non-violent over military power. We were moved, moreover, not simply by the courage the resister displayed, but also by the *unseen* figure, the man inside the halted lead tank. His actions, too, affirmed human dignity. Since the unification of man or his disappearance from the planet remains—and will remain, through many seasons of hope and despair—the most urgent item on the human agenda, we do well to explore with care any ethical or political perspective that gives promise of progress toward an end to war, even though we run the danger of strengthening a politics of apocalypse in so doing.

Trouble in the Central Arena

It is in regard to war, the central arena for pacifists, that the pacifist political record remains most vulnerable to criticism. Has pacifism, in our time, helped in progress toward a world that resolves international conflict without mass violence? Has pacifism, in word and deed, offered the needed moral and practical ground for such progress?

When the issue is conflict, not within a democratic polity, but rather between such a society and one that deliberately rejects democratic norms, the dilemma for the morally thoughtful pacifist is at least as sharp as that confronting the morally concerned warrior. The dilemma for those who accept responsibility for fire-bombing Dresden is clear. But so is the choice facing those who, in the name of peace, would offer no effective resistance to the politicide whereby rulers making war on their own peoples have killed more people than all the wars of the twentieth century.

Nor is it by any means clear that the pacifists' refusal to rely on war or preparation for war will in fact limit, much less avoid, the occurrence of war. For all the fearful horror of nuclear deterrence, many argue that it prevented war between the great powers long enough for Communist systems to change in ways that make progress toward international peace more feasible.

This time. Perhaps.

It could have come out differently. The hopeful moment in world history we enjoy in the late 1980s was one possible outcome. The other possibilities continue to haunt us, as more nations acquire modern technologies of war, and as the occasions for war multiply in a world that has neither the political structures essential to the peaceful resolution of international conflict nor the moral and political agreements that could bring such structures into being.

Can contemporary pacifists and pacifist organizations contribute to forming those agreements, to establishing those structures?

No, says Guenter Lewy in *Peace and Revolution*, not without rejecting the ideas and politics that for some twenty years have dominated pacifist thought and action in America. Not, says Al Hassler (executive director of the Fellowship of Reconciliation during some of the crucial years surveyed in Lewy's book), without a more fundamental turning; not without repentance for the role pacifist organizations played in the Vietnam years.

The changes in the pacifist world that began in those years are the subject of Lewy's book *Peace and Revolution: The Moral Crisis of American Pacifism*. In it Lewy traces the changes that left the major American pacifist organizations, in his view, "defending the moral legitimacy of armed struggle and guerrilla warfare" and "[praising and supporting] the Communist regimes emerging from such conflicts." By so doing, he asserts, these organizations abandoned their vocation and robbed American pacifism of its integrity and primary function.

A Scenario for Change

I believe the process begun by Lewy's book and furthered by discussions like the colloquium that occasioned this volume can lead to a reformation of pacifist thought. Such a reformation could make pacifist action a valuable catalyst in forming the agreements essential to progress toward stable international peace.

How might that come about?

It would begin, as it has, with a stable-cleaning book like Guenter Lewy's. The book would then be subjected to rebuttal by those who see developments in the pacifist world since the mid-sixties from a very different perspective. The subsequent discussion would lead to an affirmation, by and large, of the accuracy of the story Lewy tells. But that telling would be improved by a broader portrayal that places the errors recorded alongside the contributions to truth that pacifist organizations also made in those years.

In my ideal scenario, the very organizations Lewy criticizes would lead in correcting the errors he records. In the course of such an effort, very different understandings of the right relation of pacifism to politics could emerge. These would pose a challenge both to Lewy's narrowed understanding of pacifism and politics and to the particular politics that in the years surveyed dominated the pacifist world.

The good news is that many of the elements of such a scenario are now in place. Lewy's careful documentation broke through the evasions and confusions that have sheltered many pacifists from accurate descriptions of the political positions they adopted during the years under discussion. Some responsible for organizational public relations and many who are still committed to the political perspective he describes simply reject Lewy's findings. But many other pacifists, whether they agree or disagree with his thesis, are genuinely troubled by it.

Why, they ask, in a time when the moral weight of democracy was gathering force in so many parts of the world, were pacifist organizations advancing the agenda of anti-democratic forces? Why, when change in the Soviet agenda was clearly the key to progress toward peace, were pacifist organizations by and large identifying *American* policy as the primary obstacle to peace? How do they explain the fact that the peaceful resolution of conflict in so many parts of the world became possible when just one thing, Soviet policy, changed?

Why, when brave dissidents in the Communist world were beginning to challenge Marxist-Leninism itself, were pacifist organizations almost totally dominated by hostility to any form of anti-Communism? How does one speak to the profound dismay with which Armando Valladares, a Cuban Christian and democrat imprisoned for twenty-two years by Castro, recounts the fact that religious pacifists, whose support he expected, embraced not him but his tormentors?

Happily, the dominance of such positions in the pacifist world is fading somewhat. But unless the questions above are probed and resolved, the confusions they address will continue to block creative pacifist responses.

An Open-Minded Discussion

I am a partisan in the debate over the accuracy of Lewy's history. My primary interest, however, is not in the past but in the pacifist future in America. Developing it will require a shift from dominantly eristic discussions.

Some will find it surprising that the Ethics and Public Policy Center, founded by Ernest Lefever, Jeane Kirkpatrick, and the late Paul Ramsey, three serious scholars of the moral dimensions of power realism, should initiate an open-minded discussion of pacifist ideas. While we might expect the Center to provide a forum for *criticizing* pacifist thought, could we reasonably expect an honest effort to construct an open argument, one capable of *advancing* pacifist thought?

Those who know the Center's commitment—apparent in many of its publications—to a dialogue in which competing perspectives are well represented would not have been surprised by the colloquium on Lewy's book organized by Michael Cromartie in September 1988. But I was. Not so much by the quality and diversity of the disputants as by the character of the discussion itself.

You may judge the heat and utility of the presentations from the essays that follow. But you will miss the precious candor and spirit of the exchanges that took place that day. It is not just the climate in some of our finest academic centers that may no longer be described as open-minded; a similar closed-mindedness prevails in many religious and pacifist circles. I encountered that cast of mind in a phone conversation with a senior staff leader of the Fellowship of Reconciliation who could not conceive of taking part in a discussion sponsored by a "right-wing anti-pacifist organization like the Center."

That was obviously not the attitude of the pacifists, or, for that matter, the power realists, who did participate. Those who agreed with and those who challenged Lewy's thesis were open to interruption, to being required to unpack their position, to explain not just where they stood but why. In sum, the symposium could be characterized, in John Courtney Murray's fine phrase, as an honest effort "to achieve disagreement" in ways that clarify and set forward the argument. It was a remarkable day, one that considerably advanced the scenario I sketched above.

Two Obstacles to Change

Two obstacles to the unfolding of that scenario for a change in the political culture of American pacifism are worth highlighting here. First, for many pacifists, the curious structure of Lewy's argument in this volume presents an obstacle. For eleven chapters he devastatingly demonstrates and earnestly laments the process that led, in his view, to the loss of a genuine pacifist witness in the United States. Then in a twelfth chapter he gives a Niebuhrian listing of the moral and political "common fallacies" of pacifist belief. It is not surprising that many pacifists read the book backward. Beginning with its anti-pacifist rationale, they challenge Lewy's intention and good will, and see in his book one more "McCarthyite" attack on the pacifist organizations. Why, they ask, should pacifists take such an attack seriously?

To characterize Lewy's book in this way is to falsify both its intention and its contribution. Lewy's intention is scholarly rather than polemical. His success in tracing a complex history accurately may be challenged, but not his sincerity. As a non-pacifist, he genuinely regrets the loss of a pacifist higher ground above politics, one whose goals and standards, though they may never be achieved, remind us of the right direction. He knows the value of a pacifist witness against war and believes it has been damaged in the new political identity that came to characterize much of the pacifist world. Lewy deserves to be taken seriously, above all by those whose pacifist commitment is profound and who know that American pacifism has yet to make its distinctive contribution in a country capable of being a leader in progress toward a world without war.

There is another reason why those committed to such a pacifist contribution should attend to Lewy's argument. He raises many of the right questions and raises them with the kind of powerful documentation that makes it difficult to avoid a forthright answer. Answering his challenge will surely advance pacifist thought.

Lewy himself, along with many who agree with his rejection of pacifist analysis and prescription, poses a second obstacle to advancing the needed discussion. He appreciates a pacifism above politics, but he too severely restricts the possible pacifist contribution to political life. This is not the place to spell out the argument, but there are many positions between (a) his barring of a pacifist role in politics and (b) the particular politics that for a time dominated some American pacifist organizations. A more appropriate political expression of pacifist belief would connect work for peace to the well-being of our own society. It would understand why democratic government and rightly ordered political community offer one valuable answer to the problem of how to resolve political conflict without mass violence. It would demonstrate ways to form community in the course of ideological conflict.

A politics of this kind may involve a commitment to one side in a violent political dispute. But such a commitment in itself need not necessarily violate pacifist belief. Indeed, in some cases it may be required by the same affirmations that lead to a pacifist position. The issue here is not whether pacifists may take a side in violent confrontations over who shall rule, but which side is taken and what role pacifists play in both ending the killing and advancing the values and political perspective of the side chosen.

A Different Kind of Politics

A renunciation of mass violence and a refusal to support its use in political conflict develop out of a commitment to human dignity and unity. When in a political conflict one side affirms and another denies those values, the pacifist may, and I believe should, choose. So long as pacifists seek to advance their politics in ways that, across the battle lines, form rather than deny political community, and that focus, not on opposition to one side's resort to violence, but on developing alternatives to war in the resolution of political conflict, they fulfill their responsibilities as pacifists.

Lewy accurately describes the development of a very different kind of pacifist politics: one that not only chose a side but rationalized that side's use of violence and its opposition to democratic values. In so doing, however, he denies the possibility of a pacifism that, while affirming the value of a pacifist witness, involves for some pacifists an additional responsibility: to defend democratic values in political conflict and to demonstrate how it is possible and why it is necessary to advance those values by means other than violence.

In this political perspective, pacifists would, as Lewy requires, not focus on opposition to military programs; nor would they support them. All their effort would go into developing alternatives to violence. They would teach that both the decision to arm and, equally, the refusal to arm can lead to war and will continue to do so until the political conflicts that lead to military confrontations are resolved. They would demonstrate how to force, without violence, the changes that made such a resolution possible, changes that help bring into being the structures of political community that are, most fundamentally, the alternative to war.

I believe the essays in this book can launch a discussion that will help clear the ground for the development of such a pacifist politics. I commend them to you.

PART ONE

Lewy's Argument

The Moral Crisis of American Pacifism

Guenter Lewy

O VER THE PAST twenty years American pacifism has undergone a remarkable transformation. At one time pacifists were single-mindedly devoted to the principles of non-violence and reconciliation. Today most pacifist groups defend the moral legitimacy of armed struggle and guerrilla warfare, and support Communist regimes that emerge from such conflicts.

Moreover, pacifist organizations have increasingly abandoned their earlier opposition to a united front with Communist groups. This trend began during the 1960s, when pacifists and other components of the anti-war movement quite deliberately accepted the principle of non-exclusion, and it has continued. For instance, a protest demonstration against U.S. intervention in Central America held in Washington on April 25, 1987, saw the major pacifist organizations marching side by side with the American Communist party, its front the U.S. Peace Council, and the Trotskyite Socialist Workers party.

Such political coalitions predictably lead pacifists to downplay

Guenter Lewy is professor emeritus of political science at the University of Massachusetts, Amherst, and the author of several books, including *Religion and Revolution* (1974) and *America in Vietnam* (1978). This essay is adapted from Dr. Lewy's 1988 book *Peace and Revolution: The Moral Crisis of American Pacifism* by permission of the William B. Eerdmans Publishing Company.

criticism of Marxist-Leninist regimes, whether in Eastern Europe or in the Third World, since such criticism could jeopardize the carefully constructed united front against "U.S. imperialism" and could, pacifists argue, inflame the Cold War. The coalitions give Communist groups legitimacy and respectability that, in view of their tactics of deceit and deeply flawed political values, they surely do not deserve.

Having compromised pacifist principles, American pacifism has suffered a decline in prestige. Until the 1960s it enjoyed a generally undisputed reputation of moral rectitude. There was criticism here and there of the pacifists' alleged lack of political realism and of what some saw as their utopian faith in the peaceful resolution of all international conflicts, but the integrity of leading personalities in the movement was never in doubt. Rufus Jones, John Haynes Holmes, Nevin Sayre, Norman Thomas—these and other pacifist leaders were highly respected figures on the American intellectual scene, and their political influence extended well beyond pacifist circles. In 1931 Jane Addams, founder of the Women's International League for Peace and Freedom, received the Nobel Peace Prize. Emily Greene Balch, another leader of the league, received the prize in 1946, and in 1947 it went to the American Friends Service Committee. During the last twenty years, however, searching questions have been raised—from inside as well as outside the peace movement—about the intellectual honesty and integrity of the major pacifist organizations and about their political alignments.

Influence of American Pacifism

The four major pacifist organizations are the American Friends Service Committee (AFSC), the Fellowship of Reconciliation (FOR), the War Resisters League (WRL), and the Women's International League for Peace and Freedom (WILPF). (The latter organization has never held adherence to pacifism as a requisite of membership, but until the 1960s its American section embraced the pacifist tenets of opposition to all wars and a commitment to non-violence.) These groups overlap considerably in membership as well as in leadership, yet each also has its own distinct profile.

Although the pacifist movement in America has never been large, its political influence has often been extensive, reaching well beyond its relatively small active membership. Today American pacifists are the core of the peace movement in this country. The AFSC, for example, with its large headquarters in Philadelphia, aided by ninety full-time staff members in thirty-three regional offices nationwide, was the driving force behind the movement for a nuclear freeze that during the early 1980s appeared to sweep the nation. Together with their allies in the churches and in church-related social-action groups, American pacifists today make up a grass-roots network that can mobilize substantial voter sentiment and at times have a considerable influence on Congress.

Pacifist influence is at its strongest, of course, when it can build on widespread existing political attitudes, such as the American public's growing disenchantment with the war in Vietnam in the late 1960s and early 1970s. But the peace movement itself has considerable political clout and considerable influence upon the worldview of a substantial part of the American intellectual elite. These capabilities have persisted despite many defeats and setbacks on particular issues like the nuclear freeze.

Pacifist ideas have become influential in the political thinking of the mainline Christian churches in recent years. The Roman Catholic bishops of the United States have questioned the moral acceptability of the doctrine of nuclear deterrence, cornerstone of the West's defense posture; the United Methodist Council of Bishops has rejected the doctrine completely. Today the so-called religious left, to which most pacifist groups belong, has considerable leverage with Congress, especially over Central American policy. Since 1979 an estimated 40,000 Americans have visited Nicaragua to learn about the "progress" made by the Sandinista regime. Hundreds of thousands have been persuaded by the "peace and justice" network to send food, medicine, and money to the Sandinistas and their Marxist-Leninist allies in Central America.

A better understanding of pacifist groups, their leaders, and their political ideology is, then, of more than academic and historical interest.

Development of American Pacifism

The term "pacifist" characterizes the doctrine of those who are morally opposed to bearing arms and who refuse to sanction war for any purpose, defensive or otherwise. In this sense, pacifism has a long history. Pacifist ideas can be found in many of the major religions of the world, both Eastern and Western. While the major Christian denominations today do not on principle oppose the state's use of force for national defense, minorities within the Christian community, principally the Mennonites, the Brethren, and the Quakers, continue to espouse a pacifist creed.

The theory and practice of pacifism must be distinguished from the views and efforts of those engaged in organized endeavors to prevent war. Many leaders and members of the peace societies that sprang up in the United States in the first half of the nineteenth century were inspired by religious convictions and held all war to be un-Christian. Others were more pragmatically oriented and concentrated on promoting the peaceful settlement of international disputes. Pacifist ideas as such did not seem to find a very congenial environment in America. The rugged life of the Western frontier encouraged martial rather than pacific virtues, and the rising tide of nationalism during the latter half of the nineteenth century further hampered the spread of pacifist convictions.[1]

Currents of pacifism began to gather strength following the war with Spain in 1898, and that strength increased considerably in the aftermath of World War I. Writings portraying the brutality and carnage of that conflict found a wide readership. Moreover, the rise of Fascism in Europe contributed to a wave of disillusionment with a war that, contrary to Wilsonian rhetoric, had failed to end the threat of armed conflict between nations or make the world safe for democracy. Pacifist sentiments now were encouraged, not only by humanitarian opposition to the horrors of modern war, but also by the spread of socialist ideas.

Chief among these was the idea that wars are based upon the economic rivalries of imperialistic nations and are encouraged by the traffic in armaments carried on by profit-hungry capitalists.

The pacifist organizations founded during and after World War I included a strong core of socialists, and all pacifists stressed the importance of opposing the imperialism of the capitalist order, of ending the arms race, and of achieving economic and social justice in order to remove what they considered to be the ultimate causes of war.[2] Here we find the roots of a conflict of loyalties between the pacifists' ideals of non-violence and their desire to liberate the exploited and oppressed. This conflict of moral principles afflicted all pacifist groups, though in varying degrees, from their beginning. Finally, in the 1960s and 1970s, it changed the very nature of American pacifism.

FELLOWSHIP OF RECONCILIATION

The Fellowship of Reconciliation (FOR) was founded in England in 1914 as an international Christian fellowship committed to a religiously based pacifism. Its American branch, established in 1915, had among its leaders many prominent socialists. The editors of its unofficial organ *The World Tomorrow* included such well-known socialists as Devere Allen, candidate of the Socialist party for the U.S. Senate from Connecticut, Norman Thomas, that party's presidential candidate, and Kirby Page. During the late twenties and early thirties, pacifism and socialism increasingly overlapped. For socialistically inclined Christian pacifists and anti-militaristic socialists, the FOR became the organizational tool with whose help they hoped to defeat both capitalism and war. Whether the struggle for the peaceful and classless society could be waged without the use of violence became a highly contentious issue for the organization.[3]

One of the first to explore the relation between violence and an unjust domestic social order was A. J. Muste, a Protestant minister, longtime labor organizer, and the national chairman of the FOR 1926–29. In a 1928 article entitled "Pacifism and Class War," Muste argued that it was wrong to consider only the violence of the rebels who strove to usher in a new social condition. The present system itself, he maintained, was based on violence; therefore revolutionary action to force the present rulers to give up their privileges could not in principle exclude violence. "In a world build on violence," Muste concluded, "one must be a revolutionary before one can be a pacifist."[4]

For a time Muste attempted to remain both a pacifist and a revolutionary. Then, from 1934 to 1936, he repudiated pacifism and affiliated himself with the Trotskyite American Workers party. When, after a conversion experience, he returned to being a Christian pacifist, he resumed his active role in the FOR and was its executive secretary from 1940 to 1953. Yet, while he had abandoned the Trotskyite variant of Communism, Muste remained committed to radical direct action. During the 1960s he became one of the key figures responsible for the growing politicization of American pacifism.

Niebuhr and Violence

During the early 1930s Muste was by no means the only FOR leader to accept the moral legitimacy of using violence in the struggle for a better society. Under the impact of the misery of the Great Depression, a growing number of FOR figures began to qualify their pacifist beliefs. In April 1931 the Christian socialist Reinhold Niebuhr noted that American society still maintained important ethical values "which the naïve simplicities of Communism would ruthlessly destroy and which only a primitive world can regard as dispensable."[5] At the same time, Niebuhr warned against preferring peace to justice, thus supporting an unjust status quo. He contended that religious radicals might have to abandon their "pure pacifism" and accept coercion and resistance as necessary to the social struggle.[6]

During 1933 the dispute within the FOR over the role of violence in the class conflict turned into open dissension and schism because of the views and activities of J. B. Matthews, a Protestant minister who was one of the organization's secretaries. Practically all the FOR leaders shared Matthews's strong anti-capitalism. Most, however, were uneasy over his belief that coercive rather than persuasive techniques were necessary to bring about social change, and that during the overturning of existing social controls, constitutional and legal processes could be relied upon only slightly. Matthews argued that capitalism used the educational system to prevent the spread of radical ideas. In these circumstances, pacifists, while refusing all participation in international wars, had to accept "varying degrees of coercion as regrettable necessities" in the class struggle to abolish capitalism. Pacifists should "support an advancing proletariat by more than well-wishing."[7]

Matthews's view that pacifists had a duty to give active support to revolutionary change led him into cooperation with the American Communist party. This position, too, was criticized by most of the FOR leaders. On April 5, 1933, Matthews spoke at a large Communist-sponsored anti-Fascist rally at Madison Square Garden in New York and told twenty-two thousand cheering listeners that "the dictatorship of the proletariat is the only answer to Fascism."[8] A little later he headed the organizing committee charged with planning the First United States Congress Against War. When that congress convened in New York in September 1933, Matthews was elected national chairman of the newly formed American League Against War and Fascism.

The dominant role of the Communists both in the organizing committee for the Congress Against War and at the congress itself was obvious to most observers at the time. Devere Allen, who had attended the congress, resigned from the new American League a few months later because the Communists used the organization not only to recruit and train party members but also to disrupt and attack various groups that had agreed to participate in the league, especially the Socialists.[9] Matthews's willingness to serve as head of the league, which quickly revealed itself to be a highly successful Communist front, was another issue that troubled most of the FOR leaders.

FOR Rejects Violence

The annual FOR conference held at Swarthmore College in October 1933 took up the growing dispute. John Haynes Holmes warned that pacifism was crumbling in the face of the class war.

"The end does not justify the means. The capture of power by the use of mass force is the new transfer of power. It really cannot solve the industrial problem." Professor Arthur L. Swift of Union Seminary maintained that a true pacifist rejects "the familiar platitudes which attempted to justify the world war and rejects a 'holy war' in behalf of the poor and downtrodden and for the creation of a classless society. That would be the same old cry for 'a war to end war.' A civil war is the most uncivil of all wars." Reinhold Niebuhr, on the other hand, called himself a pacifist with qualifications: "I am opposed to continuing to be true to certain principles rather than to achieve social justice. No means or ends are absolute. . . . There is no choice except between more violence and less violence." Roger Baldwin went even further. "The ethics of Jesus," he insisted, "are identical with those of communism. We are confronted today with the choice between communism and fascism, . . . between a proletarian or a military dictatorship. There can be no neutrality in this struggle."[10]

Unable to resolve the controversy, the FOR national council decided to poll its membership with a questionnaire on the use of violence in the struggle for a just social order.[11] To the key question—"Should the FOR hold on to non-violence in the class war as well as in international war?"—877 respondents answered yes, 97 no.

With this decisive mandate in hand, the council determined to employ only resolute pacifists as secretaries. By a vote of eighteen to twelve it decided not to re-engage J. B. Matthews, whose contract expired in February 1934. Following this action, several members of the organization resigned. In an article in the *Christian Century* entitled "Why I Leave the FOR," Reinhold Niebuhr acknowledged that he was a pacifist only with regard to international armed conflicts. Calling himself a Marxian and a Christian, he explained that he had left the fellowship because of his conviction that economic justice could not be achieved "without a destruction of the present disproportion of power" and without a struggle from which violence could not be excluded.[12]

FOR Rejects the United Front

The FOR's rejection of the use of violence in the class war was followed by a rejection of political cooperation with the Communists. An editorial in *The World Tomorrow* in March 1934 pointed out that the American League Against War and Fascism was primarily a supporter of Soviet foreign policy. Any group working with the league, therefore, was open to the suspicion that it was an agent of the Soviet Union, and this would destroy the effectiveness of any of its work for peace. Two weeks earlier the Communists had systematically disrupted a mass meeting called by the Socialist party in Madison Square Garden to protest the suppression of Austrian workers by the Dollfuss government. The conduct of the Communists, the editors pointed out, further confirmed the impossibility of any united front with them. Cooperation, the editorial declared, "depends upon fair play and ordinary honesty in dealing with fellow-workers. The Communists regard these virtues as bourgeois prejudices."[13]

In February 1935, FOR vice chairman Kirby Page wrote that participation in a united front with Communists was logical for those convinced that a revolution could not be carried out without the armed seizure of power, but that pacifist radicals would only weaken their efforts for peace and a non-violent revolution in America by joining forces with the Communists. "Communists have nothing but contempt for religion and for pacifism," Page declared. "They use the united front as a means of boring from within."[14] Consequently the FOR decided against affiliating with the American League Against War and Fascism, and in February 1935 it went on record against affiliation with "communistic, fascist, and other organizations sanctioning the use of armed violence in international, racial, and class war."[15]

These two principles, a firm opposition to violence in the service of any cause and to political cooperation with the Communist party and its various front organizations, continued to be FOR policy until the 1960s. Early in 1940 a statement adopted by the FOR executive committee pointed out that the Hitler-Stalin Pact, signed in the fall of 1939, had led overnight to the Communists' complete about-face on the war and on U.S. foreign policy generally. Following the line laid down by the foreign ministry of the Soviet dictatorship, the party had abandoned the principle of collective security; it now regarded the conflict between the democracies and Nazi Germany as one between rival imperialist powers. The Communists' failure to pursue a consistent policy, said the FOR statement, meant that any effort put into party-dominated anti-war organizations was to a large extent wasted. The recent collapse of the League for Peace and Democracy (successor to the American League Against War and Fascism) demonstrated the precarious existence of Communist-led anti-war groups.

The 1940 FOR statement also declared, "The Communist party rejects pacifism in principle, its basic literature is full of bitter attacks on pacifism. For the FOR to be associated with the C.P. in 'anti-war activities' could therefore only confuse multitudes of people as to our aim and function and thus stultify our efforts." The statement affirmed the FOR's strong support for the civil liberties of all Americans, including Communists, but concluded that it was sound policy "not to engage in united front activities with organizations that welcome Communists and avowed 'fellow-travelers' on their governing boards and among their officers."[16]

Non-Collaboration Continues

The FOR maintained its firm rejection of a united front with the Communists during the latter years of World War II, when the U.S. alliance with the Soviet Union against Nazi Germany encouraged a large number of such cooperative ventures, and during the heady postwar days of optimism about constructive cooperation with the Soviet Union. A statement issued by the FOR executive committee in March 1946 once again warned against united-front tactics that the Communist party used to infiltrate and take over other organizations. According to the statement, the party shifted its positions overnight in accordance with the policies of another government: "We deem it confusing, unwise, and harmful to our cause to engage in organizational collaboration with movements which one day oppose American participation in war and the next day favor it.''[17]

This and similar policy statements rejecting collaboration predated the anti-Communist fervor of the 1950s. The FOR opposed a united front with the Communists, not because it had succumbed to Cold War thinking or anti-Communist hysteria, but because it knew from experience the dire consequences of such collaboration. When the rest of the country caught up with this insight, public opinion veered sharply to the opposite extreme from collaboration. Political intolerance and attacks upon the political rights of Communists or suspected Communists became the order of the day. The FOR responded to this outburst of anti-Communist zeal, later known as McCarthyism, by reaffirming both its traditional defense of civil liberties and academic freedom and its refusal to collaborate with the Communist party and Communist front organizations.[18]

In 1948 many liberals and pacifists reacted to the outbreak of the Cold War and the growing fear of an armed collision with the Soviet Union by joining Henry Wallace's Progressive party. The FOR's official organ, *Fellowship*, in September 1948 published ''Beware the Common Front!'' by Morris Milgram, a veteran socialist and longtime executive secretary of the Workers Defense League. During the past fifteen years, Milgram pointed out, members of the American peace movement had ''found themselves the object of the most cajoling blandishments from Communists and fellow-travelers anxious to embrace them whenever the foreign policy of the Soviet Union would be aided by anti-war sentiments in this country.'' Many American pacifists—himself included, Milgram admitted—at one time or another had taken part in the anti-war efforts of organizations that included Communists:

> What they discovered was that almost invariably such organizations (the American League Against War and Fascism, the American Student Union, and the American Youth Congress, for instance) were captured by the Communists and their positions changed to suit the Communist party line. Later, when it had become clear that they were so widely known as Communist-controlled that they were no longer effective for recruiting innocents, they were disbanded.

New fronts sprang up to take their place, such as the American Peace Mobilization—which later became the the pro-war American People's Mobilization when Russia was being attacked by the very Nazis with whom she had divided Poland!

The well-meaning Henry Wallace now had begun another effort to work with the Communists in the Progressive party. From past experience, Milgram argued, the result was easily predictable:

> The machinery of the new party, already largely under Communist control, will become increasingly so, until virtually all the key non-Communists leave the organization. Wallace prefers to say what his Stalinist-engineered audiences wish to hear, as when he deleted sections of his speech slightly critical of Russia at a Madison Square Garden rally because his audience booed one such reference. Today Wallace is silent when asked his position on slave labor in the Soviet Union, and has no criticism of the USSR for its totalitarian coup in Czechoslovakia.
>
> Those who participate in the Wallace party will find themselves considered by many to be dupes of the Communists, will find their community leadership sharply weakened, and will find the Wallace party reduced to nothing when the USSR finds a change of line requires its dissolution.

Milgram concluded that the test of a bona fide anti-war person was whether he opposed militarism and imperialism by *all* nations. "Anyone who welcomed Hitler backers into FOR groups during World War II would have weakened the FOR. Similarly, anyone who welcomes Stalinists into the peace movement, or who works with them, weakens his cause."

"Red-Baiting?"

The editors of *Fellowship* ran Milgram's article accompanied by an editorial statement headlined "Red-Baiting?": "*Fellowship* believes in free speech, for Communists as for anyone else. It deplores the present anti-Communist hysteria and in no way condones attempts to persecute and harass people for their political beliefs. All of that does not change the facts of life as they relate to Communist political action."[19]

There were those in the FOR who disagreed with this stand. A letter to the *Fellowship* editor published in February 1949 argued that anything said against Communism at that time, true or untrue, added to the flames of hate and fanaticism and to the "crazy witch hunt" that was ruining the careers of both Communists and their innocent associates. Communists were idealists, in their own way seeking to make the world a better place. The letterwriter suggested "that we turn on Communists and Russians a constant stream of good will. . . . Let the Fellowship of Reconciliation publish all those facts and arguments that will reconcile—only them, and lots of them."

The editor of *Fellowship* in 1949 was Alfred Hassler, later an executive secretary of the FOR, who in the quite different political climate of the early 1970s was to lose his leadership role because he opposed the kind of thinking exemplified in this letter. An editorial statement, unmistakably reflecting Hassler's views, responded to the letter by pointing out that neither *Fellowship* nor the staff of the FOR had any wish to add in any way to the prevailing hysteria about Communists and suspected Communists. However, "one is not necessarily a saint because one is persecuted." Often the common fronts sponsored by the Communists, the editorial statement maintained, have actual purposes vastly different from their professed ends. "No FOR member, however deep his concern to avoid war, would have suggested in the pre-war years participation by the Fellowship of Reconciliation in anti-war activities of the German-American Bund. For exactly the same reasons, the FOR cannot cooperate with far more skillfully devious Communists and Communist-inspired efforts of the present, no matter how noble-sounding their stated purposes may be."[20]

Acting in the same spirit, the FOR shunned participation in Soviet-sponsored peace activities, which it saw as serving the interests of the Soviet Union rather than the cause of peace. A statement issued in May 1951 suggested that "the best way to test any 'peace' project or joint effort which is proposed" is to discover whether its promoters clearly stated "that it is opposed to militarism and war preparations *both* in Russia and in the United States, that it is critical of the foreign policy of both countries, and opposed to all forms of totalitarianism, including the Communist."[21]

1962: Peace Congress in Moscow

In July 1962 the World Peace Council, an organization that since its founding in 1950 has consistently promoted the foreign policy of the Soviet Union, convened a congress on peace and disarmament in Moscow. Because of the history of such "peace conferences," most major American peace organizations, including the FOR, declined to send representatives or even observers. Disturbed by this snub, Professor J. D. Bernal of Great Britain, president of the presidium of the World Peace Council, promised a group of people active in the American peace movement that they would be given an opportunity to present a statement before a plenary session of the congress.

Eager to improve communication and understanding between the peace movements of East and West, the American peace groups drafted a declaration that was read to the congress by Erich Fromm, psychoanalyst and writer, and Homer A. Jack, national director of the Committee for a Sane Nuclear Policy (SANE) and a prominent FOR member. Fromm and Jack explained that they had come to Moscow as individuals and not as official representatives of American peace organizations because of the difference that they and the other signers of the declaration saw between the American peace movement and the organizations associated with the World Peace Council:

> We of the U.S.A. peace organizations openly criticize and oppose policies of our own government with which we do not agree. We maintain our independence and our opposition. When government policies emphasize military measures, we oppose them. When government policies represent a turn toward peace, we praise and support them. We try to use the same criteria and principles in judging all governments. We do not believe in having one standard for judging ourselves and another standard for judging others. Everything must be examined in terms of a single standard of loyalty to the principle that above all nations is humanity. . . .
>
> We feel that the first job of the peace movement is to challenge governments to put peace as the first item on the agenda. We do not believe that we can challenge other governments effectively until we have first spoken clearly to our own government. We believe that this is the basic difference between the Communist peace movement and our U.S.A. peace movement. The peace movement in the

United States speaks *to* its government; the World Council of Peace speaks *for* government. The peace organizations of the Soviet bloc espouse the policies of their governments, whether those policies happen to be developing greater bombs or calling for disarmament. This difference makes it difficult for us to enter with you into any joint effort.[22]

1963: Peace Confederation in Oxford

Alfred Hassler, executive secretary of the FOR, defended the same position at the first meeting of a new international peace organization, the International Confederation for Disarmament and Peace (ICDP). Forty-four peace organizations from eighteen countries were represented at the first meeting, held in Oxford, England, in January 1963. In a discussion of whether to admit ten observers from the World Peace Council, Hassler took issue with the tendency of many Americans, revolted by the excesses of McCarthyism, to reject automatically anything that sounded as though the State Department might agree with it. "Confronted by an official America that argues that nothing the Communists say can be believed, the peacemaker is tempted to act as though nothing the Communists say may be disbelieved. . . . Official America seeks to exclude Communists from everything; therefore, a 'sincere' peace movement may exclude them from nothing."

Hassler argued that the minimum standard the new confederation had to uphold as a requirement for membership was a "clear opposition to war and preparations for war on the part of any government, including one's own."[23] Despite opposition from some of the American delegates, Hassler's views opposing the anti–anti-Communism growing in the ranks of the American peace movement prevailed, and the ICDP declined to seat the observers from the World Peace Council.

WOMEN'S INTERNATIONAL LEAGUE FOR PEACE AND FREEDOM

During the years prior to 1965, other American pacifist groups experienced the same controversies that afflicted the FOR, and by and large they, too, rejected any compromise of the principle of non-violence. Most forthright in seeking the social and economic transformation of society in the direction of greater social justice, yet refusing to enter into a united front with the Communists, was the American section of the Women's International League for Peace and Freedom (WILPF).

The WILPF developed out of the International Congress of Women that met in 1915 at the Hague in Holland "to protest against the war, to stop the slaughter if possible, and to take counsel together on ways of preventing future wars." Four years later, at a meeting in Switzerland, the International Congress of Women adopted the name Women's International League for Peace and Freedom. In an action that showed the strength of the French and German delegations, who wanted active cooperation with revolutionary mass movements, a resolution rejecting violence in the struggle for social justice passed by only one vote. After recognizing "a fundamentally just demand underlying most of these revolutionary movements," the women of the congress went on to "reassert their faith in methods of peace," and said it was their "special part in this revolutionary age to counsel against violence from any side."[24]

At the 1934 congress of the WILPF, the French and German sections succeeded in passing a statement that made it the "first duty" of the league "to facilitate and hasten the social transformation" that would inaugurate a new system of social, economic, and political equality. However, the Franco-German statement did not receive the two-thirds majority necessary to effect a change in the constitution. A compromise statement of aims was finally adopted that remained official WILPF policy until 1959:

> The primary objects of the Women's International League for Peace and Freedom remain: Total and universal disarmament, the abolition of violent means of coercion for the settlement of all conflicts, the substitution in every case of some form of peaceful settlement, and the development of a world organization for the political, social, and economic cooperation of peoples.
> Conscious that these aims cannot be attained and that a real and lasting peace and true freedom cannot exist under the present

system of exploitation, privilege, and profit, they consider that their duty is to facilitate and hasten by non-violent methods the social transformation which would permit the inauguration of a new system under which would be realized social, economic, and political equality for all without distinction of sex, race, or opinion.[25]

The American Section

From its beginnings the American section of the WILPF tended toward an absolute pacifism, though adherence to pacifism was not a requisite for membership. Many of the group's early members were Quakers who exerted a decisive influence. Among them was the suffragist and peace activist Mildred Scott Olmsted, who joined the staff in 1922 and played a prominent role for more than forty years. Another strong voice for nonviolence was the social worker and feminist Jane Addams, first president of the WILPF and a future Nobel laureate. Writing in 1922, Addams stressed that social advance depends as much upon the process through which it is secured as upon the result itself. "[We] believe that we are not obliged to choose between violence and passive acceptance of unjust conditions for ourselves and for others; [we] believe, on the contrary, that courage, determination, moral power, generous indignation, active good will, can achieve their ends without violence."[26]

The depression of the early 1930s strengthened the conviction of WILPF members that a real and lasting peace could not be achieved under the existing capitalist system and led to the league's sympathetic involvement with various radical causes. After some initial hesitation, the national board of the WILPF authorized its executive secretary, Dorothy Detzer, to participate in the newly organized American League Against War and Fascism. Detzer soon developed serious concerns about the Communists' mode of operation within the organization. In her memoirs she recalls, "Communists imagined that if five of them yelled louder than twenty other members of a subcommittee, the noise they made constituted an affirmative vote on a given question. Or that it was perfectly ethical to postpone a vote on a motion until most of the non-Communist members present had to leave to catch trains." Finally, in 1937, the WILPF withdrew from the American League. Experience had shown, Detzer concluded, "that there is no basis for co-operative ventures where there is no basis of moral integrity. The clash of ideas, the conflict of thought can be healthy adjuncts to human effort, but only, I am now convinced, when they are secured by the veracity of the pledged word."[27]

During the 1950s the WILPF opposed NATO and the Korean War. It then came under attack for its alleged softness on Communism, and there were charges of Communist infiltration. Nevertheless, a statement called "WILPF and the Cold War" adopted in August 1960 reaffirmed the league's policy of open membership: "We use acceptance of WILPF's principles, policies, and methods as the sole criterion for membership." However, to avoid subversion, "we put new members in policymaking or program-making positions only after they have given ample evidence that they sincerely support all our principles and policies and the non-violent, democratic methods of promoting them which we advocate."

At the same time, the WILPF reiterated its long-standing opposition to totalitarianism of any kind. Because it insisted on the right to criticize government policy, it had no sections in countries where this freedom did not exist. Also, "WILPF does not collaborate with organizations such as the World Peace Council and the Women's International Democratic Federation, even though they support some of the same specific proposals for peace that we have always favored." To build contacts across ideological lines, the WILPF sometimes sent non-participating observers to Soviet-sponsored international conferences, but, the statement continued, "WILPF does not co-sponsor conferences in which Communist organizations take the initiative, like the Youth Congresses in Moscow and Vienna, nor participate by sending delegates."[28]

In 1961 the WILPF began a program of meetings between small groups of American and Soviet women. Most league leaders knew that the Soviet women had been carefully picked by their government for their political reliability and could be counted on to defend official Soviet positions. Dorothy Hutchinson, WILPF president 1961–65, recalled years later that the

Soviet women assumed all concessions on disarmament had to be made by the United States because the USSR, being a "peaceloving" nation, had an entirely correct position on disarmament. American women, they believed, should cooperate with their Soviet sisters by working for changes only in American foreign policy. Hutchinson said she was reminded of the joke in which an American and a Russian argue about the status of civil liberties in their countries: "The American says, 'I can frankly tell President Kennedy at any time that I don't like what he's doing.' The Russian enthusiastically replies, 'It's exactly the same with us! I can tell Mr. Khrushchev frankly that I don't like what President Kennedy is doing!' "[29]

AMERICAN FRIENDS SERVICE COMMITTEE AND WAR RESISTERS LEAGUE

Prior to 1965, similar views about Soviet foreign policy and the sincerity of the Communist party's concern for peace existed within the American Friends Service Committee (AFSC). This Quaker organization was founded during World War I to give conscientious objectors an alternative to military service by allowing them to aid civilians. The AFSC quickly developed into a large organization with a wide variety of far-flung relief services and educational programs. Its concern for eliminating the deeper causes of war drew it more and more into political, economic, and social issues. As in the Fellowship of Reconciliation and the WILPF, divisions emerged over tactical questions.

When the peace section of the AFSC held a retreat in October 1933, one of the main issues discussed was: Should Friends cooperate with groups like the Communists, who advocate the forceful overthrow of the capitalist system in order to do away with the causes of war? Devere Allen, who a month earlier had attended the First United States Congress Against War and Fascism, felt that if enough pacifists stayed in such organizations they could outvote the Communists and thus create a useful public platform for pacifist ideas. Moreover, he argued, "all the violence that Communism in this country advocates and desires is as a drop in the creek as compared with the violence which

we live under in the present economic system." Pacifists cooperated with those who maintained the status quo; why not
cooperate, he asked, with those who sought to change the
capitalist system?

The opposing view was defended by Vincent D. Nicholson,
chairman of the AFSC peace section. Nicholson maintained that
in view of the Communists' methods of operation, to work with
them was "destructive of the whole principle of life for which
the best people of the Society of Friends have stood." Friends
would not cooperate with bootleggers who favored prohibition
because they made money out of it. Similarly, Friends should
not cooperate with Communists, because they were "bootleggers in the cause of peace." More important than achieving
immediate political gains was "the slower but much more important and fundamental task to change people's basic attitudes."[30]

Nicholson's rejection of a united front with the Communists
continued to be AFSC policy for the next thirty years. In May
1941 the AFSC board laid down a case-by-case approach to
possible coalitions but also insisted that cooperation was possible only with "organizations whose fundamental purposes and
methods of work are in accord with our ideals."[31] In 1951, a
leftist group misused a prayer for peace by Clarence Pickett,
executive secretary of the AFSC. In response Pickett stated the
AFSC policy on cooperation: "The use of other people's names
as fronts or the active participation with groups whose ultimate
objectives are short of the universal and religious ones which
are ours cannot be permitted. Our own concern for peace stems
out of our deepest religious convictions and our 300-year testimony along this line, and has no temporal relationship to the
political platform of any one country or party which currently
happens to use the same words."[32] Stewart Meacham, another
AFSC official, was a signer of the declaration read at the
congress of the World Peace Council held in Moscow in July
1962, a declaration that dissociated the American peace movement from government-sponsored peace groups in Eastern Europe.

The WRL and A. J. Muste

During the early 1960s two pacifist organizations began to
assume somewhat different positions. The War Resisters League

(WRL) was the U.S. branch of War Resisters International, a secular pacifist group opposed to any kind of war, international or civil. After World War II, the WRL had experienced a large influx of young conscientious objectors, radicalized by their experiences in civilian public-service camps and prisons, and the organization increasingly came to favor a sweeping political, economic, and social transformation, albeit by non-violent means.

The Committee for Non-Violent Action (CNVA) was organized in 1959. It and the WRL cooperated closely and finally merged in 1968. Playing an important role in changing the political outlook of both groups was A. J. Muste, a member of the executive committee of the WRL and the national chairman of the CNVA.

Back in 1949 Muste had insisted that pacifists had to "condemn Russian militarism and Communist violence as unconditionally as any other" and should not collaborate with the Communists.[33] Members of the Communist party, he argued, "use deceit and violence at the behest of the party; they do conceal and lie about membership in the party; they do penetrate organizations of all kinds for ulterior purposes and without hesitating to resort to the most egregious chicanery."[34] In 1956 Muste had declared that Communists are human beings whom Christians are to love as they love other children of God, but said this did not mean "that we have to work with them politically or be sentimental and naïve about certain aspects of their behavior and strategy."[35]

A year later, in 1957, Muste organized the American Forum for Socialist Education, which brought together Communists and non-Communists in a series of conferences and debates held in various cities. Muste was criticized for this move by many members of the democratic left. Norman Thomas argued that the American Forum would help the Communist party, severely weakened after Soviet suppression of the Hungarian revolt of 1956, to revive itself and confuse people politically. "The forum gave some of those Communists the false impression that they could remain in the party and still be accepted in the community.

The Communists don't belong in jail, but they also don't belong in any party with which I want to be connected."[36]
Another rejection of collaboration came from Roy Finch, a leading figure in the WRL. Finch had attended the 1957 convention of the Communist party as an observer. He reported in *Liberation*, a magazine with financial support from the WRL, that the Communists were eager to overcome their isolation from American life. "Non-Communists and anti-Communists will rightly be skeptical of such professions. . . . Labor and liberal organizations have been inoculated against popular fronts. That tactic will not work again."[37] Finch resigned from the editorial board of *Liberation* in 1961 because he objected to the magazine's favorable attitude toward Castro's Cuba, an indulgent position shared by Muste. Other WRL leaders joined in the criticism of Muste's new views. Tracy Mygatt wrote Muste in 1961 after reading several of his articles in *Liberation*: "The curious thing to me is that it was in part some of your very own words . . . some years ago that made me anxious to keep myself from any cooperation with communists."[38]

PACIFISTS AND WORLD WAR II

Unlike the war in Vietnam in the 1960s, World War II did not give rise to an organized anti-war movement, but had there been one it is doubtful that many pacifists would have joined it. The idea that pacifists should not merely refuse to fight in a war but actively try to stop it had not yet taken hold.

Before World War II broke out, American pacifists actively sought to keep the United States out of the threatening European conflagration. In 1936 the AFSC served as a kind of sponsor of the Emergency Peace Campaign, an effort to pull many anti-war groups and individuals together in a broad coalition. The aims were to oppose increased military appropriations and to promote a nationwide propaganda campaign against the idea of collective security. Even after Hitler had demonstrated his aggressive designs by swallowing Austria and Czechoslovakia and attacking Poland, pacifists continued to make common cause with isolationists and argued against U.S. involvement on the side of England and France.

In *How to Keep America Out of War*, a book published cooperatively in 1939 by the AFSC, the FOR, the WRL, the WILPF, and other anti-war organizations, Kirby Page contended that Hitlerism could not be stopped by war and that, on the contrary, a long war would lead to the entrenchment of wartime dictatorships and spread totalitarianism over the entire globe. The war in Europe was "not a war between democracy and totalitarianism, but a death grapple between rival imperialisms, with aggressors arrayed against oppressors." Britain and France were fighting for empire and continued domination far more than for liberty. The most pressing task, Page maintained, was to remove the causes of international hostility, to build a new economic order and a true democracy free from the stranglehold of financial oligarchies.[39] For A. J. Muste, similarly, the war was a struggle, not between aggressors and peacelovers, but between satiated powers determined to preserve their privileges and another set of powers equally determined to change the imperialist status quo. It therefore made no difference which side won.[40]

Yet, while American pacifists thus denied the moral legitimacy of the war against Hitler and for the most part refused to bear arms, they did not publicly demand an end to the war. Still less did they engage in activities for the purpose of causing their country's defeat. To some extent, this stance was dictated by prudential considerations, especially the fear of a violent backlash. Many pacifists also gradually came to realize that in fighting the Nazis the United States was fighting an evil that had no precedent. But most pacifists also thought it would be undemocratic to obstruct the nation's war effort and to prevent their fellow citizens from fulfilling their patriotic duty. "We seek to wean our fellows from the desire to make war," wrote Muste in 1941, "not to interfere from without with their war efforts or to destroy their property." If pacifists' non-cooperation with the war effort were to have a decisive effect, this would be the result, not "of a position and deliberate destructive act on our part, but of our inability to cooperate with what seems to us an evil and ruinous course."[41]

Pacifists became even more determined not to engage in direct opposition to the nation's war activities after the Japanese attack upon Pearl Harbor and America's formal entry into the war. On December 9, 1941, the FOR went on record disclaiming "any purpose to sabotage or obstruct the war measures of our government or any officials, soldiers, or citizens in the performance of what they regard as their patriotic duty."[42] "The people of our country—through their elected representatives—had spoken by a declaration of war," recalled Dorothy Detzer in her memoirs. "Therefore, in this terrible ordeal for our nation, we would do nothing that would circumvent the will of the people."[43]

A few Quakers were concerned that the Society of Friends had merely protested against the war in general terms and advised its members to refuse to fight but otherwise had made no attempt to end the war. In 1943 Dorothy Hutchinson, a member of the Society of Friends and later a prominent leader of the WILPF, urged her fellow Quakers to work for a prompt negotiated peace with the Axis powers. But even as Hutchinson argued that Quakers should go beyond a mere personal peace testimony, she insisted that they "work in a spirit of love and with the purpose of converting rather than coercing other men":

> In working for a prompt peace-by-consultation we must, of course, avoid active obstructionism of the war effort. We must work in the spirit which has always restrained us from sabotage and rioting in war-time as well as in peace-time. . . . Until such time as our fellow Americans are converted to our program, we must accept the continuance of the war. But we must strive to change the will of the American people so that they may express their will within the democratic framework by peaceful methods.[44]

Harbingers of Change

This commitment to the democratic process and unequivocal anti-Communism that had characterized American pacifism for several decades began to be called into question in the late 1950s and early 1960s. Once again, as in the 1930s, some pacifists started to deride what they saw as America's pseudo-democracy. Pacifist journals began to run articles by such persons as C. Wright Mills and Sidney Lens, progenitors of what soon became known as the New Left. These persons called the United States a status quo power that ignored the new revolutionary forces of anti-colonialism and national liberation in the Third World.

The Soviet Union and Communist China were still occasionally criticized as totalitarian powers that had betrayed the humanistic essence of socialism, but writers like Lens assigned responsibility for this development, not to Leninist theory and practice or to Stalin and Mao, but to the Western democracies. "The West likes to shrill about Soviet and Chinese terror," wrote Lens in *Fellowship*, the official FOR organ, in 1959. "But it does not concede its own role in this terror. If it were not for the anti-revolutionary activity of the West for more than a century, and now the policy of military encirclement, the East might have been won over to a democratic course. Britain, France, the United States, and others have never accepted their share of guilt for the crimes of Stalin; nor their role as accessories to the Chinese totalitarianism."[45] Lens conceded in 1961 that Cuba had become part of the Soviet bloc, but the "basic humanism of Castro's revolution . . . remains predominant." It was America's "vulgar and sterile anti-Communism" that threatened to consolidate Communist rule in Cuba.[46] In May 1962 *Fellowship* announced that Lens had become a member of the FOR.

During the early 1960s, views such as these—blaming the United States for most of the world's problems, casting an admiring look at Third World revolutions—gradually spread into the larger pacifist community. This development was encouraged by the Soviet "thaw" after the death of Stalin in 1953, which weakened the old anti-Communism and undermined what came to be called deprecatingly the "Cold War mentality." There was also the impact of the civil-rights movement in the South, which by exposing the injustice of racial segregation encouraged a more critical attitude toward American institutions generally. The fear of nuclear war and concern about nuclear fallout from testing of nuclear weapons contributed to the spread of "nuclear pacifism" and to the growing tendency to hold the Soviet Union and the United States equally responsible for world tensions and the arms race.

In this political climate many pacifists, left-of-center liberals, and the emerging New Left increasingly embraced the same political agenda. Mass organizations like the Committee for a Sane Nuclear Policy, founded in 1957, enabled pacifists to break out of their political isolation and gain a wider, sympathetic audience for their demand for disarmament. Radical pacifists like A. J. Muste and Dave Dellinger developed a following among young people who had not experienced the politics of the 1930s and who did not share the pronounced anti-Communism of the older generation of pacifists. Indeed, for many of these young people the excesses of "McCarthyism" in the 1950s had discredited the very idea of anti-Communism; they quite deliberately embraced the doctrine of anti–anti-Communism.

VIETNAM AND AFTER

When in 1965 America became involved in armed conflict in a faraway land ruled by a clique of generals, and large numbers of students faced the prospect of fighting and perhaps dying in a war with an ambiguous rationale, the stage was set for a mass movement of political protest that eventually was to create a symbiotic relationship of pacifism and New Left politics. By the time "the Movement," as it became known, had run its course some ten years later, American pacifism had assumed a new political identity. The American Friends Service Committee, the Fellowship of Reconciliation, and the War Resisters League today are an integral part of the New Left—an amorphous collection of political groups that regard the United States as an imperialist nation responsible both for the poverty of the Third World and for starting and maintaining a dangerous arms race that threatens nuclear catastrophe. Members of the Women's International League for Peace and Freedom laud the peaceful intentions of the Soviet Union and defend its foreign policy at every step.

All these organizations now affirm their solidarity with Marxist-controlled guerrillas in various parts of the world. They defend the violence carried out by these guerrillas as inevitable when the oppressed struggle against the violence of an unjust status quo. While American pacifists continue to affirm the moral superiority of non-violence, they support these so-called liberation movements by actively pleading their cause before the American people and by seeking to prevent U.S. military aid to the governments under attack.

After such liberation movements succeed in seizing power, pacifist organizations praise the new societies that are being created and deny their totalitarian character. Whether in Cuba, Vietnam, or Nicaragua, the socialism of these regimes is seen as indigenous and unique and is often held to be superior to the capitalist way of life prevailing in the West.

Double standards abound. The pacifists' friendly disposition toward so-called national liberation movements does not include movements seeking liberation from Communist domination. Few pacifists show much sympathy for the Afghan *mujaheddin* fighting the Soviet occupation of their country, for Angola's UNITA struggling against Cuban-aided Communist rule, or for the various groups opposing the Sandinista regime in Nicaragua. It is permissible for leftist guerrillas to use violence in the pursuit of their goals but impermissible for lawfully elected governments to defend themselves against foreign-sponsored subversion. Pacifist organizations endorse the Sanctuary movement for politically motivated refugees from El Salvador and Guatemala; they ignore the almost 200,000 Nicaraguans who in recent years have fled to Honduras and Costa Rica. Pacifist groups decry the imperfect human-rights record of U.S. allies like Israel and South Korea but find few words of condemnation for the far worse record of Communist-ruled states like North Korea and Ethiopia. The pacifist community is concerned with the oppressed people of this world, but by its definition there are no truly oppressed people in socialist countries. The term "socialist" suffices to legitimate every revolutionary cause and regime, no matter how brutal and repressive.

As we have seen, it was not always so. Until the early 1960s American pacifists identified with the democratic values of the

United States and opposed totalitarianism of every kind. Pacifists refused to make common cause with Communist-led peace movements, which they criticized as political instruments of the Soviet Union. While personally unwilling to bear arms, American pacifists respected the democratic process and did not attempt to prevent their fellow citizens from fulfilling their patriotic duties.

The Turning Point

As the war in Vietnam dragged on with rising American casualties and no end in sight, Americans of all political persuasions began to question the wisdom of the U.S. involvement. Many of these questioners became the foot soldiers of a burgeoning anti-war movement that from the beginning was led by the Left. The leaders of this movement exploited the growing desire of the American people for an end to the killing; their primary goal, however, was not peace but a victory of the NLF and the North Vietnamese Communists. After it was all over, Fred Halstead, one of the leading figures in the anti-war movement and a member of the Trotskyite Socialist Workers party, revealed that slogans like "Victory to the Vietnamese Revolution" were ineffective in mobilizing the masses of Americans: "Our central task . . . was to put maximum pressure on the United States to get out of Vietnam. That would help the Vietnamese revolution more than anything else we could possibly do."[47]

American pacifists who saw an opportunity to break out of their political isolation quickly assumed a prominent leadership role in the anti-war movement. Many of them undoubtedly believed the claims of the NLF to be a broadly based movement of national and social liberation. The pacifist movement had always been attracted to socialist ideas; sympathy for the underdog now facilitated identification with these courageous Asian revolutionaries who had taken on the world's leading capitalist and military power.

As the U.S. involvement deepened and the anti-war movement failed to achieve its goal of an immediate and unconditional U.S. withdrawal, anti-war activists became increasingly disillusioned with the struggle for votes and took their protest to the streets. Demonstrations conducted under the principle of non-exclusion attracted all kinds of militant fringe groups and often turned violent. At times, pacifists were able to restrain their more impatient allies and impose a non-violent discipline. In many other instances, however, they failed to prevent provocations and clashes with the forces of law and order.

Frustrated by their inability to end the war on their terms, pacifist groups became radicalized and began to use the vocabulary of the extreme left. The war in Vietnam was seen not only as a mistake of U.S. foreign policy but as a necessary outcome of a corrupt and decadent system that had to be fundamentally changed if not destroyed. Allegations that U.S. troops intentionally killed Vietnamese civilians and engaged in other atrocities fell upon fertile soil and became the staple of anti-war propaganda. Elite groups—the media, the churches, business and professional leaders, Congress—became more and more disenchanted with a war that did not work.

At the same time, public opinion polls indicated that if there was anything even more unpopular than the war, it was the anti-war movement. The movement's hostility toward American society and its militant tactics of disruption antagonized middle America. As a result, beleaguered pacifists moved ever closer to their extremist allies. By the time the U.S. role in the war in Vietnam ended in early 1973, organized American pacifism had become a major component of what was known as "the Movement"—a conglomerate of leftist groups united by their alienation from American society, their infatuation with Marxist-led liberation movements, and their search for "communism with a human face."

A Few Exceptions

A few American pacifists unsuccessfully fought the drift to the left. Alfred Hassler, Charles Bloomstein, and Robert Pickus strongly opposed what they saw as an unacceptable compromising of pacifist principles. In 1975 Hassler concluded regretfully that pacifism itself had become "one of the casualties of Vietnam."[48] Because they resisted the abandonment of non-violence, these men either were eased out of or voluntarily left the leadership positions in the pacifist community they had occupied for many years. Other dissenters like Daniel Seeger and James Forest have remained in their organizations but are unable to exert any real influence. The tiny Catholic Worker movement founded in the 1930s by Dorothy Day and Peter Maurin has resisted the temptation to glorify revolutionary violence.

The major pacifist organizations, however, have continued on the political course charted during the Vietnam war. Pacifists who disagree with the prevailing leftist orthodoxy either have dropped their membership or resignedly retain it out of a reluctance to break the associational bonds of a lifetime. Dissent has virtually disappeared; for the most part, the voice of principled pacifism is no longer heard.

The armed conflicts in Central America have given organized pacifism another opportunity to line up with Communist-led revolutions. Pacifist groups today are in the forefront of those who support the Sandinista regime in Nicaragua and seek to end U.S. aid for the centrist Duarte government of El Salvador, which is battling an insurrection supported and sustained by the Soviet bloc. Once again the pacifists' strategy is to try to get the United States off the backs of their revolutionary friends.

A moral case can be made for armed rebellion and revolution. In some situations no peaceful recourse is available against tyranny and oppression, and resort to violent struggle, if successful, may actually save lives and reduce human suffering in the long run. But such a pragmatic calculation is forbidden to the true pacifist, who must oppose the use of force for any and all purposes. Still less can a real pacifist adhere to a "just war" or "just revolution" philosophy, and pick and choose the rebels he will support—Marxist guerrillas in Southeast Asia and Central America, but not the Afghan *mujaheddin* or Angola's UNITA.

The Pacifist as Gadfly

There have been pacifists who have adopted an ethic of consequences and have conceded that in the imperfect world in which we live, it may be possible or even necessary to defend values by using force. Bertram Pickard, a British Friend, observed in 1942 that, as long as the modern state is composed of citizens the majority of whom do not share the pacifist gospel of altruistic love, "coercive force not only will but must be used in the creation and maintenance of order. The fact that we ourselves feel unable, because of a special contribution we feel called upon to make, to cooperate in the application of such force, is not affected by our admission."[49] Another leading British pacifist, Cecil John Cadoux, a founding member of the British Fellowship of Reconciliation, wrote in 1940 that a pacifist can even approve of certain wars waged for good causes without contradicting "his own refusal to participate in any such war himself."[50]

This "realistic pacifism" bears some resemblance to the position of contemporary American pacifists who endorse the violence of the oppressed without themselves participating in hostilities. In both cases, armed conflict is no longer seen as the supreme evil. On the other hand, Pickard and Cadoux were convinced democrats who had no sympathy for the totalitarian left supported by today's American pacifists. They also were fully aware that the pacifist has no program for the political world of power and states that now exists, and that his main function consists in bearing witness to the values of non-violence and reconciliation. The American Quaker theologian David Elton Trueblood wrote in 1966 that the pacifist, by his extreme position, "is helping the state to avoid settling back into a mood in which war and the preparation for war are taken for granted. He is the gadfly of his civilization, somewhat as Socrates was the gadfly of the Athenian civilization."[51]

In the final analysis, then, there is no such thing as a truly pacifist political position. The pacifist is committed, in the words of the German sociologist Max Weber, to an "ethic of ultimate ends" that affirms the sanctity of human life. He feels responsible, not so much for the political consequences of his actions, but primarily for seeing that the flame of pure intentions is not squelched. This is the purpose of his exemplary acts, his protest against violence, his refusal to kill. The possibility that good intent may lead to bad results is essentially irrelevant.

Pacifists, committed to the supreme value of non-violence, remind the rest of us of the link between means and ends. Their personal "No" to killing carries an important ethical message. The pacifist vision of a world free of the threat of war can help build support for the development of an ordered political community at the international level, able to resolve conflicts peacefully and justly.

The Pacifist as a Policy Proponent

However, at the moment that pacifists enter the political arena to seek to influence the policies of their nation, they cease to speak as pacifists and become subject to what Weber called the "ethic of responsibility," which takes account of the realities of power and the likely consequences of political decisions. The *personal "No"* of pacifists, representing an act of conscience, is morally unassailable if this act of refusal does not jeopardize the survival and well-being of others. Since pacifists are usually a small minority of a country's population, this condition will be met in most cases. But the *national policies* proposed by pacifists must, like all other policies, be judged in terms of foreseeable results. As the Catholic theologian George Weigel has pointed out, "the morality of political judgment must include a consequential criterion. To argue, for example, that unilateral disarmament is the sole moral option, even if its results would be to make war more likely, is not an act of prophetic witness, but a moral absurdity."[52]

The pacifist, like any other citizen, is entitled to participate in the political process and to propose policies. He should recognize, however, that when entering the policy arena he must adopt standards of judgment distinct from those he applies in his personal life. He should not urge a course of action that, if implemented, would leave his country undefended or would tip the balance of power in the world in favor of expansionist and aggressor nations. As Reinhold Niebuhr argued during World War II, it may be noble for a person to sacrifice his life rather than participate in the defense of order and justice, but one cannot ignore the "distinction between an individual act of self-abnegation and a policy of submission to injustice, whereby lives and interests other than our own are defrauded or destroyed."[53] Individual perfection is not a basis on which to build a political platform. Pacifists have every right to avoid the moral dilemmas posed by the world of statesmanship and statecraft and to seek individual salvation through ethical absolutism and purity, but they have no right to sacrifice others for this end.

American pacifist organizations today do not adhere to these principles. Worse, they are less than candid about the muddled Marxist ideology that they have embraced and that they clothe in innocent-sounding humanitarian slogans. Pacifist groups counsel policies couched in the language of peace and justice that are in fact supportive of some of the most brutal and ruthless forces in the world. Instead of openly acknowledging that they have become partisans of Communist revolution in the Third World, they call themselves "progressives" and say they are working to establish a new economic order. Instead of admitting that they seek the unilateral disarmament of the United States, they criticize the use of money for defense rather than social welfare. Seeking to convince themselves and others that national defense is no longer possible, they paint hysterical scenarios of total war in which any recourse to force leads to nuclear Armageddon.

To soothe the country's concern about the military might of the Soviet Union and its messianic drive for world revolution, the spokesmen for American pacifism attack what they call "the myth of the Soviet threat." In 1940 Niebuhr criticized the American churches and their periodicals for not telling the true story of Japanese aggression and of German tyranny in Europe for fear of arousing the "war spirit." Similarly, American pacifist organizations today decry talk about Soviet expansionism on the grounds that it may stimulate a new cold war.

Since pacifists do not want to use force in defense of the society in which they live, they argue that American democracy is not worth defending. American society is described as militaristic, unjust, and repressive, and is seen as the root cause of evil in the world. During World War II Niebuhr forcefully argued against the pacifists' perfectionism, which he criticized as "unable to make significant distinctions between tyranny and freedom because it can find no democracy pure enough to deserve its devotion. . . . If it is not possible to express moral preference for the justice achieved in democratic societies, no historical preference has any meaning."[54] Today's generation of pacifists is even more alienated from American democracy; instead of simply counseling surrender to tyranny, these pacifists deny that our Communist antagonists represent morally evil principles. Our own society is measured by utopian standards of perfection; socialist states are judged by promises and postdated checks. No recognition is given to the fact that societies calling themselves socialist have, according to all available empirical evidence, consistently performed worse than liberal democracies, both in providing economic well-being and in protecting human freedoms.

While the major American pacifist organizations today accept the use of force in the struggle against pro-American authoritarian regimes, they continue to adhere to pacifist principles with regard to wars between nations. To solve the conflict between the United States and the Soviet Union, pacifists counsel disarmament—unilateral if necessary—and a less assertive U.S. foreign policy. Peace at any price is their demand.

To Regain the Moral High Ground

If American pacifists today were to practice clear thinking, they would acknowledge, first of all, the distinction Max Weber drew between the ethic of ultimate ends and the ethic of responsibility. In the best of all possible worlds, pacifist activity could be both morally pure and politically relevant. In the real world, that is usually not possible. When pacifists present their language of the heart as a political alternative to the pressures and compromises of the political order, they, as Niebuhr noted, "invariably betray themselves into a preference for tyranny." For the moral ambiguities of history and world politics, Niebuhr insisted, ambiguous methods and answers are required. "Let those who are revolted by such ambiguities have the decency and courtesy to retire to the monastery where medieval perfectionists found their asylum.''[55]

To regain the high moral ground pacifism once occupied as a keeper of the humanitarian conscience, American pacifists would have to return to the democratic values they espoused until the early 1960s. When they found themselves outvoted, they would have to abandon their routine resort to civil disobedience and other tactics of resistance to democratically enacted law. They would have to cease blaming the United States for all the ills of the world and end their coalition with the totalitarian left. The American Communist party today may no longer pursue as aggressively as it did in the 1930s its policy of infiltrating and seeking to take over other organizations. However, the party's role as an apologist for the Soviet Union continues unchanged, and cooperation with the party cannot be justified either politically or morally.

Nobody will expect pacifists to be active supporters of nuclear deterrence, of the use of force against terrorists, or of military aid to weak regimes facing the threat of foreign-sponsored subversion. But neither should they try to obstruct all such policies that the democratically elected government of the United States pursues as it attempts to assure the country's survival as a free society. When the pacifist's conscience does not allow him to support policies that use force or the threat of force, the proper course for him is to remain silent. A historical precedent is the withdrawal of Quaker politicians from the government of Pennsylvania in 1756 because they wanted to be neither an interference in nor a party to war against the Indians.

In 1941 Percy Hartill, chairman of the Anglican Pacifist Fellowship, criticized English Christians for harping upon the evils of the Nazi system and the crimes of Hitler and his henchmen. Anyone studying church pronouncements, he complained, would find plenty said about the ''duty of saving the victims or potential victims of Nazi sins; he will find even more about the need for crushing or restraining the Nazis. But he will find very little indeed about saving the Nazis from their sins; very rarely will he find these leaders urging their flocks to pray for the conversion of Herr Hitler; most rarely of all will he find them suggesting that the right way (because it is God's way) of meeting sin is by forgiveness, even unto seventy times seven."[56] By ignoring this utopian perfectionism and resisting Hitler to their utmost, the people of Britain were able to survive as free men and women.

American pacifists' flight from reality is no less pronounced than Hartill's; their abandonment of the fundamental values of Western civilization is one of the great moral tragedies of our age. Our free society can afford to tolerate those who seek to undermine our will to resist our adversaries. But, like the people of Britain during World War II, we must recognize that the successful defense of freedom requires the repudiation of advice that would pave the way for the triumph of tyranny.

PART TWO

Fifteen Responses

.

1

Misplaced Crisis

Charles Chatfield

A T OUR HOME we flew the American flag throughout the Vietnam war—not proudly but loyally. I was supportive of students opposing the war, but I counseled them against being co-opted by extremists or diverted from political effectiveness. My own contacts enabled me to appreciate the aptness of Tom Hayden's description of the fate of the radical left in that period:

> We had become isolated, self-enclosed in a universe of political rather than human life. In this sealed universe, social relationships were contained within organizations, language turned to jargon, disputes were elevated to doctrinal heights, paranoia replaced openness, and the struggle to change each other became a substitute for changing the world [*Memoirs*, p. 435].

On the other hand, my professional work on the history of pacifism gave me enough perspective to know that Hayden's description could not be applied indiscriminately. It seemed important to speak both against the war and against the prevalent reductionism that leveled the sacred and the profane, disdained rational distinctions, and equated difference of judgment with moral crisis.

Charles Chatfield is professor of history at Wittenberg University, Springfield, Ohio. He is the author of *For Peace and Justice: Pacifism in America, 1914–1941*. This essay, written without scholarly citation for reasons of space, is grounded in archival research for the forthcoming *Ordeal for a Nation: The Antiwar Movement of the Vietnam Era* by Charles DeBenedetti, for which Chatfield is the assisting author. The author reserves all rights to this essay.

It is this last concern especially that impels me now to disagree with Guenter Lewy's interpretation of recent American pacifism. Although readily conceding his sincerity and the real importance of the issues of which he writes, I believe that his account *distorts the historical context and confuses differences of judgment with moral crisis*, yielding a polemical construction of both ethics and history. The ethical issue is: What is the proper role for a pacifist engaged with civic problems, specifically war and revolution? The historical issue is: In what respects have pacifist answers to that question changed since 1965, and why? There have indeed been changes in pacifism; but they are not the changes Lewy purveys, and they are related to changes in the world and in worldviews beyond pacifism and beyond the United States.

PACIFISM AND SOCIAL ETHICS

"Pacifism" is a tricky word. It was invented in Europe at the turn of the century in an attempt to give a positive tone to the advocacy of peace and internationalism. At that time, war was widely glorified as the essence of national identity. Advocates of peace were generally disdained as being unrealistic and probably disloyal. One is sorely tempted, in the light of Lewy's book, to ask how much has changed.

One thing that changed was the word "pacifism." The men and women who first referred to themselves as pacifists fell within what we know as the just-war tradition. They were advocates of peace, but, with few exceptions, they did not discount the possibility of a justified war; they were internationalists, but they were very much a part of their national cultures. When World War I broke out, many pacifists—capitalists and socialists alike—supported their national governments, and most of those who challenged the war did so on the basis of their judgment of its merits.

In Great Britain and the United States especially, the word was narrowed to refer to persons who would not support even that war, which was widely regarded as just (after it was declared). "Pacifist" became a term of derision, and it was only then that the word acquired the sense in which Lewy uses it exclusively, to refer to "those who are morally opposed to bearing arms and who refuse to sanction war for any purpose, defensive or otherwise." Then, as now, polemic usage confused the refusal to sanction any war with opposition to a specific conflict, and principled rejection of military service with the advocacy of peace.

There was, of course, an ancient tradition of refusing military service on the grounds of principle, a tradition as old as the early Christian Church. It was revived at about the time of the Protestant Reformation and became associated especially with the so-called historic peace churches: the Society of Friends (Quakers), Mennonites, and Brethren. Within these associations there developed a tradition of *non-resistance*—that is, refusal to engage in the violent coercion that was understood to be the way of the world from which the non-violent communities must withdraw in loyalty to their religious principles. This view formed the original basis for legal exemption from conscription in Britain and America. It is from this tradition that Lewy derives what he regards as an authentic pacifist ethic: the refusal to sanction violence under any circumstance—*and* the consequent withdrawal from political life.

From the seventeenth-century Friends to nineteenth-century peace advocates, however, there was a parallel growth of peace advocacy in the just-war tradition that converged with both capitalist and socialist internationalism. Accompanied by an emphasis on domestic social justice, these movements flowered early in the twentieth century. The international challenge to World War I drew upon the combined strands of peace thought. It was pacifist in both the absolute and the relative sense. The organizations that Lewy depicts were formed in this period and out of this complex tradition. They were very different from one another, and they continued to develop in various international associations. As they evolved, they explored a tension between their twin commitments to non-violence and social justice; but they did not attempt to resolve this tension by withdrawing from political conflict.

The Four Organizations

The Fellowship of Reconciliation (FOR) originated as literally a *fellowship* of people who had in common only their opposition to war and commitment to justice on Christian grounds. During the interwar years it developed as a formal *organization*. Several of its leaders were oriented toward democratic socialism, and they wrestled with the tension between social justice and peace. By 1965 they had developed ideas and programs of direct but non-violent action for justice. In the 1930s this was expressed as a preference for a general strike against war and fascism. Thereafter it was applied most fully to civil rights, drawing heavily on the example of Gandhi. Well before 1965 the FOR had taken the position that in the case of a conflict between social justice and social order, non-violent but direct civil disobedience was a legitimate ethical form of political action, as well as a matter of individual conscience.

This was even clearer in War Resisters International (WRI) and its U.S. section, the War Resisters League (WRL). These were loose *associations* that came to represent especially secular war resisters, and they attracted people who tended to equate militarism with state centrism. In Europe in the 1930s, where WRI was closely associated with democratic and anarchistic socialism, war resisters encountered the repression of Stalinism and Nazism. There the claims of non-violence were clearly paired with those of revolutionary justice, and when the pairing broke down the claims of justice often predominated, as in the case of Romain Rolland. By 1965 pacifism had come to be defined in the WRL as both individual witness and political action—a form of social revolution, ethical insofar as it was non-violent.

The American Friends Service Committee (AFSC) was formed as an *agency* to provide alternative service to draftees, out of respect for the central Quaker tenet that an individual should follow the inner light of conscience in his or her service to humankind. In this sense the AFSC ministered to the morality of the individual pacifist in the midst of war. After World War II it expanded with wide-ranging services to victims of social injustice and war in Germany, the Soviet Union, and elsewhere. It did not have a membership. It operated programs of mercy regardless of politics and also advocated peace and internationalism irrespective of ideologies. In the 1950s it helped to form a coalition in opposition to atmospheric testing of nuclear weapons, a campaign in which it supported both traditional political action and symbolic civil disobedience.

The Women's International League for Peace and Freedom (WILPF) was not really a pacifist organization in Lewy's sense. Its American section did draw heavily on persons opposed to war in principle, but even here it eschewed absolute pacifism, notably in World War II. The WILPF was an early *international non-governmental organization*, essentially an expression of internationalism. Its national sections differed over the strategy of a popular front against Fascism in the 1930s, and in that context the WILPF defined its aims at Zurich in 1934. It welcomed women "from different political camps" as long as they were in harmony with the aims of the WILPF, which were to abolish violent coercion and economic inequity—its objective was peace and justice—and to facilitate "social transformation" by "non-violent methods." Those principles were updated in the still operative 1959 statement of aims. In 1965 they defined the social ethics of not only the WILPF but the AFSC, WRL, and FOR as well.

Thus Lewy's narrow reference point for pacifist ethics is not historically characteristic of these organizations. None of them avowed absolute pacifism to the exclusion of social justice and political action. By 1965 all of them in quite different ways had encountered the tension between peace and justice, and all had more or less distinguished between individual morality and public ethics.

Individual Morality vs. Social Ethics

This latter distinction is critical for an understanding of the ethical issue of the role of pacifism. It was made most sharply by Reinhold Niebuhr in the late 1930s. He argued that individual morality might appropriately reflect absolute principles such as the total rejection of force or coercion, but that social ethics requires that political choices be weighed against alternative principles of goodness and against consequences. Individual morality may be grounded in absolute, fixed truth; social ethics is relative and proximate.

Taken as a relative, in-so-far-as distinction, Niebuhr's point is valid and important. It requires clarity about the relationship of means and ends, assumptions, and conclusions. Taken as an absolute dichotomy it is fallacious, ignoring the fact that any individual (or group) may in fact act in several roles. Many pacifists did so, even in Niebuhr's time. As individuals they abjured violence and war altogether, but, at the same time, as citizens they challenged specific foreign policy on the grounds of realism and social values.

Any number of pacifists and non-pacifists confused their roles and principles before and during the Vietnam war, and it was precisely that confusion which Niebuhr had hoped to avoid. To write a book clarifying this issue—the relationship of individual morality and social ethics—in its modern context would be altogether appropriate. Unfortunately, *Peace and Revolution* is not that book. It obscures ethical issues by its narrow reference point and its either/or dichotomies, and it stereotypes the four peace groups in a way that makes a case for the author's own version of pacifist morality.

PACIFISM AND MORAL CRISIS IN AMERICA

Prior to 1965, most of the American members of the major pacifist organizations had not faced a situation where the policy of their own nation seemed unequivocally unjust and their own government virtually unaccountable. Some had: Alice Hertz, a WILPF member and the first American to commit self-immolation during the Vietnam war, had faced Nazism in the 1930s, along with other German pacifists. Some of them had gone into exile; others had joined the resistance or had merely endured. For American pacifists, though, the Vietnam war presented a new ethical context. After 1965 and especially after 1968, there was a growing conviction that the war waged by the United States was both politically unjustified and immoral. Whether or not this was so can be debated, but leading pacifists assumed it was the case. Overwhelmingly and consistently they opposed the war in Vietnam for this reason, and not (as Lewy insinuates) in order to make possible a Communist victory. The likelihood that this would happen, combined with the repugnance of the American war, intensified their differences of judgment as well as their common feeling that they were citizens of a nation in moral crisis.

Political Judgment vs. Moral Principle

For pacifists and non-pacifists, critics and supporters, the war in Vietnam clouded distinctions between political judgment and moral principle. In part this was due to the kind of coalition that gathered in opposition to the war, but in large measure it was a function of the lack of governmental accountability with which the war was conducted. Throughout the decade following 1965 the executive branch was neither candid nor credible, and it attacked and harassed its opponents, often illegally. Numerous opponents of the war came to despair of the political system itself.

The more desperate pacifists felt, the more they became vulnerable to divisiveness and extremism, and this at a time when a series of cultural and social movements independent of the war—most notably the racial crisis, but also a revival of radicalism and a counterculture—were generating enormous social dissonance. The war attracted all these elements. They saw in the anti-war coalition potential leverage with which to advance change, and they thereby attached their causes, rhetoric, and internal factionalism to it. No account of the period can be satisfactory that does not take into account its confusion and complexity, all compounded by a terrible sense of urgency and mounting frustration with what seemed to be an infinitely protracted and immoral war. Fatigue itself seriously affected the anti-war movement. It was a prime consideration in, for example, Al Hassler's withdrawal from FOR leadership.

Distinctions between political judgments and moral principles were clouded also because the national debate over the war was conducted on the level of political symbolism. In some large measure the Johnson and Nixon administrations contributed to this. Both of them deliberately obfuscated issues with appeals to national symbols—preeminently the flag and the POWs (when politically convenient), but also verbal symbols such as Americanism, anti-Communism, loyalty, victory, and (when victory became hollow) honor. Again, pacifist challengers were vulnerable because they depended for political leverage on a coalition they could not dominate, one whose rhetoric often employed symbols of resistance that fastened a radical and "anti-American" stereotype on the movement.

In fact, for all but small and peripheral factions of the anti-war movement, symbols such as draft-card burning, street theater, even the occasional unfurling of Vietcong flags expressed anger at what was perceived as a distortion and betrayal of traditional American values. No account of the period can be satisfactory that does not put anti-"American" in quotation marks, because overwhelmingly that which was opposed was the draping of a contested war in the garments of patriotism. This is not to defend the style or politics of the anti-war coalition or of the pacifist elements in it. It is, rather, to establish the historical setting for intense contests of judgment that often were depicted (and are so used by Lewy) as issues of principle.

Issues Dividing Pacifists

What issues divided pacifists, then, and what was their historical significance?

There were almost as many issues as there were pacifists. Very often they were matters of priority in the allocation of scarce resources and energy, especially in the FOR and AFSC, where anti-war work competed with other programs. Again the controversy in the FOR comes to mind because Lewy interprets it as exclusively a contest over principle. In fact, it involved also questions of administrative style and, especially, the priorities of competing FOR and IFOR (the international body) programs. Al Hassler came to place a high priority on IFOR work not directly related to the war, and on support of Vietnamese Buddhists within it. Allan Brick and Ron Young, who are portrayed as Hassler's antagonists within the FOR, worked on programs he valued. Notably they helped to develop connections with Buddhists (each of them led trips to Vietnam), although they differed with Hassler on questions of priority and strategy. Ignoring the question of priorities, Lewy constructs his account around strategic issues, especially (1) anti-war coalitions with radical groups, (2) the equal and universal condemnation of violence, and (3) attitudes toward the U.S political system.

1. *Coalition Politics.* The so-called anti-war movement was an eclectic, loosely aligned coalition of disparate groups that differed about the significance of U.S. policy and about strategy to reverse it. The coalition was never built; it simply assembled. It was organized at the national level but was not controlled from there. The most effective coordination came at the local level, as in the New York Fifth Avenue Parade Committee. In a very rough sense the movement was divided between liberal and radical elements, each in turn a loose alignment that changed over time. Pacifist groups were composed in various proportions of liberal and radical pacifists, with the former predominating in the AFSC and the latter in the WRL. Coalition among them and with other groups was a necessary political strategy, given their felt imperative to challenge the war and their very limited constituencies. The divisive issue, therefore, was not so much the coalition as the terms of coalition, particularly with respect to public demonstrations.

On one level the contest took the form of which groups to cooperate with. Given pacifists' experience both with guilt by radical association and with the internal disruption engineered by radicals in the 1930s and 1950s, many were reluctant to cooperate with any semblance of a Communist organization. They were countered by others who argued that radicals in the 1960s did not have the organizational base or foreign connections of the old left (and indeed the FBI and CIA reached the very same conclusion after exhaustive efforts to prove the contrary). Moreover, some insisted, the only responsible test of coalition was its central purpose—to halt an unjust war. Indeed, they added, to exclude groups on the basis of ideology was to succumb to the very ideological polarization that had led to Cold War interventionism itself. "Inclusiveness" was held by the

New Left to have a value in itself, to be a test of an open society. The issue was further complicated by the fact that Communist party strategy was attuned to traditional political work rather than mass demonstrations, and that the strategy of the Trotskyites' Socialist Workers party was oriented toward disciplined, single-issue demonstrations. Ironically, therefore, the anti-war groups least acceptable in the political lexicon were politically among the most responsible.

On another level the issue of coalition took the form of slogans and policy positions, notably whether to withdraw from intervention immediately and unilaterally or gradually through negotiation. This was in part a matter of factional loyalty and in part a matter of serious debate. As the war continued, especially after 1968, liberals gravitated toward withdrawal either immediately or by a specified date. By the time the FOR and the AFSC adopted unilateral withdrawal, the position had been accepted by the Committee for a Sane Nuclear Policy (SANE) and Americans for Democratic Action (ADA), among several liberal groups adamantly opposed to cooperation with the radical left. Accordingly, the terms of U.S. withdrawal defined groups only at given points in time, and placed at least the FOR and the AFSC in the liberal, not the radical, camp.

On a third level, the elements in coalitions were distinguished by three alternative forms of action: (1) the orderly expression of opinion, (2) direct non-violent confrontation and civil disobedience, (3) deliberate disorder and property destruction. In part this was a matter of principle for pacifists committed to an ethics of non-violence, and they divided over whether non-violence should be extended to confrontation or even to extra-legal actions. In part it was a matter of political judgment, since the media and the executive branch tended to highlight, even exaggerate, confrontation and disorder so that protest, rather than the war being protested, became the public issue.

At the outset, in fact, the AFSC, WILPF, and FOR (as well as SANE) were reluctant to cooperate in demonstrations called by groups such as Students for a Democratic Society (SDS) or the radical coalitions behind the various Mobilizations. Cooperation increased from 1965 to 1967, as demonstrations proved to be relatively trouble-free and increasingly impressive, and as the war escalated. Often coalition was informal, through local groups or individuals influential in but not formally representative of the nationals. From 1968 to 1971 demonstrations were marred by disorder and even violence, but by that time the moral crisis of America at war was so intense that some sort of coalition was widely assumed to be necessary, and so the question of the *terms* of cooperation became ever more important.

Largely under pacifist influence a distinction came to be made between ideology (expressed as slogans) and behavior (expressed as forms of action). By 1969 there were large-scale programs to train marshals in the use of non-violent crowd control as well as to train select contingents in disciplined civil disobedience. Demonstrations were divided into three kinds: orderly demonstration, symbolic non-violent civil disobedience, and non-violent confrontation. Pacifists like Ron Young and Stewart Meacham, and after 1968 the pacifist leaders in the National Action Group (NAG), played key roles in imposing control and discipline on coalition demonstrations. They were enormously frustrated by militant non-pacifist radical factions— and by the government. Meacham eventually withdrew from coalition activity and took an AFSC position outside the country.

If one assumes *a priori* that coalition effort with radicals violated pacifist principles, as Lewy does, then its advocacy by Young, Meacham, or Dave McReynolds can be used to illustrate the point. If, on the other hand, one understands the issue to be the *terms* of coalition, then the roles played by Young and Meacham in seeking to make coalition demonstrations responsible and effective, and the instances when McReynolds refused to support them, illustrate the attempt of even radical pacifists to exercise responsible judgment.

The most divisive aspect of coalitions was the extent to which they infused organizational factionalism into the anti-war movement. In particular this was a result of a pervasive attempt to construct a radical coalition that would use the war issue to mobilize the transformation of domestic social institutions. Radical pacifists such as Sidney Lens and Dave Dellinger reflected this view. For the most part, though, pacifist efforts were directed toward assembling various constituencies of disaffected Americans in opposition to the war. In any given mobilization the two strategies converged, however, and nearly all of them were marred by the chaos of conflicting goals and organizational infighting on the left.

By 1973 radical extremism had dissolved, and there was a broad consensus among pacifists that multi-issue coalitions had been divisive and distracting—a serious diversion of limited resources from the war issue. Accordingly, even to the extent that participation in radical coalitions was an issue of pacifist principle as opposed to a matter of judgment, it was widely rejected by the end of the war in favor of other forms of action.

2. *Condemnation of All Violence.* A second issue with which Lewy tests the moral conscience of pacifists is their willingness to apply non-violence universally. The argument here is that pacifist groups increasingly romanticized and identified with violent revolutionaries and isolated America for attack. The most articulate appeal for equal condemnation of violence on both sides came early in the war in a 1965 article by Robert Pickus, who equated universality with pacifist principle. Even then the issue was not new, for it had divided pacifists in their opposition to the nuclear-arms race.

One case in point was the support given to Buddhists. Al Hassler, working through the FOR and IFOR, took the lead in this effort. As noted above, he worked with Allan Brick and Ron Young in developing connections with Buddhists. Moreover, the AFSC also facilitated an early tour by Buddhist emissary Thich Nhat Hanh and maintained contacts with neutralists in Vietnam throughout the period. The large bulk of its medical assistance programs went to civilian victims of the war in the South (contrary to Lewy), although it did mount a drive to rebuild a major hospital in Hanoi that was destroyed by Nixon's bombing campaign. After 1973 the pacifist coalition worked more and more closely with South Vietnamese exiles in a joint attempt to cut off military assistance to the Thieu regime (the form of intervention to which Lewy refers on page 109 is a mystery).

On the other hand, there was a divisive issue in the Buddhist connection. Much more forcefully than anyone else, Hassler pressed support for the Buddhist Third Force as a political alternative. That this was a matter of political judgment is clear in a long correspondence between him and McReynolds. The question turned largely on the political viability of Buddhist leadership, which McReynolds doubted. But there was another point, and it was a matter of principle. For Hassler, the alternative to a neutralist solution was North Vietnamese domination, and he was convinced that this would lead to another form of victimization in the South. For McReynolds, to advance even a Third Force solution as a point of official negotiations was to introduce yet another, if more benign, attempt to construct Vietnam from America. As the two old friends agonized over the alternatives, Hassler acknowledged that pacifist ethics itself offered no answer to the dilemma. It was not pacifism that divided them; it was political principle and judgment.

The question of a ceasefire took a similar turn. Early in 1971 Hassler responded to a Buddhist appeal for help by promoting through the IFOR an "Appeal to All Combatants to Stop the Killing." The appeal for a ceasefire was taken up later in the year by Mary Temple and others, who formed a committee of notables. They were attracted by the fact that the IFOR appeal did not single out the United States as solely responsible for the continuing war. The universality of the appeal was consonant with Hassler's understanding of pacifism, but at least equally important, it reflected his judgment that a ceasefire was the only possible way of stopping the killing, given what seemed to be Nixon's mounting control of events. McReynolds and Richard Fernandez of Clergy and Laity Concerned (CALC) disagreed, arguing that the killing would not end until the conflict in Vietnam was resolved. This could not happen so long as the United States provided political and military support to Thieu. Only the Vietnamese could resolve the issue, they argued, although neither of them was sanguine about a North Vietnamese victory.

McReynolds and others repeatedly voiced private apprehensions about the Communists, but they rejected appeals by Pickus and others to level public condemnation equally at the United States and North Vietnam. In the first place, they argued, the sheer destructiveness of the American war effort was out of proportion to that of the North. Moreover, their moral responsibility for political impact lay primarily with their own government. Finally, condemnation of North Vietnam was gratuitous and would contribute to the American war effort until the United States was out. Then and then only, they argued, would it be appropriate to hold the Vietnamese up to pacifist standards.

There were innumerable variations on this debate, and they merged with the controversy over coalition with political radicals who often did romanticize the Communist revolution and who were unilaterally strident in their attack on U.S. policy. The relationship with radicals compromised pacifist efforts insofar as it obscured the thrust of their protest. Pacifists overwhelmingly agreed that the war was a moral crisis for America. They differed primarily over the context and consequences of their political choices—over judgments—even though they often couched their arguments in the rhetoric of principle (and of course there is a real relationship between principle and its application). Given the tenet of an ethical responsibility to engage in political action for peace and justice that characterized the four peace groups at the outset of the war, differences were inevitable. Disagreement, even acrimonious dispute, was part of sharing the American dilemma in Vietnam, not a moral crisis distinctive to pacifists. Moreover, the fact that they were confused or divided in their judgments did not indicate that they had abandoned their principles.

3. *Political Direction.* It is not the case, as Lewy would have us believe, that the pacifist organizations became ever more radical in the sense of rejecting the U.S. political system and its symbols or in identifying the United States as the source of all the world's ills. The contrary was the case in three respects.

First, from the mid-sixties to the mid-seventies the AFSC and WILPF especially, but also the FOR, cooperated with liberal groups such as the Friends Committee on National Legislation (FCNL), ADA, SANE, and CALC to influence policy through traditional congressional and electoral politics. They also coop-

erated with liberal groups to form networks of alternative exper-
tise and authority on both the academic and the popular level.
These efforts were initiated, in fact, before 1965, and they
continued beyond the 1973 peace acccords. They were concomitant with (though much less visible than) the mass demonstrations and direct actions in which pacifists also cooperated in
varying degrees.

Second, the emphasis of pacifist effort shifted between 1965
and 1971 from peace advocacy through traditional political channels to mass demonstration, direct action, and adversarial confrontation; but from 1971 to 1975 it shifted back again to traditional pressure and electoral politics. This is the significance of
the broad Coalition to Stop Funding the War. Whatever one's
judgment on the validity of this coalition's goals—to cut off
military assistance to the Thieu and Lon Nol regimes—its politics were thoroughly affirmative of the American system. The
McGovern campaign of 1972 enticed even anarchists in the WRL
into the mainstream of politics. The Indochina Peace Campaign
of Tom Hayden and Jane Fonda developed an explicitly and
affirmative "American" style.

Indeed, by 1973 there was a widespread pacifist consensus
that the earlier and confrontational opposition to the war had
been counterproductive. By this time, moreover, the pacifist
groups loosely connected through the National Action Group
(NAG) had begun to broaden their agendas from the Vietnam
war to issues such as the arms race, policies on Third World
nations, and détente. Whatever one's judgment on these matters, their emergence was part of the reevaluation of Cold War
liberalism that underlay the whole Vietnam crisis. By the end of
the war, pacifist organizations were converting to their traditional role as advocates for peace and internationalism as an
extension of American values.

Third, even in the most radical, let us say confrontational,
phase of the anti-war coalition—from 1968 to 1971—pacifists
acted to impose such discipline and issue-oriented focus as they
could. This is the significance of the NAG. It was created by
Stewart Meacham and others out of the debacle of Chicago in
1968 precisely to give guidance and form to the movement.

Although its discussion of strategy that October was "inconclu-
sive" (as Lewy notes on page 37), the group attempted to
develop a relatively disciplined set of demonstrations during the
following two springs, and nurtured the shift to traditional politics thereafter. The NAG group never controlled the anti-war
coalition or its demonstrations, even in 1970–71, and within its
pacifist constituency there was a great deal of division over anti-
war strategy and the meaning of the war; but these were matters
of conflicting judgments about how best to respond to the war.

By polarizing issues associated with coalition politics, by
citing views expressed by individuals as though they represented
organizational positions, by concentrating on rhetoric to the
exclusion of roles played, and by focusing on confrontation to
the virtual exclusion of other forms of political protest—in all
these ways Lewy plays on a stereotypic image of the anti-war
movement that obscures its larger relationship to the American
political system and symbolism. Pacifist groups (and the
WILPF) never really abandoned the American system. If in the
depths of the war they despaired of it, they were functioning
more surely in it than ever during the counterfeit peace between
1973 and 1975.

PACIFISM AND MORAL CRISIS IN THE WORLD

The issues that divided pacifists during the Vietnam war had
less historical significance than those on which there was a large
measure of consensus, because the latter led more surely to the
future. These were preeminently matters of principle—the twin
commitments to non-violence and to peace and justice. Neither
was abandoned, but both were further developed in the context
of a significant change in the pacifists' political situation.

1. *Non-Violence.* The major pacifist groups maintained their
commitment to non-violence during the war, but they emerged
from it with a somewhat chastened understanding of non-violent
action. Violence against *persons* in the wartime crisis had been
directed primarily *at* protesters. Violence against war-related
property, on the other hand, accompanied protest. Insofar as it
involved pacifists, it came largely from radical Catholics who

interpreted it as an extension of non-violent direct action. At first it was undertaken in full compliance with the law (as in the case of the Berrigans' action in Catonsville); but as respect for lawful authority declined, it became extra-legal.

This development divided the pacifist community. Although the major pacifist groups expressed respect for the inner convictions motivating radical pacifism, they often explicitly rejected its tactics. In any case, the main source of protest-related violence was from non-pacifist extremists, although it was indiscriminately and often deliberately attached to the anti-war stereotype. The groups described by Lewy, while recognizing the rule of individual conscience, rigorously affirmed non-violence as a principle of their effort. Indeed, in the midst of the war the FOR and IFOR even extended programs of non-violent action for justice in Latin America. In the United States, however, the early confidence in direct action that accompanied the civil-rights movement was constrained by the experience of wartime protest. Pacifists seemed to emerge with a greater sense of the limitations of direct action as a force for change in American society.

More precisely, they were more ready to advocate change within the channels of the political system. Partly this reflected a stronger understanding of the extent to which foreign policy was institutionalized in society. In large measure, however, it mirrored a change in American society, where citizen action had mushroomed during the war and where a cluster of advocacy groups remained to address a wide range of issues. These included SANE, CSFW (Committee to Stop Funding the War, under several other names as well), Common Cause, Clergy and Laity Concerned, and a host of social-ethics nuclei among the professions. There was a new constituency for social- and foreign-policy issues in the Congress and the Democratic party. Perhaps most important, there was much experience at the local level throughout the nation; henceforth peace advocacy would be more decentralized than ever before (a development that Lewy seems not to appreciate). In the 1980s this was illustrated in the organized promotion of a nuclear freeze and in the protest of the Reagan administration's Central American policy. Pacifist groups participated in but did not direct these broadly based actions. The fact that they were no longer politically isolated signaled a major change in their situation.

2. *Peace and Justice.* Their wartime experience gave pacifists not only more access to the public but also a greater appreciation of social and international systems, and this affected the way they pursued their commitment to peace and social justice. As they regrouped following the war and reoriented themselves to the role of peace advocates, they addressed issues in more systemic terms. Hassler had in some respects led the way with his promotion of Dai Dong, a worldwide network that linked environmental problems to war and social injustice in the context of a global system. As the AFSC and SANE cooperated to challenge the arms race, they monitored and addressed it in economic terms and tried to interpret national security as a function of international order. As pacifists worked with the independently mounted nuclear-freeze movement, they addressed nuclear issues in strategic terms and in relation to popular European apprehensions. Whatever one's views of the freeze movement, there are no reasonable grounds on which to interpret it as subversive, and there is much basis for understanding it as an expression of legitimate national and international concern.

As it addressed conflicts in the Third World, the peace-education division of the AFSC found itself involved in the study of transnational corporations and development theory. Accordingly, its AFSC-approved 1976 report *The United States and Latin America Today* attempted to treat the U.S. role in functional, not ideological, terms—in relation to the structure of the international economy and regional societies—and it recognized the complexities that accompanied the paradoxes of the region. In this respect the AFSC report continued a series of analyses from 1949 to 1955 (*Speak Truth to Power*) that had sought to "transcend the conventional wisdom of the Cold War." The 1976 report was new in that it addressed the emergence of the Third World as a critical policy arena.

The pitfalls of military intervention in the tumultuous changes of the Third World had been dramatized in Indochina, and this concern was extended to Latin America (in the case of Chile, even before the war ended). The region was not new to pacifists: leaders of the FOR had challenged intervention in Nicaragua in the 1920s, and even earlier peace advocates had opposed neo-imperialism there. They then had begun to explore the relation between injustice and violence, and they were not at all unique in doing so. Through the 1970s, U.S. intervention in Central America was understood primarily in economic terms, and it became interpreted in the context of a larger North-South debate. In the following decade, as American intervention took an increasingly military cast (notably with respect to Nicaragua and El Salvador), pacifist concern was incorporated in a broad non-pacifist coalition for political action that drew explicitly on the national memory of intervention in Vietnam. Whatever one's view of this protest movement, there is no evidence to link it with external subversion and much to commend it as a legitimate challenge to executive policy in the region.

With respect to the Third World, pacifists faced the limits of non-violence as a force for constructive change that they had encountered in Vietnam. Once again they entered a new and perplexing world context. Once more, along with the American people, they had to sort out reality from reality. As they encountered another series of armed revolutionary movements apparently rooted in popular resistance to oppression, they again experienced a sharp tension between their pacific ideals and engagement in a warring world.

In the spirit of William James, pacifists addressed these contradictions by drawing distinctions: they acknowledged that repressive injustice would result in violence without conceding the legitimacy of violence itself; they condoned social transformation without knowingly cooperating in revolutionary violence; and they actively sought to succor the oppressed without supporting armed rebellion itself. In sum, they conceded the relative justice of armed resistance to oppression without abandoning their personal commitment to non-violence. They did not concede the relative justice of military intervention. Whatever one's views of social-justice movements in the Third World, and whether or not pacifist judgments were sound, there is no ground for interpreting them as a deviation from historic principle.

Pacifists interpreted not only the Third World but also the Eastern-bloc Communist nations as dynamic societies. They promoted peace and justice (notably human rights) across ideological boundaries. Far from being a deviation from historic pacifism, this was an extension of the efforts for international reconciliation and problem-solving that had spawned the IFOR, AFSC, and WILPF in World War I and had defined much of their program in the 1920s. Whereas then pacifists addressed Europeans, now they addressed primarily Americans. This was a recognition of changes in world power. In different, far less politically open terms, they also addressed the Soviets. That was the point of WILPF contacts with the East. If they subverted anything, it was the rigidity of the Eastern bloc, for their extension of Western idealism and internationalism reinforced independent citizen efforts there. In all these respects the AFSC, WILPF, and FOR sought to broaden their roles as international non-governmental organizations, part of a rapidly expanding network that has significantly supplemented intergovernmental organizations and moderated the nation-state system.

War and Injustice: A Moral Crisis

As noted above, one of the reasons for wartime tension in the FOR was precisely the priority that Al Hassler gave to the systemic problems of the globe. Once the American crisis in Vietnam had passed, the major pacifist groups (along with a fresh group of non-pacifist ones) elevated that priority. Political scientist Robert Osgood wisely included ideals in his definition of national interest, and one might well include also worldviews. The programs undertaken by pacifists after the Vietnam war were responses to a perception as old as all the strands of thought from which pacifism had grown: the sense that in war and injustice the world faces a moral crisis that undermines human well-being and even national security.

Whether or not one agrees with this view, it lies at the base of pacifist social ethics. Here is precisely the *interaction* of intrinsic values and pragmatic calculations. That is what Lewy apparently does not understand. By limiting pacifism to a morality that repudiates force absolutely, he would take it out of politics, but his statement that "there is no such thing as a political position that is truly pacifist" (p. 241) is facile. Al Hassler confessed as much to Dave McReynolds in a probing exchange of letters during the war. He did not conclude that pacifism was irrelevant, only that it was not per se a political solution. That is to say, there was no political alternative that measured up to the absolute values of pacifism. Hassler neither abandoned pacifism nor quit his efforts to make a political difference. He continued to work for the Buddhist "Third Solution" and for *Dai Dong* because those were political courses that in his judgment came closest to a relative approximation of pacifist ends. McReynolds and others differed in their political judgments, not their pacifist ends. Insofar as pacifism *qua* pacifism can be extended to political action, then it offers a standard against which to measure relative possibilities.

The crux of the matter is revealed in Lewy's statement that the public citizen "must adopt standards of judgment distinct from those he applies in his personal life" (p. 242). The point is the standard and the assessment of what violates it. The real basis for Lewy's allegation of a moral crisis in pacifism is, in fact, that in his own judgment the essential foreign-policy goal is neither to "leave the country undefended" nor to "tip the balance of power in the world." His book is an attempt to interpret the recent past in such a way as to make the case that four pacifist groups did just that—violated his own view of the challenge for U.S. foreign policy. That is not a moral crisis or an ethical dilemma. It is a political judgment miscast in historical interpretation.

The ethical question is: In what respects can pacifist principles be extended from personal witness to political action? To what extent can the moral crisis of the world be addressed realistically? The answer is: Insofar as pacifist values and worldviews can be understood as standards against which to make judgments in the relative, contingent ethic of consequences. It would be worthwhile to clarify how pacifist values impinge on political judgments, but Lewy's book does not do that. In fact, by denying the validity of the effort, it obscures the intense wrestling with this issue over the past quarter century. Lewy attempts not only to take pacifism out of politics but to take it out of history.

A MISPLACED CRISIS

Clearly the account I have given here differs sharply from Lewy's. It is reasonable that a subject as complex as this should bear various interpretations. What gives Lewy's book its distinctive force, however, is precisely the fact that it oversimplifies the issues and events involved, reducing them to an arbitrary moral polarity. The process by which he does this involves some technical elements that affect the reader's judgment.

Although the book is based on archival and other primary materials, there is nonetheless a problem of selective use of evidence. In part the difficulty derives from the choice of published and archival sources: the papers of the FOR, AFSC, and WILPF are cited, although within these papers there is only a limited attention to correspondence; but there is little reference to the records of the WRL or other anti-war groups. Largely, however, the problem is the selective use of evidence within the sources. It is aggravated by the use of extended quotations that explain the positions of partisans with whom the author agrees, in contrast to limited quotations from others that serve mainly to document their deviance from allegedly authentic pacifism. There is a major problem in citing individuals as though they were representative of organizations when they were not. There are other difficulties. The AFSC policy statements on Central America are so selectively used as to be unrepresentative, for example. The allegation that Hassler was "eased out" of FOR leadership in 1971 is unfounded even in terms of evidence presented, and is incorrect in the light of other sources.

There are occasional factual errors, such as the account of administrative experimentation in the FOR (it was reversed in October 1972, not May 1973), the assertion that AFSC relief aid was directed primarily to the North (it was not), or the allegation that the People's Peace Treaty was "drawn up in Hanoi" (it was carried to Hanoi and Saigon by American students). Lewy's account of the nuclear-freeze movement is based on erroneous analysis of evidence and is tangled. The allegation that CISPES (Committee in Solidarity with the People of El Salvador) was founded with Communist funds has been refuted by the Senate Select Intelligence Committee; the evidence cited for the statement has been shown to be spurious, and the FBI has acknowledged that its investigation was not merited. Such errors are very difficult to avoid, as all scholars understand. In themselves they do not invalidate the book's thesis. They do suggest that the research was driven by the argument, however, and this feeling is reinforced by the construction and language of the account.

An author's selection of substance inevitably creates a biased historical context. That is true both of this essay and of Lewy's book. As Lewy tests pacifist morality by adherence to his definition of pacifist principle, he minimizes the importance of several contexts: the real political issues associated with the Vietnam war, the distinctive moral crisis that it posed for pacifists, the evolution of their protest in the social climate of the 1960s, their despair, and the range of their peace and anti-war activity. The dimensions of pacifism are further narrowed by the exclusion of concomitant programs of advocacy, support for conscientious objectors, and non-war concerns such as the FOR's *Dai Dong* or the AFSC's relief work elsewhere in the world. Similarly, Lewy distorts the post-war role of the WILPF by limiting attention to its pacifist participation in Communist bloc–related international forums and by waiving the historical context of international relations.

Another form of historical bias is the confusion of effect with cause, or the treating of concurrent developments as though they reflected cause and effect. This underlies Lewy's willful supposition (most blatantly stated on page 167) that the AFSC advocated U.S. withdrawal from Vietnam *in order* to support the Communists there. Other examples are the erroneous account of the AFSC's relationship with the freeze movement, the imputation of a causal role in the anti-war movement to the Vietnamese National Liberation Front (NLF), and the alleged support of the WILPF or AFSC for Communist goals. In a related way, there is in the book an obscuring of contemporaneous events that form the background for disputes it cites, such as U.S. post-1973 intervention in Indochina or post-1975 policy on Vietnam, not to mention the policy of Vietnamization.

Finally, the author somewhat arbitrarily adapts to his purpose both historical allusions (like those to the Spanish Civil War or Munich) and narrative (as in the contorted account of recent events in El Salvador). Once again, all scholars face the difficulty of selecting and summarizing events, and how they do it is a matter of judgment. The way in which this book is written reinforces my sense that the author's interpretation determined his selection of historical substance.

The language of *Peace and Revolution* includes several forms of innuendo—that is, the use of concepts in a way that preempts serious consideration. In Lewy's lexicon, terms such as "anti-American," "Communist," "anti-war," and "anti–anti-Communism" are used to connote something bad, or at least suspicious. "Revolution" implies mainly violent change. "Unilateral withdrawal" is a synonym for defeat; the issues are never discussed. The New Left is fallaciously stereotyped without distinction among its adherents or phases, and its initial critique of American policy and society is treated with disdain. Similarly, there is no differentiation between the Communist party, Progressive Labor party, Socialist Workers Alliance, or the New Left generally.

Given the unexamined but negative connotations of these labels, the often unexplained association of pacifists with them amounts to what used to be called guilt by association. In a related way, a number of concepts (such as economic transformation, imperialism, and social revolution) are referred to as though they have no legitimate meaning and only convey a repudiation of American values, although all of them were discussed during the period precisely in terms of preserving national values. In any case, the power of the argument derives at least as much from the arbitrary use of language as from the selection of evidence. It conveys the strong convictions of the author more than it illuminates the subject.

Guenter Lewy is a man of deep sincerity and a competent scholar. He addresses important issues. He organizes his argument and marshals his evidence effectively. He cites his sources with apparent meticulousness. All this does not in itself validate his thesis, any more than the devotion of pacifists in itself validates their judgments. The difficulty, in my view, is that technical scholarship is used to construct an arbitrary and, I think, erroneous interpretation of pacifist history that cloaks differences of judgment in the guise of moral deviance.

The crux of the problem of interpretation is the author's disagreement with leading pacifists about the challenges posed to the United States and the world. However pacifist judgments are weighed in this regard, they do not add up to a moral crisis. On the other hand, the polemical construction of history obscures both ethical and political issues, and contributes to a crisis in public understanding, democratic process, and national purpose.

2

Five Theses for a Pacifist Reformation

George Weigel

ALTHOUGH I am not a pacifist, I must decline to be disinvited to the debate over the future of pacifism. The matter is too important to be left to pacifists alone, just as the future of just-war theory is too important to be left to just-war adherents alone. Any tradition of moral reflection, no matter how secure its own self-understanding may be, benefits from the friendly criticism of other traditions. Moral traditions whose self-understanding is undergoing ferment should be even more open to a widened circle of critical conversation. Since American pacifism is in a period of perhaps unprecedented ferment, the time is right for a candid exchange between pacifists and non-pacifists on the future of the pacifist conscience and pacifist politics.

There are four other reasons why I, a non-pacifist, lay claim to being part of the discussion.

First, the pacifist conscience (in a variety of forms) animates an increasing number of American Christians today, and can be expected to have a discernible effect on future public life. Anyone interested in the intellectual and moral health of the

---

George Weigel, formerly president of the James Madison Foundation, became president of the Ethics and Public Policy Center in June 1989. He is the author of *American Interest, American Purpose* (1989), *Catholicism and the Renewal of American Democracy* (1989), and *Tranquillitas Ordinis: The Present Failure and Future Promise of American Catholic Thought on War and Peace* (1987).

debate over ethics and U.S. foreign policy must be interested in the debate over the pacifist future.

Second, the pacifist conscience has had a demonstrable impact on the conduct of America's business in the world. Pacifists and foreign-policy realists alike persistently minimize this impact. But the historical record shows that one cannot understand the terms of the debates over isolation-and-intervention in the 1930s, over nuclear testing and related issues in the 1950s, over America's role in Vietnam in the 1960s and 1970s, and over U.S. policy in Central America today without taking serious account of the role that pacifist individuals and agencies have played in shaping the public discourse. Pacifists have always been a small minority in the U.S. population, but their influence has been greater than their numbers suggest.

Third, I take an active interest in the future of pacifism because mainline/oldline Protestantism and Roman Catholicism now recognize the legitimacy of the pacifist conscience within their traditions. Those who think that American pacifism is still largely confined to the historic peace churches have not been paying close attention to the American religious scene over the past generation. The emergence of a significant pacifist presence within the mainline/oldline churches and within Roman Catholicism has not been without its theological difficulties; witness the *sotto voce* argument between the Vatican and the drafters of the U.S. Catholic bishops' letter "The Challenge of Peace" over whether there were indeed, as the bishops had claimed in their second draft, "two traditions" of Catholic moral reflection on war and peace, the pacifist and the just-war tradition.[1] But the pacifist presence has been a source of light as well as heat. Pacifist theologians of the intellectual stature of Stanley Hauerwas and John Howard Yoder have enriched the ecumenical theological dialogue for almost a generation now.[2]

My fourth reason for wanting to be a part of the debate is that I have learned much from some pacifists of deep moral conviction and impressive political sophistication, and I hope to make some small recompense in what follows.

As a theologian, I do not regard the pacifist conscience as inherently superior morally. And as a student of modern history, particularly of the modern quest for peace with freedom, I have considerable misgivings about the pacifist record in world politics. But I do regard the pacifist conscience as a legitimate expression of Christian moral conviction.

Moreover, the dilemma of the pursuit of peace and freedom is so pressing today, the inadequacy of so much of what passes for moral argument within that dilemma is so painful, the need for fresh thought, drawing on the full resources of the Christian tradition, seems so clear, that I think it behooves all of us to widen the circles of discourse within which we usually operate, so that a new conversation, ahead of the barricades, might have a chance of forming, and, having formed, just might lead to moral wisdom in the quest for peace and freedom. And I believe that American pacifism can make a distinctive contribution to the effort to bring about a world in which conflict is resolved without mass violence.

FOUR INTELLECTUAL PROBLEMS

Although I may not agree fully with this or that judgment offered in *Peace and Revolution*, I believe that Guenter Lewy's chief critical contention is true: over the past two generations, pacifist organizations have tended to abandon pacifist commitments in world politics for the sake of what they judged to be higher moral goods. The organizations in question deny this, but they do concede that pacifist self-understanding and pacifist politics have "developed."[3] Everyone agrees, then, that something has changed. The real argument focuses on the moral evaluation of that change, and whether it is a consequence of flaws in the pacifist conscience itself.

I find four intellectual problems in contemporary pacifism:

1. Misperceiving Totalitarianism.

Even those who, as I, believe that the pacifist conscience contains important insights about world politics, ought to concede that American pacifists have never been particularly astute at reading world-historical realities in the short and medium term. This critical judgment is supported, I think, by a careful reading of the standard histories of American pacifism.[4] Most (though not all) pacifists were wrong about the intentions of Adolf Hitler and National Socialism. Most pacifists were wrong about the domestic and international politics of Joseph Stalin, and about the goals of Ho Chi Minh (although, again, others were not). Most pacifists today, I believe, are wrong about the ideological commitments of Daniel Ortega and the core of the Sandinista leadership of Nicaragua.

Pacifists have not been alone in these erroneous judgments. Charles Lindbergh and Senator Burton K. Wheeler were wrong about Hitler; Franklin Roosevelt and a generation of American intellectuals were wrong about Stalin; Lyndon Johnson was wrong about Ho Chi Minh (whom he somehow thought susceptible to the kind of rhetorical massaging that had once worked wonders in the Senate cloakroom); and in my judgment, virtually the entire Democratic leadership of the Congress has mistakenly read the Sandinista project for Nicaragua and indeed for all of Central America. Whatever else might be said about them, Lindbergh, Wheeler, FDR, LBJ, and Jim Wright were or are not pacifists. In short, pacifists have not been alone in their misperception of the forces chiefly responsible for the brutalization of international public life in the twentieth century.

A remarkable bond of misperception has linked pacifism to traditional isolationism (as in the 1930s), or pacifism to neo-isolationism (as in the 1960s, 1970s, and 1980s). There is something quintessentially American about this pattern of analytic folly. It has to do, I think, with our character as a people. Americans are, for good and for ill, a "liberal" people. Immune (thus far) to the direct havoc that totalitarian politics has wrought on countless millions of human lives, we find it hard to imagine that people could commit mass murder for the sake of political power. That might be called "naïveté," or "innocence," or, more charitably still, the reflection of a fundamental decency in our society. Americans tend to be myopic about the ideological passions that have made an abattoir of the mid- and late-twentieth century.

Naïveté or gullibility about the bloodymindedness of totalitarian politics is not, therefore, a failure peculiar to pacifism: it is shared by our political culture as a whole. But it is a failure against which pacifism has failed to armor its adherents. And it renders more difficult the pursuit of the pacifist's entirely admirable goal: a world in which international conflict is resolved without the use or threat of organized mass violence.

2. Importing Alien Views.

To say that American pacifism has failed to perceive the realities of totalitarian ideologies is not to suggest that it has been non-ideological. On the contrary, the pacifist misperception of Hitler in the 1930s and of totalitarian forces today is in part the result of alien ideological currents imported into pacifist thought.

The pacifist case against Western rearmament in the 1930s was buttressed by the "merchants of death" analysis of progressive historians seeking an explanation for the First World War—an analysis that had little or nothing to do with pacifist moral convictions *per se*. Similarly, the pacifist interpretation of post-colonial revolutionary politics in the Third World has been deeply influenced by the redefinition of "violence" proposed by Franz Fanon and a host of liberation theologians. This redefinition, in my judgment, threatens the core integrity of the pacifist conscience.

The intellectual move here is familiar enough. A "first violence," usually identified as the "violence" of "sinful social structures," must be redressed before there can be a meaningful moral address to revolutionary or "second" violence. The most simplistic response is for a pacifist organization to say that it does not have the right to cast moral doubt on the politics of those who seek to redress the injustices perpetrated by the sinful social structures of colonialism, neo-colonialism, racism, imperialism, and rapacious capitalism—even if that redress takes the form of "second violence." More subtly, and therefore more dangerously, pacifists may argue that the greater good of the just cause being pursued requires building coalitions with those who choose revolutionary violence. This is, after all, only "second violence," and in time there may be opportunities to make the case for non-violent resistance to others in the coalition. That there is, to my knowledge, precious little empirical evidence to support this strategy of post-revolutionary conversion does not seem to have hindered the argument in certain pacifist circles, a judgment sustained by Lewy's documentation.

The problem here seems clear, on two levels. First, in the order of morality, to compromise the pacifist conscience by adopting the "first/second violence" concept is to subject the rigor of the pacifist commitment to the death of a thousand cuts. In this sense, the moral strength of pacifism comes precisely from its absolutism on the question of violence. Just as there can be no such thing as demi-virginity, surely there can be no such thing as demi-pacifism. One either abjures violence—the deliberate infliction of pain, suffering, and even death—in the pursuit of political ends, or one does not. If one does abjure violence, then one cannot make common cause with the violence of others. Christian moral discourse about whether a resort to violence is possible in the defense or pursuit of moral goods is weakened by such obfuscations.

Second, in the order of political reality, weakening the definition of violence inevitably weakens the presumption against its use. The notion of the "violent system" against which the revolutionary struggle is being mounted, and the parallel notion of morally justifiable "second violence," have led to atrocities ranging from the Weather Underground's bombing of the University of Wisconsin math lab during the Vietnam troubles to the brutal practice of "necklacing" in South Africa. Violence begets violence, a truism captured most powerfully in the classic film *The Battle of Algiers*. The presumption *against* violence, and *for* non-violent means of conflict resolution, is a fragile and precious reed in the construction of an international public order fit for human beings. That this presumption, fragile as it is, is being further weakened by pacifist individuals and organizations is a moral and political tragedy.

And it need not have happened. There is no *necessary* connection between the pacifist conscience and the enthusiasm for revolutionary violence of the Franz Fanons and Camillo Torreses of this world. The connection was made when ideological themes alien to the pacifist conscience were imported into pacifist thought. Over time, these themes blurred the pacifist conscience to the point where it compromised its most fundamental convictions. Some pacifists resisted this, as Guenter Lewy demonstrates. Non-pacifists sympathetic to pacifism, such as Thomas Merton, warned against the dangers of moral syncretism for the future of peacemaking. But the resistance was largely unsuccessful, and the warnings seem to have gone largely unheeded.

3. Practicing Gnostic Politics.

The pacifist failure to confront adequately the brutalities of modern totalitarian politics, and the American pacifist tendency to import alien ideological themes into pacifist thought, taken together amount to a kind of "gnostic politics." This manner of thinking fails to take account of the truth that altered facts, not altered intentions, are the fundamental stuff of change in international politics.

Pacifists correctly argue that non-violent struggle has made a difference "on the ground" in modern politics. As prime examples they point to the Indian independence movement, the American civil-rights movement, the overthrow of Marcos in the Philippines, and the democratic transition in South Korea. I do not want to gainsay the importance of these examples for the evolution of a humane politics within and among nations.[5] But their distinctiveness must be confronted: In each, non-violent resistance and non-violent direct action were successful in a society in which the rule of law was acknowledged, in however tenuous a form. While we may all hope and work for the day when international law has the kind of restraining force that domestic law (and the moral understandings that sustained it) had in Lord Halifax's India and even in the Philippines of Ferdinand Marcos, the plain fact is that such restraints simply do not exist today. There has been some progress toward that goal, but a prudent reading of contemporary history suggests that in this matter we have just begun to traverse a long road.

But even if the desired end—a world in which "international political community" is a reality rather than a dream—were to be achieved, conflict and the clash of interests would remain the order of the day. To pursue a world without conflict is to pursue a chimera. To envision a world in which "national interest" is no longer a category of statecraft is to engage in gnostic fantasizing. Men and nations are limited in their capacity for goodness, fallible in their perception of the good. While we work to enlarge our individual and civic capacities to discern, choose, and act on the good, the fact remains that multiple definitions of "the good" will always be in play in our world. This means that conflict and the pursuit of interest are a normal, not aberrant, reality of political life. The root of the pacifist failure to take adequate account of this is, as root problems usually are, theological.

4. *Minimizing Sin.*

That contemporary American religious pacifism need not be allied to the political agenda of the secular left is made clear by the work of Stanley Hauerwas, a stringent critic of that temptation to concubinage. That the temptation is all too infrequently resisted is the judgment of Guenter Lewy's study, and is one that my own experience amply confirms. Why has this happpened, this curious bedding-down of the pacifist conscience and the politics of the Rainbow Coalition? I suggest that *theological* failures and miscues are, at the deepest level, at fault.

Closely related to the American liberal sentimentality noted above (i.e., our incapacity to comprehend the murderousness at the heart of totalitarianism) has been a tendency in religious pacifist circles to minimize the abiding fact of sin and brokenness in this world. Yet the mainstream of Christian theology, from the Fathers to today, has insisted that the doctrine of original sin is not merely a statement about Adam and Eve and the unhappy events in their garden. Rather, it is a perennially valid description of us and our garden and the gardens of our children and their children. This world, short of the Kingdom, will never attain perfection. Schemes based on a belief in mundane perfectibility not only are liable to frustration; worse, they can become instruments of further suffering if they lead us to ignore the harsh realities of a broken world in which the evil one is always prowling, seeking someone to devour (I Pet. 5:8).

In less explicitly biblical terms, the human condition is fundamentally marked by pathos, irony, and tragedy, to use Reinhold Niebuhr's triad.[6] Recognizing this, Niebuhr argued, is not an argument against the Christian's involvement in politics, but a warning against the dangers of a utopianism in which human pretensions masquerade as virtue. I do not share Niebuhr's conclusion that pacifism is not a legitimate Christian option.[7] But I do believe that a failure to confront Niebuhr's critique of this-worldly schemes of human perfectibility lies close to the heart of the pacifist tragedy that Lewy sketches.

Post-Niebuhrian pacifism has also been susceptible to another theological failure that, in technical terms, I would describe as a collapse of eschatology into apocalyptic.[8] The harsh reality of life under the threat of nuclear holocaust has foreshortened the horizon of moral judgment so that our times are thought to be the end times in some absolute sense. The result is that consequential criteria, practical reason, and the virtue of prudence are deemed of little or no moral account when judgments are made about world politics. During the nuclear-freeze debate of the early 1980s, for example, religious pacifists adopted survivalist language from Jonathan Schell (*The Fate of the Earth*), arguing that man's nuclear folly threatened God's sovereignty over creation. This too-easy resort to apocalyptic intensifiers overwhelmed not merely classic Christian eschatology but the rest of the Creed as well.

There is no need to marry the pacifist sense of urgency about the mortal threat under which we live and the pacifist conviction that, come what may, God's purposes will be served, to a secular apocalypticism and survivalism run riot. Yet this is precisely what the Methodist bishops of the United States did in their 1986 pastoral letter "In Defense of Creation." I take it as a sign of hope that perhaps the most trenchant critique of that particular collapse of moral imagination and Christian orthodoxy was mounted by a pacifist, the aforementioned Stanley Hauerwas.[9]

THE DIFFERENCE IT HAS MADE

While the guardians of establishment opinion on public opinion and U.S. foreign policy would almost certainly regard all of the above as a kind of alley-fight among sectarians, marginal to the larger opinion process, I would argue that these developments within pacifism have had an important impact on our public discourse, and consequently on world politics.[10] These are necessarily matters of impression rather than of statistically significant survey data, but I would judge that the dominant teachings of American pacifist agencies have had at least three crucial effects on the public debate over war and peace and America's role in world affairs.

First, they have reinforced the classic American tendency toward isolationism.

Second, they have reinforced the anti–anti-Communism of the post-Vietnam cultural and political elite.

Third, and perhaps most importantly, they have reinforced in the religious community a diminished sense of the possibilities of American leadership for peace, freedom, and security in the world.

All these reinforcements increase the difficulty of making the United States a leader in the pursuit of a world in which conflict is managed by peaceful means. The isolationist reinforcement is the most obvious barrier toward that leadership: leadership requires the United States to be actively engaged in world politics and economics, which is precisely what isolationism seeks to avoid.

Why is anti–anti-Communism a problem? Because Marxism-Leninism is incompatible with the construction of an international political community based on those democratic norms whose deepest roots lie in Jewish and Christian understandings of the human person, human society, and human destiny. And while there are intriguing empirical grounds for arguing that the Marxist-Leninist project is spent as a moral and intellectual lodestar, this does not minimize the danger that Communist states and movements still pose to the pursuit of peace and the advance of human rights.

And then there is the problem pacifists have with America. Pacifists (and others, of course) cannot teach the American people both that (a) their political community and their economy are a (if not *the*) primary source of the world's suffering, and that (b) America ought to be actively engaged in the pursuit of peace. The quite logical conclusion of blaming America first is to try to get the United States out of world politics and economics. If one denies, as a matter of principled moral and political judgment, that the United States is, in however manifestly flawed a way, still an experiment in the peace of dynamic and rightly ordered political community, then one's public task is clear: impede the impact of American policy on world politics and economics. A diminished sense of the moral importance of the American experiment in ordered liberty thus coincides, as a matter of practical politics, with neo-isolationism.

The impact of pacifist neo-isolationism and anti–anti-Communism, and pacifist disdain for the American experiment, is being felt not only in the realm of ideas but in human lives: lives in Southeast Asia, in Central America, in a dozen other conflict arenas around the world. Pacifism does not, of course, bear sole or even primary responsibility for the continuing tragedy of the boat people of the South China Sea, or for the fact that over one-fifth of the population of Nicaragua is now in exile from that unhappy land. But although rigorous pacifists may decline to apply a consequential criterion in their personal moral-political judgments, their teachings and actions do have consequences, and the responsibility for those consequences ought to be faced.

Theses for a Reformation

My theses for a pacifist reformation are considerably fewer than ninety-five. There are, in fact, five.

1. A reformed religious pacifism will be marked by a sense of theological modesty.

In an age in which the boundaries of Christian conviction seem to become ever more porous, I would be the last to urge that pacifists abandon the conviction that theirs is the more excellent way. The rigor of the pacifist conscience ought to be a considerable part of its claim to the attention of the entire Christian community.

Still, the pacifist must contend with the fact that, throughout

Christian history, his position has been a decidedly minority one.[11] To be in a minority on a matter of moral judgment does not mean to be wrong. Yet it ought to give one pause that the weight of Christian history lies so heavily in favor of the just-war tradition. In any event, pacifists should not see themselves as a community of the elect, set over against all those others who have failed to grasp the fullness of Christian truth. (The obverse of this is true, too, of course: pacifism should not be regarded by the majority of Christians who are not pacifist as the private preserve of a small band of cranky sectarians.)

The contemporary case for pacifism is best made, I believe, not by literalist appeals to certain biblical texts, but by the kind of "narrative" approach to Christian moral life developed by Stanley Hauerwas. Hauerwas argues that Christians who "live within the story of Jesus" are *already* living "within the Kingdom," and this precludes the resort to violence in the defense or pursuit of moral goods. John Howard Yoder has argued that such an approach to the moral life is most definitely not to be understood in sectarian terms. While Yoder does not satisfactorily settle the question of pacifism-and-sectarianism, I think we must take seriously the claims of Yoder and Hauerwas that pacifism need not take the Christian decisively out of the affairs of this world.

Hauerwas's pacifist theology is particularly striking in its combination of intellectual rigor, ecclesiological modesty, and political sophistication. The latter characteristic, I fear, cannot be attributed to Yoder or Duane Friesen, who seem more tempted to marry pacifist theology to mainline/oldline Protestant politics.[12] What is needed, though, is a theological dialogue in which pacifists are in forthright conversation with adherents to the just-war tradition. The purpose should be, not to find some (probably spurious) "higher viewpoint" in which differences are too easily resolved, but to foster the evolution of both traditions.

2. A reformed religious pacifism will have recovered a sense of the moral importance of democracy.

If memory serves, it was John Howard Yoder who coined the phrase "doing ethics for Caesar" as a rhetorical put-down of (among other things) the just-war tradition. Without question, that tradition has at times been used to rationalize depradations committed by the principalities and powers of this world. But no serious student will argue that this is either the intention of the tradition or the structure of its reasoning.[13] Yoder's *mot* is best considered a warning, rather than a service ace.

Moreover, is "doing ethics for Caesar" precisely the same as "doing ethics for James Madison" or his successors? The Christian holds all principalities and powers under transcendent moral judgment, to be sure. But some emerge from that scrutiny with considerably stronger claims to moral approbation than others.

The moral claims of democracy, though not absolute, ought to be especially compelling to the pacifist, since democracies are the premier example of successful non-violent conflict resolution in our world. Even under rigorous moral scrutiny, the United States, with its luxuriantly plural racial, ethnic, and religious strains, is a remarkable example of how democratic law and democratic politics can resolve conflict without the use or threat of mass violence.

The historical record also shows that developed democratic nations do not go to war against each other, preferring to settle their differences through negotiation and arbitration. The advance of democracy throughout the world is good news precisely for the cause of peace.

Unless the pacifist wishes to argue that "wars will cease when men refuse to fight"—to argue, in other words, for religious or moral conversion as the only effective means of peacemaking—the question of the political organization of peace must be forthrightly engaged. The available evidence shows that democracies do well by peace and non-violent conflict resolution, domestically and internationally, and that democracies are the most effective guarantors of those basic human rights with which pacifists are justifiably concerned (including the right of conscientious objection to military service). These facts ought to bear on the moral evaluation of democracy by pacifists, and might even lead some pacifist theologians to construct a pacifist moral defense of democracy.

3. A reformed pacifism will develop a new style of religious "witness" in the public arena.

"Witness politics" today means left-liberal political posturing far more that it means public actions that testify to those transcendent moral norms by which politics ought to be judged. When a convent of nuns in Michigan declares itself a "nuclear free zone" and sends a notice of its "witness statement" to the local Associated Press stringer,[14] we may be reasonably sure that what is going on here is not religious witnessing to the truth that makes us free. Yet these Dominicans are not alone in their well-intentioned, if pathetic, adoption of such tactics. The hard truth is that declaring a convent a nuclear-free zone is more a typical than a marginal expression of what is often thought to be "religious witness" today.

Although some American pacifists have resisted the Gadarene rush to the politics of the cost-free gesture, "witness" actions against nuclear weapons and U.S. policy in Central America have become a staple of religious activism in the 1980s. However we judge their moral persuasiveness or political integrity, though, we should all acknowledge that we lack a *concept* of "religious witness" that can withstand the ever-present danger of identifying the fullness of religious and moral truth with one's prudential political judgments (on MX missiles, *contra* supplies, or whatever). Even to sketch such a concept is beyond the scope of this essay, but a few markers can be laid down.

a. First, a true "religious witness" takes as its primary theological intention the affirmation of God's sovereignty over all creation. It does not root itself theologically in tendentious readings of the Sermon on the Mount, nor does it assume that the evangelical counsels can be applied in one-to-one correspondence to the exigencies of public life. Thomas Merton put it well when he wrote that "non-violence [and, by extension, all true religious witness] is not primarily the language of efficiency but the language of *kairos* [conversion]. It does not say, 'We shall overcome,' so much as, 'This is the day of the Lord, and whatever may happen to us, He shall overcome.' "[15]

b. The second theological task of a true "religious witness" is to stand as a reminder that the Kingdom of God will come in God's time, not our own, and is ultimately a work of God's hands, not ours. In this sense, religious witness is the eschatological prod to the community of faith and conscience that is the Church, and through the Church to the wider public arena. The Kingdom enters our lives, not as an instruction kit for mundane policymaking, but as a horizon toward which human history is pointed and against which the present moment (with its myriad political failures) is measured.

This witness to the Kingdom is sullied, often beyond recognition, when it is confused with the making of policy judgments that, according to classic Christian moral understandings, must be guided primarily by the virtue of prudence. The pacifist engaging in religious witness plays a vital role in reminding the wider religious community that "prudence" can degenerate into excuse-making for the status quo. But that is a debasement of prudence, the moral skill that allows us to work for change in and among nations without making matters worse than they already are. As such, it is a virtue that ought to be affirmed, and indeed celebrated, by pacifists.

c. As for the public character of "religious witness": civil disobedience, properly understood, has a long and honored tradition in both Christian social ethics and American democratic theory. By "properly understood" I mean civil disobedience that affirms the rule of law, is aimed at changing unjust laws rather than at sedition or anarchy, accepts the legal consequences of the action, and is intended to call the republic to an awareness of its failure to incarnate, in law and policy, a truth it holds in principle. The strategies and tactics pioneered by Bayard Rustin and Martin Luther King, Jr., in the 1950s and early 1960s fit this pattern; the theory and practice of civil disobedience exemplified by the leadership of the sanctuary movement today does not.

d. Further, a genuine "witness for peace" must address the use of violence by all parties in a conflict, not just the violence of those deemed the "oppressors." When the members of Witness for Peace act against U.S. policy in Nicaragua but fail to address the question of Sandinista responsibility for Nicara-

guan civil war, what they are bearing witness to is not peace but
Sandinista policy. When religious activists strike out against
U.S. nuclear force modernizations but fail to address, even
rhetorically, the Soviet military build-up, what they are bearing
witness to is not peace but a particular view of the dynamics of
international politics. To those who respond, as happened so
often during Vietnam, that "it is our responsibility to confront
our government," the appropriate answer is that our address to
our government inevitably has its impact on the calculations of
other states. A true "witness" addresses the full range of the
problem in question, not simply one of its parts.

e. In practical terms, I believe that these considerations require pacifists, if they claim to draw solely upon pacifist moral
warrants, to eschew military prescriptions. Pacifism diminishes
its witness when it engages in lobbying about weapons systems:
one cannot reject the legitimacy of the resort to armed force and
at the same time try to design the structure of America's armed
forces. The pacifist who argues, on pacifist grounds, for six
carrier battle groups rather than twelve, or for C-4 rather than
D-5 missiles for Trident submarines, is demeaning "religious
witness" and confusing the public-policy debate. Here Yoder's
warnings about "doing ethics for Caesar" might be more appropriately addressed to Yoder's pacifist brethren.

There is a wide scope for pacifists to engage in the debate
over the right ordering of international public life, in ways
congruent with pacifist understandings. Pacifists should be in
the forefront of efforts to reform today's decayed and debased
international legal and political institutions. (Why shouldn't
pacifists have led, rather than resisted, the attempt to reform
UNESCO?) Pacifists should be, as some have been, vigorous
defenders of religious liberty for persecuted believers. Pacifists
should support non-violent resistance in a host of situations. But
a pacifism that urges non-violent resistance in Chile and Para-
guay while failing to see its importance in Czechoslovakia and
Nicaragua has formed its witness by what Bonhoeffer aptly
called "cheap grace." A pacifism that holds to a single standard
on human-rights issues not only is more morally intelligible but
also serves to remind government officials that this single stan-

dard is what the United States is committed to, even when circumstances make it difficult to act on that standard.

4. A reformed pacifism will forthrightly and unambiguously reject the Marxist-Leninist project and its inherent violence.

This was once bedrock doctrine in American religious pacifism; Guenter Lewy amply demonstrates that it is no longer. We now find ourselves in the bizarre situation in which Mikhail Gorbachev is saying tougher things about the Soviet system than some American pacifists of the past generation have been able to bring themselves to say. The pacifist absorption of the New Left current of anti–anti-Communism has been particularly distressing, given the unarguable fact that Marxism-Leninism has been the most systematically brutal political force in the twentieth century.

At the level of political and economic theory, much less moral theology, those who have not yet been convinced to date of the failure of Marxism-Leninism are probably beyond hope of conversion. I do not think American pacifists fall, in the main, into that category of invincible ignorance. But American pacifism, with some notable exceptions, has been slow to seize the opportunity presented by the emergence in Eastern and Central Europe, and indeed in the USSR itself, of an independent peace movement—sometimes informed by the pacifist conscience and sometimes not—for which the right of conscientious objection to military service is a priority. Here, then, is a grand opportunity for coalition-building across the iron curtain. Whether that opportunity will be seized will tell us much about the degree to which American pacifism has rethought its approach to Communism. So will, of course, the future pattern of pacifist activism on Nicaragua, where an avowedly Marxist-Leninist regime is trying to consolidate its power.

5. A reformed pacifism will have disentangled itself from the politics of the Rainbow Coalition and be hard to locate in a standard ideological slot.

There is no reason why pacifists should find their primary political allies in the forces of the New Left and related points on the American political spectrum. What is now assumed to be a natural affinity is really the result of the ideological deconstruction that Guenter Lewy believes American pacifism has suffered over the past generation.

There is no necessary reason why pacifists as pacifists should support racial quotas, and the consequent Balkanization of American life; why they should not be at the front of welfare-reform efforts that emphasize character development; why they should support the feminist agenda as defined by NOW and Molly Yard; or why they should not be leaders in the movement to marry international education to a reformed civic education in our schools. There is also no reason why pacifists as pacifists should indulge in Tercermundismo, anti–anti-Communism, and blaming America first.

An attempt has been made to construct a new moral/political coalition around Cardinal Joseph Bernardin's image of the "seamless garment" of "life issues," or as the cardinal puts it, around a "consistent ethic of life." The coalition, called Just-Life, includes a number of prominent pacifists. Unhappily, JustLife's 1988 voters' guide is as egregious an exercise in theological and political confusion as similar efforts by the religious New Right to create "biblical" scorecards for assessing congressional candidates. This is not the direction in which a reformed pacifism should be marching.

What that direction is, I leave for pacifists to define. A pacifism truly committed to religious, moral, and political renewal will broaden considerably the ideological range of its interlocutors. I doubt that there will ever be any one "pacifist approach" to public policy, domestic or international. But I suspect that I can make a fair guess at the seriousness of such efforts by the difficulty I will have in placing them in the regnant media-generated left/right pigeonholes.

Will It Happen?

Will there be a pacifist reformation in America? I doubt it. The reception given to Guenter Lewy's study does not suggest that the chief pacifist organizations are ready to engage in the radical self-criticism that is essential to their reform. Men and women of conviction and honor will continue to work in these organizations, calling them back to their fundamental principles. But these men and women will most probably remain an embattled minority. I say that, not with any sense of satisfaction, but with a sense of sadness.

Why, then, bother to write this essay? Because pacifism is here to stay. If its time of reformation is not now, then perhaps what we do now will be helpful to those who come after us. The pacifists of the twenty-first century ought to know that such men as Alfred Hassler, Daniel Seeger, Robert Pickus, Gordon Zahn, and Stanley Hauerwas have modeled an alternative. Such persons, and doubtless hundreds of others like them, ought to be supported in their efforts to call American religious pacifism back to its originating moral insights. I choose to stand with them in their fight (if such it may be deemed). They should be supported because the cause of peace and freedom requires it— but most of all because the cause of the Gospel requires it. And that is what is most fundamentally at stake in the reformation of Christian pacifism in America.

3

An Attempt to Silence Pacifists

John N. Swomley

A LTHOUGH Guenter Lewy raises some important points that should be duly considered, it is difficult for me to take his attack on pacifist organizations seriously. He omits important material that does not support his thesis, quotes out of context, distorts major pacifist decisions, and in general uses a "smear" technique unworthy of a person with academic credentials. My judgments are based largely on my analysis of what he says about the Fellowship of Reconciliation (FOR), an organization in which I have been active for fifty years.

1. Lewy uses extreme statements that cannot be based on any research. For example, "Despite all this negative publicity [about Cuba], most American pacifists appear to have remained loyal to Castro." How many of the more than 100,000 American pacifists did he interview? And what does "loyal" mean? He tells us nothing except to give some adulatory quotations from one mimeographed statement by a short-term pacifist executive. He omits references to pacifist articles critical of Castro, including some that also contain positive statements about some Cuban achievements.

John N. Swomley is professor emeritus of social ethics at St. Paul School of Theology, Kansas City, Missouri. His book entitled *Liberation Ethics* (1972) analyzes revolution and violence from a pacifist perspective.

Lewy says: "In a rare instance of candor, *Fellowship*, the magazine of the FOR, recently opened its pages to an American official of Amnesty International (AI) who accused Vietnamese military and civilian officials of playing a role in political arrests and torture. . . ." Either he did not examine or he preferred to ignore the numerous reports in *Fellowship* over the years since the war; the subjects of these included arrests of Buddhists reported by AI (July-August 1978), the torture of Buddhist monks (November 1978), Hanoi's "systematic expulsion" of people, creating more than 42,000 refugees known as "boat people" (September 1979), and a letter from exiled Buddhist leaders in Paris that commended AI and the International Fellowship of Reconciliation for their intervention in the release of four Buddhist leaders and listed thirty-seven monks still in detention (March 1979).

Lewy writes: "All the major pacifist organizations had gradually come to support the armed struggle of the National Liberation Front of South Vietnam." Neither in logic nor in fact does opposition to U.S. intervention in Vietnam or a belief that the Vietnamese should determine their own destiny lead to a conclusion that pacifists supported armed struggle as a method.

2. Lewy misrepresents the statement "Violence and the United States," adopted in 1970 by the FOR National Council, which he says "reflected the bitterness, extremist language, and New Left vocabulary of the radical anti-war movement of which the FOR had become an integral part." In discussing the statement he omits its crucial part; this could only be deliberate. That statement begins with these sentences:

> The major violence of American society today is that practiced by the government of the United States against the people of Southeast Asia in a war suddenly escalated again by the invasion of Cambodia, and the resumption of air strikes against North Vietnam. There is no domestic violence taking place within the United States—however extreme or critical it may be—that can compare with the daily annihilation of Vietnamese, Cambodians, and Laotians by B-52 raids, massive artillery fire, search and destroy missions, and direct massacres of villagers by U.S. troops and their allies.

The statement refers to "oppressive police, right wing, and racist practices" in the United States, such as "police killings of black people in Augusta and at Jackson State College in Mississippi and the National Guard killings at Kent State University," as "recent examples." It then asserts, "It is such government-supported violence against *people* by which violence done to property must be measured." There was reference to students' burning of a branch of the Bank of America in Santa Barbara as a "mild act of violence in comparison with, for example, the dropping of 12,000 tons of bombs on South Vietnam by the American high command."

Lewy, in summarizing and quoting from that statement, characterized it as one of "indulgence for revolutionary violence." He could do this only by omitting the next few crucial sentences:

Yet the rhetoric and practice of violence—even when the violence done is simply against property—can lead to increased violence. The use of bombs against vacant edifices of injustice can escalate to the use of bombs against certain unjust people, which can in turn lead to the massive use of bombs against populations in war. . . . Thus the practitioners and justifiers of violence must be seen on a continuum at the end of which are the very war criminals of our own society.

After this unethical omission of the heart of the statement, Lewy castigates as a "lame afterthought" the conclusion of the statement: "We deplore any apology for violence used for any ends, however good they may be."

3. Lewy distorts and misconstrues measures taken by the FOR National Council in dealing with ideological differences among senior members of the FOR staff. Alfred Hassler, FOR executive secretary, proposed endorsing an end to the war in Vietnam by a ceasefire and negotiated withdrawal of U.S. forces to ease the transition to an independent Vietnam. Allan Brick and Ron Young wanted an immediate unilateral withdrawal of U.S. troops, which Lewy characterizes as an effort to give North Vietnam victory. Lewy asserts that the FOR National Council did not confront "the basic issues of principle and strategy that divided the FOR" and that "a majority of the Council had agreed to dismiss Hassler." This is simply not true.

As Hassler's predecessor, I had decided in 1960, when I left the FOR staff, not to serve on the National Council so as not to appear to be influencing his decisions. In late 1970 Hassler called me to say that he needed help in dealing with staff differences in ideology and asked if I would run for election to the Council. I was elected in 1971.

During the 1971 council meeting, in a fifteen-hour executive session, we decided not to dismiss anyone from the staff and acknowledged that "there is room for a variety of program thrusts." There was no repudiation of Hassler or his ideology. We decided that, since he was three and a half years from the normal retirement age, we would search for a co-secretary who would meet two needs. One was to put less emphasis on political anti-war activity and more on work with churches and religious organizations. The second was to bridge and heal "the clash of personalities" (Lewy's phrase) by bringing in someone not involved in the staff decision. I was made chairman of the search committee and Hassler was *ex officio* on the committee. I wrote Hassler in November 1972 that we did not expect him to adhere to a legalistic interpretation of the retirement age, saying, "It may be that you ought to continue longer than that if we have not resolved some of our problems." Brick and Young had sent letters of resignation to Hassler in early 1972.

Hassler decided to retire in the summer of 1974, and Barton Hunter was chosen as executive secretary, with Hassler's full approval. The two were in basic ideological agreement.

The 1971 council meeting also adopted policies within which all staff would be expected to work. Those policies clearly repudiated any identification of the FOR "with any war-making activity" and rejected any "idea that we seek either a ceasefire or a complete withdrawal in order that the North Vietnamese and/or the National Liberation Front or the Saigon government shall win a military or political victory."

Lewy's conclusion, contrary to fact, is that "the politics of the FOR became virtually indistinguishable" from other groups that "defend the moral legitimacy of armed struggle." Lewy has read the council minutes, was aware of the fifteen hours of executive session, but never checked his interpretation with Robert Moon, the council chairperson, or with me. This is unheard of in responsible research. In short, he distorted what happened so as to sustain his thesis.

4. Lewy commends Gordon Zahn, "one of the few leading members of the FOR to express his unease over the new indulgence of revolutionary violence." He claims that Zahn's essay in the June 1977 *Fellowship* "had been subjected to criticism by two authors" who reflected the "political preferences of the journal's editor" and "the strength and support that these rival positions had achieved in the FOR." Lewy, again, does not give an accurate picture either of the *Fellowship* editor's "political preferences" or of the response to Zahn's article.

The editor, Richard Chartier, is thoroughly committed to nonviolence, and did not choose authors who espoused violence. I was one of the two authors Lewy did not name. I called Zahn's article "an excellent statement of the case against acceptance of the violence of liberation movements" and said, "With the main thrust of his article I have no disagreement." However, I said that "moral outrage will not suffice" and suggested the need for a "convincing analysis and strategy for achieving liberation" without violence. My article included an outline of such an analysis and strategy.

In my comment on Zahn's article, I said that "my opposition to violence does not mean that we should be neutral in the struggle between the oppressed and their oppressors when both are using violence." I cited the example of the Hungarians' use of violence in 1956 to gain freedom from Soviet control, and insisted that I wanted them to gain their independence. Does Lewy, who is very anti-Soviet, think that I should have no moral preference or desire for Hungarian freedom?

Lewy apparently sees no distinction between a moral desire that an oppressed or colonial people gain their freedom, and support for the methods they use in seeking that freedom. In other words, he appears to be asking pacifists by silence to consent to the superior power of the oppressor. Thus by implication he asks pacifists to condone left-wing as well as right-wing oppression.

A. J. Muste in a 1928 essay wrote that we should not preach

"non-violence to the underdog unless and until we have dealt adequately with the dog who is chewing him up." Speaking of World War I, Muste added: "No absolutist pacifist in America would have felt justified in exhorting Germany to lay down its arms while saying and doing nothing about America's belligerent activities. We should have recognized instantly the moral absurdity, the implied hypocrisy of such a position. Our duty was to win our own 'side' to a 'more excellent way.' "

In Central America, American pacifists ought not to oppose Nicaragua's defense against the *contras* while remaining silent about the CIA-sponsored violence. To do so is to condone the U.S. war against Nicaragua while telling Nicaraguans they alone are wrong in using violence. On the other hand, it is important for Americans to go to Nicaragua to demonstrate, with more than talk, the use of non-violence against the *contras*; this they can do by standing unarmed vigil on borders or in peasant communities, as many pacifists have done. Regrettably, Lewy disapproves of such non-violence; he attacks the FOR for supporting "Witness for Peace," members of which, he said, stood on the Honduran border "in order to provide a protective shield for the people of Nicaragua against *contra* attacks."

It is also important, wherever possible, to discuss with government personnel and citizens the theory and practice of non-violence, as I have done in Nicaragua, and as I did in Prague with representatives of the NLF during the war in Vietnam.

Pacifists must not fall into the ideological trap Lewy has set for us in this book: Pacifists believe violence is always wrong; therefore they can never espouse the cause of any oppressed people who use violence; however, when the United States uses violence to maintain control or oppression, "the proper course for [the pacifist] is to remain silent." In other words, Lewy is proposing a course that is ideologically functional in maintaining and expanding U.S. military or other control over Third World countries.

5. Lewy professes to have respect for pacifists and their leaders as they were prior to the war in Vietnam but claims they changed their principles during that war. This too is a mispercep-

tion. There have been at least four main streams of pacifist thought and action in American history. The first, non-resistance to evil except for personal refusal to participate in war, has been held historically by Mennonites, Amish, Dunkard Brethren, and some other groups. Adherents to that kind of pacifism, which Lewy obviously believes is valid pacifism, generally did not engage in legislative or electoral politics or in public protest about foreign policy.

The second type was exemplified by Quakers who served as legislators and governors and in other political roles in Colonial America and subsequently.

The third type, in which the Quakers also engaged, is non-violent resistance, including civil disobedience, refusal to pay taxes, public demonstrations, and other radical activity. Their action against established churches, the swearing of oaths, and military service, and their aid to runaway slaves through their underground railroad, is so evident in history that Lewy's overlooking this type of pacifism is a serious failure in research and reporting.

A fourth type was different only in degree from such non-violent resistance. Henry David Thoreau, who inspired Gandhi, added the dimension of revolutionary non-violence to achieve justice and good government. He wrote in his "Essay on Civil Disobedience" that a minority "is irresistible when it clogs by its own weight."

All these types of pacifism have been practiced to a greater or lesser degree for more than a hundred years by "peace churches," abolitionists, prohibitionists, some labor unions, anti-war and anti–civil-defense movements, and blacks and whites demanding civil rights.

Lewy, who is a German Jewish immigrant, could be unfamiliar with Christian pacifist resistance in early America; or perhaps he simply failed to do adequate historical research. A third possibility is that he has a bias so great that it leads him to ignore any interpretation other than his own as to what pacifists should do and think.

The Vietnam war was so clearly a manifestation of a great power's seeking to control a small country by chemical poison, saturation or serial bombing, terrorism, and barbaric brutality that even American soldiers engaged in "fragging" (shooting their own officers). Even without the help of the news media, many soldiers were informing the people back home of their opposition to continuation of the war. It was almost inevitable that hundreds of thousands of Americans, some of them led by pacifists, should revolt against that war, and hold different positions on how it should be ended. Lewy's simplistic analysis neglects and is insensitive to the political atmosphere in the United States at the time.

Pacifist action against that war was not different in kind from pacifist action in earlier centuries or even following World War II. What was different was the larger number of people who accepted militant pacifist leadership and who also did not follow those who urged violence on the American scene.

If Lewy had thoroughly analyzed pacifist history, he would also have known that the diversity of views about "enemies" and political tactics that he criticizes during the Vietnam war was not unique to that war but was evident during the U.S. War of Independence, the Mexican War, the Civil War, and earlier wars against Central American nations. Unlike Communism and Fascism, pacifism is not marked by obedience to a party line; it welcomes diversity and dialogue. There will always be pacifists who do not seem "typical," or whose failure to keep silence will irritate those who justify invading other sovereign nations.

6. Lewy says pacifists "praise and support the Communist regimes emerging from [armed] conflicts." He supports this blatantly unjust McCarthyist type of blame only by selective quotations from some pacifists during the war in Vietnam and by statements taken out of context. Lewy overlooks pacifist support during the Vietnam war of the non-violent resistance by Czechoslovakia to the Soviet invasion and to the suppression of Czech efforts to gain internal freedom. He also overlooks subsequent pacifist contacts with Soviet and Hungarian "dissidents," the critical dialogue pacifists have had with the Soviet Peace Committee about Afghanistan, the leafleting in Moscow's Red Square by U.S. pacifists critical of Soviet violence, and other similar actions.

A good illustration of Lewy's selective out-of-context statements is his description of A. J. Muste's organization of "the American Forum for Socialist Education, which brought together Communists and non-Communists in a series of conferences." What Lewy didn't report was a previous series of dialogues between five pacifist leaders and five top Communists over a period of two years, as a result of which three of the Communist participants decided to leave the Communist party. Muste and I, as FOR executive secretary, arranged the dialogues, which took place in his and my apartments.

The American Forum for Socialist Education was Muste's response to a statement by John Gates, editor of the *Daily Worker*, that the three did not want their exit from the Party to be interpreted as a betrayal of all forms of socialism and a retreat into reactionary politics. Muste, a person of integrity, never publicly announced that the Forum was a face-saving device for those leaving the Party. He also hoped that others would leave the Party and form a new democratic socialist organization. This never happened; the idea did not get off the ground, and the Forum was abandoned after a two-year trial. Although I decided not to support the Forum, I defended Muste's integrity in setting it up when Norman Thomas and Roger Baldwin came to talk with me about it. Good research would have noted the absence of my involvement and led to questions why.

7. Another flaw in Lewy's analysis is his view that all pacifists must be strongly anti-Communist to be adjudged pacifists of integrity. His book is full of the dangers of silence about Communism, but is strangely silent about the dangers of open or tacit support of right-wing dictatorships.

Lewy uses the term "Communism" and assertions about collaboration with Communists very loosely. For example, he said "the AFSC [American Friends Service Committee] decided to seek allies wherever it could, and that included the Soviet Peace Committee and the World Peace Council." I wrote in the margin of the page at this point: "When, where, and by whom was the decision made?" Lewy doesn't tell us. Nor does he define the term "allies" except in saying that one staff member was an "observer" at a World Peace Council meeting and urged future attendance in order to "challenge them in the area of values and commitment at the very center of their ideological justification for violent struggle." This is not the usual definition of "ally"!

Lewy would apparently object to FOR discussions with the Soviet Peace Committee about efforts to gain recognition for conscientious objectors in the Soviet Union, or other forms of purposeful contact. In 1966 Heinz Kloppenburg, the West German FOR secretary, and I initiated discussions with the Communist secretary in charge of church affairs in East Germany to get permission for West German churches to send religious books and periodicals regularly into East Germany. We succeeded. Was it wrong to try, and could Lewy with his hostility to Communists and to any contact with Communists have done as well? Do I misread Lewy in believing that he thinks pacifists and others should not treat Communists with the respect normally given to human beings with whom one disagrees?

8. Lewy indicates that "there is no such thing as a political position that is truly pacifist" and quotes Niebuhr as saying that when pacifists propose political alternatives to the existing political order, they invariably betray themselves into a preference for tyranny. Otherwise Lewy believes they are politically irrelevant.

Lewy forgets that a pacifist-led campaign in India was the catalyst for non-violent campaigns in numerous countries that led to the end of colonialism for more than a billion people, without violence. American and British pacifists participated in some of those campaigns. He forgets also the civil-rights campaign led by FOR members, of whom Martin Luther King, Jr., was one. That campaign accomplished major political changes in the opposite direction from tyranny. Could Lewy or Niebuhr have done as well by their methods? FOR members in the Philippines, including visiting American members, had for more than a decade been organizing and educating for the non-violent overthrow of the Marcos dictatorship. Was this a mistake when it actually happened? It was certainly a surprise to many of us who had been involved, because we do not view pacifism as necessarily or even usually successful.

Lewy is too interested in discrediting pacifism to acknowledge these and other important political contributions of pacifist groups.

9. The charge that the FOR did not immediately plunge into an effort to protest civil-liberties violations in Vietnam after the war is, in part, accurate. It was not, however, because of the "dominance of New Left ideology in the Fellowship," as Lewy charges, but for three other reasons. First, the FOR decided as the war ended to concentrate on other issues. Second, it also wanted to put the controversy over Vietnam to rest. (Jim Forest, as Lewy indicates, apparently decided unilaterally to raise post-war issues, without seeking advance staff or council approval.) Third, in the confused post-war period there were conflicting reports about the internal actions of the Vietnam government. Therefore the FOR staff, as Lewy notes, decided—perhaps too cautiously—to ask Amnesty International "to explore the truth or falsity of the allegations being made."

Unlike some to whom Lewy referred, most of the FOR Council had no illusions about the Vietnam government; it was clearly totalitarian. Nor did we expect it to act as a civil-liberties model. When the evidence became clear to more than those who had direct contact with Buddhist monks in Paris, the FOR did work to gain release of prisoners and for the end of torture.

Organizations, even small ones, never work as efficiently or achieve goals as lofty as their leaders and members would like. One of my own regrets is that the public furor over the Vietnam war and the conflicting views among FOR staff did not permit the kind of closer and continuing relationship with the Buddhists of Vietnam that Al Hassler urged and many of us wanted. The Buddhists have been more consistently vocal for peace than Christians and Jews over the years, although that record is flawed in some countries.

I conclude with certain generalizations about the FOR, in which for some years I have had no official position. All representatives of the FOR during the Vietnam period held to pacifism and non-violence as our central position; all agreed that we are opposed to totalitarianism of both right and left. The FOR is a religious fellowship rather than a political movement, and therefore could not accept either a "New Left" or an anti-Communist or an anti–anti-Communist label. However divided people in or out of the FOR have been or may be, it is central to our faith that we respect individual personality and work for political arrangements that permit freedom of speech, religion, assembly, and conscience.

There is no evidence since the war that either the FOR staff or the Council has departed from our central positions of non-violence and reconciliation, no evidence of support for totalitarian governments or for the assumption that authoritarian governments are good, just, or free from the structural violence that exists everywhere in the world. I did not check Lewy's references to other organizations as I did his generalizations about the FOR. In general I regret that he paid no attention to the Buddhist, Catholic, Jewish, and various Protestant denominational pacifist fellowships that are key parts of the FOR. I hope this was not an intentional omission because he could not find among them illustrations of his thesis.

My primary concern is not to defend the FOR but to demand accuracy and integrity in publication. I have my own criticisms of the FOR and other pacifist groups, which I share with them from time to time. The FOR will not live or grow or die because of attacks from defenders of U.S. military policy. Its future depends on its commitment to its reason for existence and on creative action and education.

If Lewy's book assists in the FOR's self-examination and self-criticism, I will consider that a net gain. I regret that it was written not to be helpful to the pacifist organizations in their self-examination but as part of a continuing attack by someone who wants to "silence" pacifists on the major issues of U.S. foreign and military policy.

4

At Ease With Violence?

James Finn

THE HISTORY of peace movements reveals a recurring pattern. In periods of relative peace, pacifists are a numerically small group of principled people who cultivate their conceptual gardens with little public attention. When noticed, they are generally praised for their witness for peace, their moral integrity, and their active concern for the destitute, but they are more admired than emulated.

As war threatens, however, pacifists gain converts and sympathizers, and—at some costs to conceptual purity—the "peace" camp grows. But when war actually breaks out, people are moved to support their country's declared cause and the peace ranks shrink. As the war winds down, the pacifists are gradually reduced to their former status of principled, admired, but marginalized dissenters from the national consensus on the use of armed force.

This pattern seemed to be developing in the sixties as the United States became ever more deeply engaged in the conflict in Vietnam. As the "peace movement" expanded in numbers and influence, long-standing pacifist organizations were perceived as valuable resources. They provided meeting places, reading material, seasoned counseling, communal support, and reasoned analyses of the conflict at hand. But, unlike past

James Finn is editorial director of Freedom House in New York City, editor of its magazine *Freedom at Issue*, and the author of *Protest: Pacifism and Politics*.

American peace movements that had contracted as the U.S. engagement increased, the movement inspired by the war in Vietnam continued to grow as the conflict grew. Pacifists and their organizations became a significant component of the movement that strove to halt the war.

As the war ended, the anti-war movement broke up into its various components: pacifists, political "realists," summer soldiers, and ideological partisans. But—at least if we concur with the findings of Guenter Lewy—in the case of the pacifists the anticipated pattern did not fulfill itself. Pacifists did not return to their former status. The major pacifist organizations had been traveling on a two-way street. They not only had contributed to the anti-war movement but also had absorbed into themselves some elements of the movement that would previously have been regarded as alien to the pacifist spirit.

Lewy makes the charge in his opening sentences:

> Over the past twenty years pacifism has undergone a remarkable transformation. While at one time pacifists were single-mindedly devoted to the principles of non-violence and reconciliation, today most pacifist groups defend the moral legitimacy of armed struggle and guerrilla warfare, and they praise and support the Communist regimes emerging from such conflicts.

Later he asserts, "The ideological assumptions which led American pacifists to become closely enmeshed with the radical anti-war movement and to support revolutionary violence still govern the political thinking of the major pacifist organizations." The importance of this is that "together with allies in the churches and numerous church-related social action groups, American pacifists today constitute a potent grass-roots network that can mobilize substantial voter sentiment and at times have considerable impact on Congress."

What Is Pacifism?

I am persuaded that Lewy's principal contentions are correct, but on one major point I—and a number of pacifists, I am sure— differ with him. It is a point that is bound to bedevil the argument, as Lewy himself is quite aware. The question is what we mean when we speak of pacifism. Lewy characterizes pacifism as "the doctrine of those who are morally opposed to bearing arms and who refuse to sanction war for any purpose, defensive or otherwise." We must distinguish pacifism, he says, from "the views and efforts of those who are engaged in organized endeavors to prevent war."

Perhaps Lewy has the right to define pacifism as he intends to use the term in his study, but it can also be argued—more convincingly, I believe—that pacifists and pacifist organizations have the right to say how they understand the term under whose banner they operate. Lewy's definition is a common one that many non-pacifists readily accept. But for many pacifists, the refusal either to bear arms or to sanction the use of armed force represents only the negative, if essential, aspect of their position. There is also a positive component: the effort to prevent war, to diminish and alleviate its horrors when it takes place, and to heal the wounds and reconcile the warring parties after it ends.[1] The effort to inhibit armed conflict may include, as the American Friends Service Committee puts it, making "common cause with those who are oppressed."

For a number of pacifists this positive element is not merely an appealing adornment but an integral part of their belief. Ideally, these negative and positive aspects would run in tandem. Alas, in the real world they sometimes pull in different directions. And even if one does not accept Lewy's definition of pacifism, one must ask whether these positive elements have subverted the necessary negative element of pacifism. Those who thoroughly disagree with Lewy will dismiss or attempt to refute his evidence.

Those of us who agree with a great part of what he says must have a different agenda. We must first try to understand why and how the transformation took place, then ask what can be done to counteract or at least challenge the harmful consequences of that change.

HOW THE SIXTIES AFFECTED PACIFISM

I believe it is possible, though not simple, to identify the principal forces that transformed self-proclaimed pacifists into post-war partisans of causes, regimes, and leaders that support armed violence. (It is not accidental, as good Marxists might say, that a number of these regimes and leaders are inimical to the United States and its interests.) The wellspring of those forces must be found in the period we have agreed to call the sixties, though it does not correspond exactly with that chronological decade. The central event was, of course, the war in Vietnam, but a number of other social forces are relevant to our analysis.

In the mid-sixties, many people asserted that what came to be called the Movement should embrace both the fight for civil rights and the fight against the war. Some people also thought that the tactics and lessons learned in the civil-rights struggle could be applied in the anti-war protest. The early days of the civil-rights movement, when the non-violent resistance of young people roused the national conscience, and black and white worked closely together, set a high-water mark of politically effective idealism. Membership of civil-rights groups, religiously inspired groups, and peace organizations frequently overlapped. The various groups inspired and learned from one another.

Losing Faith in Non-Violence

But as the growing Movement met greater resistance, faith in non-violence declined. Rap Brown declared violence to be as American as apple pie, Stokely Carmichael called for the "execution" of white people in the streets of the United States, and Martin Luther King, Jr., not long before his assassination, declared the United States the greatest purveyor of violence in the world. The principal resistance to the civil-rights movement and the strongest opposition to the anti-war movement were thought to be lodged in the same place—the governing structures of the United States. The "system" was at fault and the system must be changed. If non-violent means would not do it, then other measures must be found.

And now the learning process was, in a sense, reversed. Where previously advocates of non-violence had drawn others into their ranks, now the audience for the gospel of violence included pacifists and pacifist sympathizers active in the civil-rights and anti-war movement. Because there were shared goals, those who rejected violent means were often reluctant to criticize those who accepted them. And there were long and passionate debates about what constitutes violence, which tactics were acceptable and which not, and to what degree pacifists should cooperate with other groups. As often happens, there were fewer people in the two polar groups—absolute pacifists and hawks—than at points in between.

A related stream that fed into the discussion of violence had to do with other countries deemed to be in a "pre-revolutionary condition." Since, the argument went, the oppressed in these countries were attempting to throw off an oppressive yoke, those who wished to side with the oppressed should support their revolutionary efforts. But for the pacifist, the inevitable question arose: Can I side with those who adopt the ways of violence?

I put this question to A. J. Muste, a preeminent pacifist leader, not long before his death in 1967. He said his position was that you could not be truly non-violent if you weren't a revolutionary, because you would otherwise be condoning oppressive structures; you could not be truly revolutionary if you weren't a pacifist, because violent responses would be likely to lead to another oppressive structure.

When I resisted this, pointing out that in the world as it existed, to be on the side of revolution was necessarily to side with people who used violent means, he agreed. He added that since he believed the United States was "the main obstacle to peace and human development," he felt closer to those who radically combatted U.S. military policy. Clearly Muste believed that his pacifism not only did not preclude such political judgments but in fact led to them. This strained application of pacifism was embraced by many self-labeled pacifists in the Movement.

Lessons for Democrats and Students

There was more than one way to oppose the war in Vietnam, and one of them was to mount a domestic offensive against those political leaders responsible for the war, the liberal Democrats. They should be purged from the Democratic party, which should be returned to office only after it had undergone the necessary political catharsis. In immediate, practical terms, this meant ensuring the defeat of presidential candidate Hubert H. Humphrey. It did not matter that the alternative, the winning candidate, would be Richard Nixon, who had been the *bête noire* of those on the left for many years.

Many students in the sixties received a most potent set of lessons. Political and civil leadership, they were taught, was corrupt and undependable. They themselves were members of the brightest and most honest generation to have graced this country. When tested, the structures of authority established by their elders rang hollow. The war in which their generation was enlisted was bad in itself and the product of an oppressive system.

The result of those lessons was that in resisting the draft and opposing the war, these students were able to combine moral outrage with self-interest, a heady mixture. It happened also that this body of students was part of a prominent bulge in the demographic charts. They represented a higher proportion of the population than their age-group normally did. Their sheer numbers added greatly to their social power.

To assess the impact of the sixties on pacifism, these and other social forces—for example, the development of pacifism within Catholicism, the growing revolutionary impulses in South America—must be kept in mind. Simply to mention them, as I have done, is to omit the overheated political climate in which they were discussed and the passion that participants brought to them. This period frequently joined pacifists to violent revolutionaries and political ideologues, and separated pacifists from other pacifists. All did not march to the same drummer. Nor do they now.

The System as the Oppressor

How do all these observations relate to Guenter Lewy's thesis? Directly. In foreign affairs, the temptation of people on the right has been to focus on the role of the Soviet Union in fomenting national dissent and revolution and to overlook or minimize causes indigenous to particular countries. The temptation of people on the left is to see the "system"—and the

United States as its principal agent—as the oppressor, and national revolutionaries as the virtuous oppressed. Pacifists and peace organizations tend to be on the left. The sixties made it even more difficult for them to resist their natural temptation, and many of them succumbed. Much of what we see on the pacifist scene today has its roots in that tangled period, an assertion for which Lewy provides much of the evidence.

While recognizing the wide range of pacifist belief and practice, one can say that many pacifists see their work in highly politicized terms. After the war in Vietnam they refused to criticize the absolute horrors the Vietnamese visited upon their own people, even when the available evidence was beyond reasonable dispute. Some pacifists retain to this day the ability to explain, in the most principled way, their decision to withhold criticism of Vietnam even as they lavish criticism on the United States. Such pacifists are active in the major organizations that Lewy examined, and they exert their influence on judgments about troubled situations around the globe.

To say this is not to accuse these pacifists of insincerity. They are, if anything, true believers. As such they are unlikely to be touched by Lewy's arguments, except to have their previous convictions reaffirmed.

LEWY'S CHALLENGE TO PACIFISTS

Lewy's book should, however, be a challenge to other pacifists. I presume that many will reject his narrow definition of pacifism and insist that the negative aspect—rejection of armed conflict— is accompanied by a positive aspect, alleviation of the perceived causes of conflict. Those who follow this route must still deal with his findings. How does a pacifist relate the witness to peace and a disavowal of armed conflict with a high social involvement that has identifiable consequences subject to political analysis and judgment? And how does one justify such involvement when it aligns the pacifist with the violent revolutionary, with the "liberating" insurrectionist, with the "oppressed" guerrillas? How does the pacifist support a cause when he or she can foresee that it will be achieved only through violence? Can the

American pacifist feel at ease with organizations that usually
function as critics of the United States and apologists for countries hostile to the United States?
These are not rhetorical questions. Guenter Lewy has
amassed enough hard evidence to show convincingly that they
are valid questions and are not being adequately addressed by
major peace organizations in this country. Until they are, those
interested in the political health of our society have a right to be
wary of the direction these organizations have taken.

Looking at a Pacifist Magazine

After I read Lewy's book, I picked, quite arbitrarily, an
issue—July/August 1988—of *Fellowship*, the magazine of the
Fellowship of Reconciliation (FOR). In that issue I read first the
editorial, from which I quote: "Superpowers breed super-sized
problems. Not only corruption and scandals plague both the US
and the USSR but we both suffer from economic crises. They
still haven't figured out how to make their economy work, and
ours is in decline. Maybe we can find a way to save each other."[2]
No comment.

I then turned to a report on a trip to the USSR written by
Doug Hostetter, the Mennonite executive secretary of the FOR
in the United States.[3] I select from Hostetter's interesting article
two items only. First, he reported that the deputy director of the
Institute of State and Law of the USSR Academy of Sciences
revealed—in the new spirit of *glasnost*—that the admirable
Soviet constitution "had been little more than a piece of paper,"
and that there had been "very little constitutional, legal, or
judicial protection or recourse available to the average citizen."
Although these truths have been well documented in the West
for years, Hostetter expressed surprise at them. He had previously heard such charges, but not from Soviet legal experts;
they had come from "right wing ideologues and the émigré
groups." Is it possible, as he seems to suggest, that he did not
believe such critiques until he heard them from a Soviet source?

Later, Hostetter reports that in an extraordinary, large, tele-
vised meeting with Gorbachev, he began a question to the Soviet
leader by saying, "Now that the USSR is taking the lead in the

struggle for world peace. . . .'' The Soviet Union as the great peace leader? Does one have to be a right-wing ideologue to find this a stunning piece of nonsense?

Mikhail Gorbachev is a bold and vigorous leader. What is going on in the Soviet Union under his aegis is truly extraordinary, and no one can accurately project the full trajectory of his political reign. Restrictions are being lifted, censorship is being decreased, many dissenters are being allowed to leave, weapons are being cut back, and Soviet troops are being withdrawn from foreign lands. And when people are no longer being beaten or injected with drugs for political or religious dissent from the system, they feel better. But Moscow is still the center of an empire that keeps many nations and many people subjugated by force or wars, that has deprived them of freedom and cruelly ravaged their economies. Gorbachev is the leader of the system that maintains that empire. To regard that man as the leader in the world's quest for freedom is to indulge in political nonsense—but dangerous nonsense.

Necessity of Moral Distinctions

If we have any regard for those standards that allow us to use the term *civilization* with any validity, we must make moral distinctions. Totalitarianism is bad; it is bad for people. Democracy is good; it is good for people. With all its recent improvements, the Soviet Union is still a totalitarian empire, and with all its glaring faults the United States is still a democracy. To make statements that obscure these essential facts is a disservice to the truth and a handicap to constructive thought and action. A sound grasp of political/moral realities must be the basis of any realistic consideration of future relations between the United States and the Soviet Union, and between its peoples.

In the same issue of *Fellowship*, a college professor who works as a volunteer with the American Friends Service Committee has an article whose principal thrust is that "words like 'communist,' 'Marxist-Leninist,' and 'Soviet threat' " inhibit clear thinking in the United States.[4] In developing this thesis he invokes the authority and sometimes the words of such people as George Kennan, Conor Cruise O'Brien, J. William Fulbright,

John Oakes, Stephen F. Cohen. Fair enough. And since the author is intent on pointing out the inadequacies of the double standard that allegedly shapes U.S. policies, it is probably not surprising that his article reads like an uninterrupted litany of U.S. failures. He is, after all, trying to right what he perceives as an imbalance. But it is fair to point out that all his authorities are situated left of political center, and that his attempt to correct an imbalance creates its own highly imbalanced political picture, with all the errors assigned to the United States.

One example only from this article: "Soviet achievements—such as inclusive social services and rising living standards—go largely unreported in this country." Rising living standards in the Soviet Union? Rising relative to what? To seventy years ago? Or to the living standards of other industrialized countries? We in the West are now being taught by the Soviet leaders and their people that *glasnost* and *perestroika* have been introduced precisely because long-promised increases in living standards have not materialized. The failure of the Soviet system is finally being acknowledged, officially and publicly, but not a word of this most remarkable shift seeps into this article.

Guenter Lewy has been accused of reducing his charges against the pacifist organizations he examines to an agenda of anti-Communism. The charge is unjust. As this single issue of a leading publication of one of those organizations confirms, the Soviet Union continues to be the major concern of U.S. foreign policy. Other pacifist organizations provide additional confirmation that they recognize this fact. The importance of the Soviet Union in world affairs is not, then, in question. What is in question is how we evaluate the Soviet Union and its declared and actual policies. And on the evidence they generously proffer, many of those who are most responsible for making this evaluation for the pacifist organizations Lewy discusses are not reliable.

This judgment leaves completely untouched many of the valuable programs in which these organizations are heavily engaged. To highlight these programs refutes neither the charge that the organizations favor policies that inevitably involve siding with violent forces, nor the charge that those forces are frequently inimical to the interests of the United States. Guenter Lewy's charges should be taken seriously.

5

Quaker Service at the Crossroads

Charles Fager

THERE'S AN OLD Quaker joke: a young woman attends her first business meeting as an adult member, looking to make her mark, and sits next to a weighty older Friend in a grey bonnet who is knitting quietly. When an agenda item comes up that requires nominations to a new committee, the young Friend eagerly raises her hand and offers a name.

The older Friend listens without looking up from her knitting, then says quietly, "*That* is a name that would not have occurred to me." Nothing more is heard of the upstart newcomer's suggestion.

If I were looking for someone to make a detailed critique of the American Friends Service Committee, Guenter Lewy is a name that would not have occurred to me. Partly this is a matter of jurisdiction: I would prefer that such an examination be done first from within the Society of Friends, as a species of "family business." But another reason is that over the last decade or so, I have perceived an increasing sense of concern and uneasiness

---

Charles Fager is editor and publisher of *A Friendly Letter*, an independent monthly Quaker newsletter. Among his books are *Uncertain Resurrection: The Poor People's Campaign in Washington* (1969) and *Selma* (1974). He edited *Quaker Service at the Crossroads*, which deals with some of the same issues as the present volume; it is available from Kimo Press (Box 1361, Falls Church, Va. 22041).

about the AFSC's evolution among many Friends who had once staunchly supported it. So there were also Quaker voices to be heard on the subject.

But Guenter Lewy, a non-Friend and retired political science professor, also had concerns about the AFSC, and his book got done first. As a result, Quakers who have concerns about the AFSC have to deal not only with that organization but also with Guenter Lewy.

We may not want to admit it, but his achievement is sufficient to merit at least three responses from concerned Friends. First, we owe him a vote of thanks for providing the incentive for some critical Friends finally to begin saying aloud what was on their minds about the AFSC. A few have raised their voices before, usually in private; but some have hung back out of a combination of sloth and timidity that does us no credit. The truth is that, while liberal American Quakers denounce what they consider problems and sins in our government at the drop of a broadbrim hat, we are often rather slow and fainthearted about facing up to problems and sins in our own ranks. I gather from Matthew 7:3-5 and other sources that Quakers may not be unique in this respect.

Lewy has not suffered from these defects, and his book was the scholarly equivalent of a swift kick in the pants, one well deserved and long past due, in my judgment.

Second, we should admit that Lewy has saved us a lot of work by his research into AFSC history, particularly that of the 1960s and 1970s. While he may have misidentified an occasional tree of fact in the recent landscape, there seems little doubt that he has pretty accurately portrayed the forest of organizational evolution into which the trees fit. Much of the picture he paints is not very gratifying to behold; certain of its features are embarrassing and even shameful. There is, of course, much more to be told about the AFSC, even in its recent years, and fortunately historian J. William Frost of Swarthmore College is at work on a more comprehensive AFSC history. But that project is years away from completion. In the meantime, squirm as we might, Lewy's selective sketch of the last generation is the best we have.

Finally, however, Lewy's book presents Friends with a major problem. His is an unabashedly interpretive account of the AFSC: he has an ax to grind and is not shy about grinding it, even if the blade turns out to be not so sharp as he had hoped. Yet his outlook and theses have very little in common with those of most of the AFSC's Quaker critics. He got there first, with a book too well researched and revealing to be ignored; but the material he presents must be substantially reframed before it can be of much use to Quakers for the task of examining AFSC history from our point of view.

Beginning such an attempt at reframing is my purpose here. My thesis is that much of Guenter Lewy's critique of the AFSC misses the mark, particularly as far as Quakers and their religious values are concerned. Let me try to say why I think this is the case.

Lewy's Background and Outlook

First a bit of background. Guenter Lewy was born into a German Jewish family that escaped from the Nazis just before World War II. He told me during a conversation about his book that he had seen a democracy destroyed once in his lifetime, and that this experience had left him convinced of the fragility of civilized values and democratic structures. Lewy is thus not only a non-Friend; he is a non-pacifist and very strongly anti-Communist as well, with a base of experience for this outlook that merits no little respect.

Nevertheless, Lewy was once active in the peace group SANE, when it was supporting the Limited Test Ban Treaty negotiated by President Kennedy with the Soviets in 1963. But he was among the more conservative members of the early 1960s peace movement, one of those who felt unable to tolerate the changes wrought in it by the Vietnam war and the rise of the 1960s counterculture. One gets the impression that the evolution of the movement reminded him all too much of the ordeal he had been lucky to survive in Germany as a youth. In any case, Lewy supported the Vietnam war; indeed, one of his earlier books, *America in Vietnam* (Oxford University Press, 1978), defended U.S. policy and conduct there against, among other things, the allegations of systematic war crimes that were made by some peace activists.

Like many others of similar views, Lewy is convinced that the peace groups he examines, and perhaps the AFSC above all, were pivotal in undermining America's national will to win in Vietnam. He believes furthermore that the AFSC's agitation against the war helped produce, not peace, but enormous evils in Southeast Asia, including the exodus of the boat people and the Khmer Rouge genocide in Cambodia.

Further, Lewy asserts that the AFSC's activist role in the anti-Vietnam movement was shaped by internal changes that he chronicles in detail. These changes, he argues, represented the victory of radical leftist tendencies within the organization. He traces with particular emphasis the abandonment of a longstanding informal prohibition against joining coalitions that included any explicitly Marxist groups, such as those associated with the Communist party.

In Lewy's view, the abandonment of this prohibition was perhaps the AFSC's key bargain with the devil. He sees it as leading inexorably to the effective abandonment of the AFSC's Quaker pacifist heritage, and its alignment with violent and totalitarian forces, not only in Vietnam but more recently in Central America.

Along with many other Friends, I share at least some of Lewy's concerns about the AFSC's recent attitude toward many revolutionary groups, finding it too often tilted in a simplistically leftward direction. But on two of his biggest issues, the justice of the U.S. war in Vietnam and the meaning of pacifism, Lewy gets little sympathy from me or from the other Quaker critics with whom I am familiar. Because these issues shape so much of his critique, they deserve a brief response here before the effort of reframing proceeds.

Another View of the Vietnam Aftermath

During the seminar on Lewy's book conducted by the Ethics and Public Policy Center, the author declared that "in the last analysis," the AFSC's anti-war work in this period had failed the practical test of results because of what happened after the war in Vietnam and Cambodia.

From across the table, I replied that this was by no means the last analysis—it was only his analysis. While much of the aftermath of the Vietnam war has been horrible indeed, it is not at all clear that the peace movement can be fingered with the responsibility for it.

In fact, another equally plausible "last" analysis could be that, bad as the aftermath of the war has been, the peace movement helped avoid the even worse toll of destruction and killing that was likely had the war continued for many more years with increased U.S. involvement.

Suppose the war had been escalated at the end of the 1960s, as many of the military commanders wished. Lewy evidently thinks we could ultimately have defeated North Vietnam and established a regime satisfactory to us in Saigon. But would it have turned out that way? And even if it had, "ultimately" could have been a long time. Who is to say that we might not still be bogged down there? The somber black marble of the Vietnam Veterans Memorial might now be half a mile long, still being engraved with an ever increasing American casualty list—and how many millions more Asians would have been killed since 1975?

History suggests that a continued bloody stalemate was at least as plausible as any hopes of victory. The record of the Vietnamese for fighting outsiders, be they French, Japanese, or Chinese, goes back not decades but centuries. And what risks of escalation into a nuclear confrontation with Vietnam's Soviet and Chinese allies would we have run in the meantime? These were not inconsiderable even before 1975.

Additionally, it can be argued that Cambodia's slide into savagery began with an illegal "secret" bombing campaign by the United States, followed by a CIA-sponsored coup that replaced Prince Sihanouk, the linchpin of that nation's stability, with a corrupt and doomed military junta. It is entirely reasonable to suggest that this, as well as the illegal U.S. invasion of 1970, had more to do with the victory of the Khmer Rouge than any machinations of domestic doves. Indeed, it is one of many ironies of our Indochina debacle that the Khmer Rouge massacres were stopped only by the invasion of Cambodia by another Communist army, that of the victorious Vietnamese.

The debate over the Vietnam war will certainly not be settled here; my point is simply that while Lewy is entitled to his analysis of it, his analysis is hardly the "last," or the most convincing. Those who opposed the war, including the AFSC and this writer, may occasionally have acted unwisely, even foolishly. But we are not yet obliged, even by the post-war evils, to confess that we were fundamentally mistaken and that the war should have been supported and continued.

If anything, the post-war record suggests just as plausibly that U.S. involvement in Vietnam can be compared to kicking rocks down a mountainside: it started an avalanche of evil that continued to roll destructively across the slopes of Southeast Asia long after we had left the scene.

No, my only regret as a former protester is that I did not do more (non-violently) to stop the war sooner, and I am confident that most AFSC partisans feel the same way.

Pacifism Too Narrowly Defined

As for the meaning of pacifism: Lewy believes that the AFSC's turn to the left in the 1960s led it to abandon a traditional and authentic concept of pacifism, a concept that he believes had guided it until then. But his understanding of pacifism is a very restrictive one that identifies it with what pacifists call "non-resistance," a simple refusal to take a direct part in war. This narrow definition leaves unchallenged those who *do* wish to make war.

To be sure, non-resistance is an ancient and honorable form of pacifist witness; but it is not and has not been the only one, certainly not among Quakers. After all, as far back as the Sermon on the Mount, Jesus pronounced a blessing on peace-*makers* (Matt. 5:9), and the Greek text makes it clear that the blessing is reserved for those who get results, not simply those who stand aside from the fray and pray.

To be sure, once people or groups set out not simply to avoid war but to help make peace, their choices and judgments should be subjected to rational analysis and practical criticism; to this extent Lewy is correct. The AFSC's attempts to apply its active version of pacifism may not always have been wise—indeed, I and many other Friends think some clearly were not. But they were not wrong in *principle*, a point that Lewy seems to have trouble admitting. Further, let us remember that any attempt at prudential evaluation will reflect not only the facts, which Lewy has generally gathered accurately, but also the critic's values, which are much more open to debate.

Coalitions With Communists

Finally, to the matter of coalitions that include Marxist groups. Lewy's analysis here seems to have been shaped by the traumas of the liberal left in the 1930s and 1940s. At that time many groups fell victim to a pattern of seemingly principled cooperation with Communist groups. This opened the way to infiltration of the liberal groups by Marxist cadres, followed by the groups' subversion, manipulation, and destruction.

Such things did occur during the 1960s, as the demise of Students for a Democratic Society testifies. Yet it seems to me that Lewy's analysis has missed the essence of these 1960s coalitions, both more broadly and with specific reference to the AFSC.

On the broadest level, I see the anti-war coalitions as comparing less to the Popular Front leftism of the 1930s than to the alliance of the United States and the Soviet Union against Hitler during World War II. That is, they were emergency confederations of highly dissimilar and often mutually suspicious parties, most of whom had little in common except their opposition to the Vietnam war. And like the U.S.-Soviet alliance, none of them outlasted the war, though some insignificant vestiges remain.

Whatever else can be said of these coalitions, one thing they did not do, particularly in the AFSC, was to produce a 1930s-style pattern of infiltration, subversion, and destruction. Lewy specifically acknowledges the absence of evidence that the developments he dislikes in the AFSC can be traced to direct involvement by the minions of Moscow, Hanoi, or even Managua. Yet clearly the experience left its impact, and much of it was negative. So what happened?

An *"Organizers' Subculture"*

My own sense is that rather than the infiltration-subversion model, what we have seen in the AFSC over the past generation is the rise of a new establishment, made up largely of former 1960s radicals of various stripes, who, rather than operating as a conspiracy, have more or less backed into becoming a distinct, careerist constituency that I call the "organizers' subculture."

I doubt that many of these men and women started out thinking in career terms. Their mood—mine, too—in the late 1960s was too apocalyptic for that; moreover, such long-term strategizing did not fit with the outlook summed up in the slogan "Don't Trust Anyone Over Thirty." Once they were irrevocably past that dreaded landmark, with families and possessions and debts arriving sooner than the revolution, career considerations became unavoidable. Yet many of these men and women were still alienated from "establishment" institutions and conventional career tracks. So what were they to do?

Over time, and with artful application of their organizing skills, a kind of informal network of professional activists with similar histories formed, concerned to protect and advance its members as any other such network does.

In the case of the AFSC, this evolution has, among other things, produced a dramatic erosion of its connections to the Society of Friends. For Quaker critics, this erosion is the principal underlying problem in the AFSC. It is a problem that Lewy's book, almost inadvertently, has brought into the spotlight. Yet Lewy's 1930s infiltration-subversion analysis, with its alarm about anti-war coalitions, does not offer much in the way of understanding this. My sense is that even if the AFSC had heeded Lewy-like scruples and firmly eschewed the tainted coalitions, it would not have avoided the problems it now has. There was no safe haven for it from the turmoil of the sixties.

Furthermore, I can remain convinced that it is entirely appropriate for the AFSC and others concerned for peace to maintain contacts with persons and groups from Communist countries in this effort, and that whatever the risks, Quakers can build such relationships without automatically turning into "useful idiots" and Communist dupes.

What all this comes down to is the assertion that, rather than repeating a previous generation's mistakes, these sixties activists made some new mistakes of their own. Thus Lewy's analysis of what went wrong is not all that useful, especially to the AFSC's Quaker critics.

This brings us back to the need to reframe Lewy's data for Quaker purposes. Despite their differences with Lewy over Vietnam, pacifism as non-resistance, and coalitions, Quaker critics of the AFSC will find that the book has illuminated three of their key concerns:

1. Can the American Friends Service Committee still be considered an authentically Quaker agency?

2. On the whole, is AFSC work over the past generation of a quality and direction that Quakers can be proud of?

3. What should be done to remedy any shortcomings revealed by these lines of inquiry?

Still a Quaker Identity?

As for the first query, Lewy makes uncomfortably plain what too many liberal Quakers have long known but been loath to admit, namely, that the AFSC now lacks any meaningful connection with the Society of Friends from which it sprang. Its staff is barely 15 per cent Quaker, and those few represent only the narrowest leftward slice of the Society. There are no meaningful structures of accountability between the AFSC and the Yearly Meetings that are our main organizational units. The large majority of its funds come from non-Quaker sources. Its priorities are set according to its own internal processes, which are related only coincidentally if at all to the concerns and discussions occurring among Friends at large. And, not least, the AFSC has in the last fifteen years consistently shrugged off the concerns raised by Quakers who are uneasy with some of its actions and directions.

Just how far the AFSC has moved from its origins is clearly shown by the Statement of Purpose that still opens its bylaws:

The AFSC is to work "on behalf of the participating yearly Meetings and other bodies of the Religious Society of Friends in America; and in addition . . . to promote the general objects and purposes of the participating yearly Meetings and other bodies of [Friends]."

I have been asked why this whole matter is seen to be of any great consequence. Why is a "Quaker identity" for service such a big deal in a world full of starving and oppressed people? What difference does it make what label goes on the work that is done?

The primary response to such questions can only be that many Quakers, including this one, see in Quakerism a vehicle of the Spirit of God, and this makes it valuable in itself. It has made numerous outward contributions to history through its role in the struggle for freedom of worship, and its character as the seedbed of the anti-slavery and feminist movements. But its specifically religious contributions have also been important. It has been a bearer of mysticism within Protestantism, and has carried the standard of universalism in theology and pacifism in practice when almost all other major Christian bodies had forgotten or denied that these things were ever parts of the gospel. Indeed, there are many ways in which the rest of Christianity has yet to catch up with the insights of George Fox and other members of our founding Quaker generation.

This is a very significant record for a small religious body scarcely three hundred years old, and in my view Quakerism is by no means played out. The history of such a movement is very much worth preserving and its potential well worth cultivating. Whom can Quakers expect to do that but Quakers themselves? More concretely, the idea of the AFSC as an instrument of the organized bodies of Friends once had considerable functional reality, the memory of which is both precious and poignant. A great many Friends once bore witness in many places through various kinds of service under AFSC auspices. Indeed, there was once an almost organic, reciprocal relationship between the AFSC and numerous Friends groups. But no more. The connection is now marginal at best, and many Friends whose spiritual life was immensely enriched by the relationship are grieved and quietly angry about the loss.

In any such institution, as the histories of many church-founded colleges show, as the direct involvement of the parent constituency declines, at some point its founding tradition becomes simply a relic, a vestigial organ with no real meaning. If it is difficult to pinpoint exactly when this threshold is reached, there is little doubt that it exists.

This was starkly illustrated in 1988 by the case of the YMCA in Beverly Hills, California. An advisory group had recommended that, as a religious organization, the YMCA not be given space in a proposed city-owned building. As reported in the *Washington Post* of September 3, 1988, the YMCA officials insisted that it was not in reality a religious body, even though the C in its name means Christian and its statement of purpose describes it as a "fellowship united by a common loyalty to Jesus Christ for the purpose of developing Christian personality and building a Christian society."

Beverly Hills mayor Robert Tannenbaum, who is also president of the Y's board, told a reporter that he regards the purpose statement as "institutional rhetoric that acknowledges the historical roots of the association and in no way mandates a religious commitment on the part of the Beverly Hills Family Y." He also pointed out that two-thirds of the board members were Jewish.

No doubt Mayor Tannenbaum is right, and probably the Beverly Hills Y will eventually gain its niche in the new city building. But in light of this incident, and the fact that the proportion of non-Quakers on the AFSC staff is now considerably more than two-thirds, it would be fair to ask just how much longer the F in AFSC will carry any more meaning than the C in YMCA.

A Fitting Quality of Work?

As for the Quaker critics' second question, about the quality of the AFSC's work, this is not the place to go into detail. Suffice it to say that the AFSC has issued a great deal of material in the past fifteen years dealing with various peace and justice issues, but most of it that I have seen, though I may agree with the position taken, I would not want to show to persons whose intellect, spiritual depth, and scholarship I respected. Too often the materials were simply inferior: shoddily researched, needlessly tendentious, freighted with dubious political baggage, showing little spiritual depth. There were signal exceptions, but too much of the material was just bush league.

This is an embarrassing, even humiliating admission to make. I consider Quakerism to be, if you will, a first-class religion, and want the public manifestations of my religious denomination to reflect that level of quality. *Corruptio optimi pessima.*

What Can Be Done?

The third question is the most difficult. As I see it, there are three choices: release, renunciation, or reclamation.

By *release* I mean that perhaps it is time simply to cut the few remaining organizational ties between the AFSC and the Quaker Yearly Meetings and let each go its own way. Perhaps this is not enough: *renunciation* would suggest that it is time for the AFSC to acknowledge how far it has evolved away from its Quaker identity and to drop "Friends" from its name. Or possibly the organization could be *reclaimed* from within so as to revitalize its Quaker identity, rebuild its Quaker cadre, and establish new, authentic connections with the Society.

Here again, disgruntled Quakers owe a debt to Guenter Lewy. His book, however unsatisfying in many respects, has made it more difficult for us to continue evading the hard choices. He has reminded us that the issues involved are important, that their ramifications go beyond our ranks, and that if we are unwilling to tell the hard truths and ask questions about our own religious witness as embodied in our institutions, as Jesus declared in Mark 4:22, someone else will.

6

The Muddle of American Pacifism

James Turner Johnson

THE APPEARANCE of Guenter Lewy's *Peace and Revolution* provides the stimulus to examine contemporary American pacifism, its relation to the pacifism of earlier ages, and its relation to the rival moral tradition of just war.

Lewy focuses on four organizations whose historical roots lie in the reaction to World War I. These four cover a substantial part, though hardly all, of the spectrum of contemporary American pacifism. (1) The American Friends Service Committee is Quaker and provides a link to the "peace church" traditions that originated in the Reformation as well as to a later religious tradition of social transformation through individual endeavor and witness. (2) The Fellowship of Reconciliation is nondenominationally Christian and reflects the liberal, progressivist Protestant vision of the late nineteenth and early twentieth century, for which the Gospel meant working in the world to make it more and more like the Kingdom of God. (3) The Women's International League for Peace and Freedom in its origins drew on Christian ideals at second hand, through the Tolstoyism of

---

James Turner Johnson is professor of religion and associate in the graduate department of political science at Rutgers University. His books on war and peace include *Just War Tradition and the Restraint of War: A Moral and Historical Inquiry* (1975 and 1981), *Can Modern War Be Just?* (1984), and *The Quest for Peace: Three Moral Traditions in Western Cultural History* (1987).

Jane Addams and others prominent in its early years. While this connection has long since atrophied, the league has deep roots in the soil of some of the same religious concerns that shaped the first two organizations. (4) The War Resisters League was founded to provide a vehicle for opposing war from non-religious perspectives.

Complexity of American Pacifism

A full mapping of American pacifism would need to cover considerably more ground than this list. John Howard Yoder has identified seventeen varieties of religious pacifism and suggested there are probably more; he did not even try to count the varieties of non-religious pacifism.[1] The thrust of his argument is that all the types he lists should be taken seriously:

> There is no such thing as a single position called "pacifism," to which one clear definition can be given and which is held by all "pacifists." There is rather a congeries of varied kinds of opposition to war; some of them run parallel, but some are very different from one another in accent and sometimes even in substance.[2]

Yoder's own rather general working definition of pacifism moves between opposition to Christian participation in war and opposition to war itself. These same two standards, out of all the possible ones, are put together in Lewy's definition: "The term 'pacifist' characterizes the doctrine of those who are morally opposed to bearing arms and who refuse to sanction war for any purpose, defensive or otherwise."[3] Yoder allows for a spectrum—or as he puts it, a "congeries"—of positions, all claiming to be "pacifist."

Lewy, by contrast, attempts to clarify the concept of pacifism by narrowing it down, at the expense of excluding some who call themselves pacifists as not pacifist after all. His definition excludes all four of the groups he treats in his book. It would also exclude one of the paradigmatic religious pacifist groups of the Reformation era, the Swiss Brethren, who were morally opposed to bearing arms but held that "the sword is ordained by God outside the perfection of Christ."[4] Moreover, the definition excludes some of the regularly cited examples of early

Christian pacifism, including Origen of Alexandria, a Christian father of the third century, who argued against the pagan Celsus that while Christians were obligated not to bear arms, they performed the more useful service of praying for victory for the emperor's forces—thus mixing refusal to bear arms with sanctioning war as an activity of the Roman state.[5] Though polemically useful, Lewy's definition of pacifism excludes too much for it to be more than a starting point for an analysis of pacifism.

Some contemporary pacifists would insist that a proper definition of pacifism must include a commitment to non-violence, either as a form of personal witness, or as a means of corporate social witness and protest, or as a technique for bringing about change in society, or all of these.[6] Gandhi and Martin Luther King are usually cited as the examples of this aspect of pacifism. Out of a pacifism centered on non-violence Gene Sharp has fashioned a proposal for national self-defense that relies on non-violent techniques rather than on arms.[7]

Yet others have argued that there is no real pacifism without disavowal of coercion or the threat of coercion. Reinhold Niebuhr, for example, in his critique of pacifism in the 1930s, insisted that the disavowal of coercion, and not the adoption of some technique, whether violent or non-violent, for coercing others, should be the real concern for Christians.[8]

These examples still take in only a small part of the picture. They leave out (except for the case of Gandhi) forms of pacifism rooted in non-Christian religions and non-Western cultures, which have different theoretical bases and different histories. They also omit, within Western culture, the quite substantial non-religious forms of pacifism that began to appear in Renaissance humanism, have flourished among intellectual elites since the Enlightenment, and are a prominent element in the broadened culture of non-exclusionary American pacifism today.[9]

Pacifism, in short, is not a simple phenomenon but a very complex and variable one. The non-exclusionary principle that since the Vietnam war has been widely accepted among American pacifist groups and individuals blurs the distinctions and makes it harder to analyze pacifism and its place in American political debate.[10] It also, as Lewy points out, allows pacifist organizations such as the four he treats to advance their political agenda as an implication of pacifism in general—which it is not.

BEFORE AND AFTER VIETNAM

Until the period on which Lewy focuses, which begins with resistance to U.S. involvement in the Vietnam war, pacifism in American society was simpler to identify. It is not just that, as Lewy puts it, "pacifists were pacifist," for even then there were real differences among them.

Two Pacifist Themes

These differences clustered around two themes that both Yoder and Lewy include in their definitions: opposition to participation in war, and opposition to war as such. Some groups, most notably the three historic "peace churches"—Quakers, Mennonites, and Church of the Brethren—took their stand against being compelled to participate in war. In the Civil War, such persons were often able to avoid conscription by paying for a substitute, and many did.[11] Beginning with the twentieth-century draft, the focus shifted to establishing alternative service for conscientious objectors, who were defined during most of the history of the draft as members of religious bodies that did not permit their members to bear arms. These were primarily the members of the three "peace churches," though other religious groups like Jehovah's Witnesses also came to qualify.

War itself might be abhorrent, a sign of human wickedness and a disordered world, but the pacifism that concentrated on establishing the moral right not to have to engage in military service did not challenge the state's right to make war. Indeed, pacifists of this sort depended on the laws of the state to guarantee their own right to refuse to bear arms. This position was in continuity with the sectarian tradition of pacifism exemplified in the Reformation era by members of the Anabaptist movement, including the direct ancestors of the Mennonites and Church of the Brethren. These pacifists were able to say, along with the Swiss Brethren, that "the sword is ordained by God outside the perfection of Christ," but that they felt themselves called not to bear the sword in order to live according to that ideal of moral perfection. The other major theme of pre-Vietnam American pacifism was opposition to war as such. This was expressed in various efforts to abolish war and in religious and secular visions of a world without war, often to be achieved by the transformation or end of the state. Under the umbrella of opposition to war there was great diversity, and the anti-war movement included some who justified participation in World War I as a step toward ridding the world of war. *Internationalism* in a variety of forms was prominent among those seeking to abolish war; *social transformation* was another important subtheme; and *individual moral transformation* toward peaceful behavior and universal brotherhood was another. Associated with the anti-war theme and feeding it was a view of war as inherently chaotic, disproportionately destructive of values, bestial, and reflective of something fundamentally wrong in the government of states.[12]

Mainstream American religion drank deeply of the stream of progressivist social thought during the late nineteenth and early twentieth century. The non-"peace church" Christian pacifism of the World War I era was an outgrowth of the sincere belief that, through moral transformation at the individual level leading to social transformation, the world could grow beyond war. As the renunciation of war became linked with an individual morality of love, pacifism came to be associated with non-violence.

Post-Vietnam Pacifism

During the Vietnam war era, the non-exclusionary practices of the resistance movement drew together these two major themes—opposition to participation in war and opposition to war in general—and joined them as they had not previously been joined. The breadth and diversity of American pacifism today reflects the collective inheritance of the anti-war movements of earlier periods; this latitudinarianism does not always mix well with the form of pacifism derived from the "peace churches," shaped by their long sectarian history.

I do not find anything particularly surprising in Lewy's portrait of the four pacifist organizations, except for the depth of example and documentation he provides. These groups, while not representative of the full breadth of contemporary American pacifism, well exemplify the importance of ideas developed in the historical tradition of anti-war utopianism to the "peace movement" of the last twenty-five years. These ideas include distrust of the state and its political leadership, affinity for revolutionary movements that purport to be about bringing in a new political order, attraction to socialist and Communist ideologies and politics, rejection of national defense as "militaristic," and many other characteristic attitudes identified by Lewy; they have long been present, in forms appropriate to differing historical contexts, in a tradition of thought and effort to abolish war reaching back to the Renaissance and beyond. Like the four organizations that Lewy faults for claiming they are pacifist while accepting violent revolution in the name of "liberation," this tradition, through its history, has traced most of the problems of war to the state and to the venality of rulers and has accepted the use of military force designed to right such wrongs.

The people Lewy is criticizing, as he rightly points out, are largely outside the "peace church" tradition with its conscientious refusal to bear arms. They should therefore be challenged on the ground they have chosen to occupy, not the ground occupied by persons and organizations that continue to be principally or entirely motivated by the moral claims central to the peace-church tradition.

PACIFISM AND JUST WAR

The positions taken by the four organizations Lewy treats can be challenged on political grounds and on moral grounds, and Lewy himself begins debate on both. I will here leave aside the political debate to focus on the moral, in particular the relation of the positions Lewy criticizes to the moral tradition of just war.

Two Pacifist Traditions

Historically, just-war tradition has been informed by a set of assumptions about history and the place of war that differs from

the corresponding assumptions made in either of the two traditional pacifist themes. The sectarian tradition that produced the
"peace churches" is profoundly dubious about the possibilities
of human history after the fall and "outside the perfection of
Christ." Sin is held in check within that history by civil government, and war is one of the means God allows such governments
to use to fulfill their functions. Yet the Christian should be aloof
from involvement in that world as far as possible, and this means
in particular that no Christian should consent to bear arms.

By contrast—and this is the source of some of the contradictions inherent in the broad, non-exclusionist pacifist coalition in
contemporary America—the utopian pacifist tradition has always assumed that human history is capable of being moved,
through human actions, toward a goal of perfection. War, in this
tradition, is at once a sign of evil in the world where it appears,
a source of further evil, and a roadblock to progress. War will
have no place in the ideal, global society toward which progress
tends, and the abolition of war now will hasten the progress of
human history toward such a goal. Yet before the ideal is
reached, some uses of military force may be necessary to
counteract the forces of those evildoers whose interest lies in
maintaining the status quo or in rolling back progress for their
own narrow ends.

The Just War

Just-war tradition, in distinction from both of these views,
proceeds from the assumption that human history holds the
potential for both good and evil, for both justice and injustice,
that it will be so throughout the course of history, and that
within this framework war is an instrument that may be used for
good or ill.[13] Against those who hold that participation in war is
immoral, the just-war perspective implies that there are times
when participation in war may be a positive moral duty. Against
the view of the utopian tradition that war is necessarily chaotic
and destructive of values, the just-war tradition holds that war
can and should be subjected to moral control so that it can serve
to protect and preserve values. In such cases war is justified, in
moral terms; more specifically, it is justified and may become a

positive moral duty when it satisfies certain moral criteria. These criteria define the right to go to war (in classic terms, *ius ad bellum*) and the right to set limits on what may justifiably be done in war (*ius in bello*).

Something like the criteria of the just-war *ius ad bellum* is at work in the way that Lewy's four groups justify revolutionary violence: there is an idea of just cause, right authority, right intention, proportionality, last resort, hope of success, the goal of peace. Yet the fundamental difference in perspective about the nature of history and the place of politics and war in history means there is no agreement on the content of these criteria. For example, just-war tradition defines *defense* as a justifying cause for resort to war; yet defense is limited to a response to the use or threat of imminent use of violence against the defender. The rhetoric of the groups Lewy treats rests heavily on a broadening of the concept of "violence" to include various forms of "structural violence" characterized collectively as "oppression." For just-war tradition, "structural violence" would be characterized rather as political, economic, or some other form of injustice. If it did not involve the use of armed force, the presumption would be for correcting the injustice through political, economic, or other appropriate means short of resort to armed force. There are similar divergences on all the other criteria for a just resort to force.

Justifying Revolutionary Violence

No less importantly, I do not see a sign of *ius in bello* reasoning in the rhetoric these groups use to justify revolutionary violence while they denounce counterrevolutionary use of arms. Just-war tradition sets moral limits on even the justified use of force: it must be discriminate, that is, avoiding direct and intentional harm to the innocent, and it must be proportionate. The history of revolutionary forces supported by Lewy's four groups gives cause for concern on both counts. Such revolutionary violence characteristically is justified by reference to high ideological goals, and whatever tends to support those goals is excused. Enemies are identified not by combatancy or noncombatancy but by ideological affinity, and the most elemental rights of noncombatants are thus made into nothing. Indeed, when terrorism is a part of the revolutionary arsenal, noncombatants are typically singled out as targets, for this challenges the ability of the "oppressors" to protect their own.

Of course, there are plenty of cases of genuine oppression by use of violent means that are not only unjustified but indiscriminate and disproportionate. Yet my point is that, from a just-war perspective, both these and comparable violence from revolutionaries deserve to be judged by the same moral reference points, and both sides need to be pressed to seek their ends within the moral limits set by the principles of discrimination and proportionality. There is no reason to give revolution as such a morally privileged position.

Finally, it seems to me that there is a fundamental difference over the controlling concept of war between just-war tradition and the position represented by the four groups Lewy treats. For utopian pacifism generally, war is inherently chaotic, uncontrollable, and destructive, and is the result of venality and self-interested behavior on the part of states. For Lewy's four groups this translates into opposition to military preparedness and the use of military force by the United States—or rather by its "government," depicted as an alien entity with its own purposes distinct from those of the nation at large, much as Erasmus excoriated the "princes" of his day.[14]

For just-war tradition, war may in fact be chaotic, uncontrolled, and destructive, but it can be brought under moral control so that it serves to protect and preserve values, not destroy them. The just and rightly ordered state is able to use its military arm to promote peace. In just-war terms, the United States, with its democratic political processes, its respect for human rights, and its tradition of civilian control over the military, is such a state.

On their readings of the nature of war and of the national character of the United States, then, there is simply no common ground between the just-war perspective and that of the four pacifist organizations analyzed by Lewy.

CONCLUDING OBSERVATIONS

Is there a "moral crisis" in American pacifism? I believe there is and has been for some time. While I do not grant moral superiority to the claims of conscience that prevent some people from bearing arms, I observe a fundamental difference between these persons and others who focus their concerns about war elsewhere—on the attempt to create, even by use of war, an ideal world without war. I do not think the non-exclusionary alliance between these two quite different kinds of pacifists is legitimate or morally defensible. Conscientious objectors to the bearing of arms should be morally opposed to the bearing of arms for whatever purpose, be it for a revolution or for a state. Involvement in politics should be allowed to the limits of conscience, but these limits can hardly be determined by the one-sided and question-begging criteria employed by the four organizations on which Lewy concentrates. Within American moral and political pluralism—as in few other societies of the world—there is a place for both these sorts of pacifism if indeed they are both equally well described as pacifist. It will not do, in either moral or political debate, to blur them together.

These moral tensions should be paramount within American pacifism, as they are, for example, in the cases of the dissenters identified by Lewy and in some of the recent writings of Stanley Hauerwas.[15] As yet, this internal critique has not found its full voice, and it is not clear whether it ever will or, if it does, whether it will make an institutional difference.

For persons outside American pacifism, like Lewy and like myself, the moral crisis within pacifism is less acute a problem than that of the politics with which pacifism represents itself in the public forum. While Lewy's critique of the four organizations he treats is harsh, it is less harsh than the rhetoric and decisions he subjects to criticism. The commitments behind such rhetoric and decisions need to be made plain, and their implications analyzed, in the public forum. Lewy has taken a beginning step in this direction.

7

Pacifism: A Form
of Politics

Stanley Hauerwas

I CANNOT JUDGE the accuracy of the history Guenter Lewy tells of the major pacifist organizations over the past thirty years. I have no reason to doubt that, in general, his account is right. Rather what I will do is raise some questions about the conceptual presuppositions with which he tells the story.

First I want to locate my own history in relation to the story he tells. As a pacifist I am a late bloomer. When I left graduate school armed with a Ph.D. in Christian ethics, I was a committed Niebuhrian. I became a pacifist only because I was convinced by John Howard Yoder's work that any adequate account of what it means to be a disciple of Jesus requires one to take up the way of non-violence. To try to spell out the complexities of that position would be inappropriate here, but at the very least it requires an understanding of the church as a political alternative to nations and empires. The important point I wish to make at the beginning, however, is that my own pacifism is Christologically determined in a way that also commits me to definite political options regarding the everyday life of our society.

Stanley Hauerwas is professor of theological ethics at Duke University Divinity School and director of the university's graduate program in religion. Among his many books are *The Peaceable Kingdom: A Primer in Christian Ethics*, *Against the Nations: War and Survival in a Liberal Society*, and *Christian Existence Today: Essays on Church, World, and Living in Between*.

I was not a pacifist at the beginning of the war in Vietnam, and I looked upon the protests of groups like the American Friends Service Committee with a good deal of Niebuhrian bemusement. Like Lewy, I thought they must be deeply confused: they apparently failed to understand that their pacifism should prevent the kind of preferential judgments they seemed to be making. (In fairness it must be said that those were indeed extraordinary times, and that more than a few people would like to call back some of the things they did and said during that period.)

As the war went on I increasingly read Yoder's work, and I finally was convinced that I could not be other than a pacifist. The horror of the Vietnam war had little to do with my decision, for I was convinced that in many ways it was the kind of limited war the just-war thinkers should have supported. Moreover, my conversion to pacifism at this time did not make me more sympathetic to the American Friends Service Committee and other such groups, for now I thought that their position had an insufficient theological base. They seemed to ground their pacifism in a vague humanism that led them to the kind of uncritical political judgments Lewy documents.

What bothered me most about the political activity of some of the peace groups was the kind of selective humanism it implied. Those groups were to be preferred whose oppression put them on what was considered the "right side of history." It was not just the acceptance of violence for the oppressed that disturbed me, but the fact that the oppressed turned out to be those who seemed to represent egalitarian movement within the world. Peasants who supported royalists and conservative regimes were not counted among those deserving support. Perhaps this selectivity derived from the general presumption of pacifists that their task was to eliminate those conditions that make war likely.

Lewy notes that pacifist organizations founded during and after World War I were often based upon opposition to the imperialism of capitalist orders, on the assumption that such orders were the ultimate cause of war. I think this is at least partly true; it was one of the reasons why I was somewhat critical of such groups even though I had become a pacifist. Part of what Yoder had taught me was that Christian pacifism was based upon the belief, not that war could be eliminated, but that as Christians in a world at war we could not be anything other than pacifists. It was not that our commitment to the way of non-violence promised to rid the world of war, but rather that God had given the world an alternative to war through the kind of politics present in the church, where reconciliation triumphs over envy and hate.

No Politics for Pacifists?

Putting the matter in that way, however, brings me to my primary worry about the way Lewy tells his story. In the first sentence of his preface he asserts that American pacifism has been essentially transformed over the past twenty years because pacifists have given up their singleminded devotion to principles of non-violence and have instead defended the moral legitimacy of armed struggles, particularly when they underwrite socialist or Communist regimes. In short, Lewy is suggesting that the problem with contemporary pacifism is that it has gone political.

In Lewy's view, pacifism is properly understood as "the doctrine of those who are morally opposed to bearing arms and refuse to sanction war for any purpose, defensive or otherwise" (p. 3). That is a deeply misleading account of pacifism, or at least the kind of pacifism I and many others represent. For it makes it appear that what is at stake in the pacifist witness is simply opposition to war *qua* war rather than the basis from which our pacifism arises. Lewy's account of pacifism in fact is determined by the same kind of presuppositions as those held by the pacifist organizations of which he is so critical. For pacifism appears almost as an end in itself rather than as simply one expression of a way of life that is constitutive of a whole community. The kind of pacifism embodied in Quaker meetings, in Mennonite churches, and in thousand of other expressions of people who have learned to live non-violently is made irrelevant to this abstract understanding of pacifism.

As a result, Lewy fails to see that pacifism by its very nature is a form of politics, not, as he would have it, merely the private expression of certain people's individual convictions. Such a characterization of the pacifist witness reflects his commitment to the corrupt distinction between the public and the private presumed by liberal political theory. This judgment may seem harsh, but I think it is completely affirmed by Lewy's explicit Niebuhrian acknowledgments at the end of his book. Lewy notes that pragmatic calculations are forbidden to the true pacifist, who must uphold the principle of non-violence and oppose any use of force for any purpose (p. 240). Therefore, he suggests, there can be no such thing as a political position for anyone who is truly a pacifist. Because the pacifist is committed to an ethics of ultimate ends, as characterized by Max Weber, he must avoid all forms of life that require an ethics of responsibility. It simply does not occur to Lewy that Weber's distinction not only is problematic but also is intelligible only if one assumes the normative status of social orders based on the assumption that citizens hold no moral goods in common.

Lewy's Own Assumptions

Lewy, of course, is candid in his support of liberal democracies. He applauds pre-1960s pacifists because they regularly identified with the democratic values of the United States and opposed totalitarianism of every kind. Even though they were personally unwilling to bear arms, American pacifists respected the democratic process and did not attempt to prevent other citizens from fulfilling their patriotic duties (pp. 237–38). So at least part of Lewy's complaint against the pacifists is, not that they were abandoning their traditional commitment to non-violence and becoming political, but that they were giving up a political position he himself approves. That, of course, is an ideological critique that must be justified rather than simply asserted.

Even more, Lewy owes us some account of why we should accept his understanding of pacifism, based as it is on Niebuhr's claim that pacifists must be either vocational and thus a-political, or incoherent for wanting to be politically relevant. For Lewy's (and Niebuhr's) account of pacifism is based upon the same general humanistic presuppositions held by many of the kinds of pacifists he criticizes. Such an account hardly does justice to the pacifist witness as embodied in Christian tradition.

Certainly Christians called to non-violent witness have often found themselves in tension with the surrounding political order. That is not a sign that they have withdrawn from the political order but rather a clear indication of their understanding that the kind of non-violent witness Christians make is clearly political. Lewy, of course, can respond that he is suggesting, not that pacifists cannot be political, but that they can be so only to a point. Moreover, when entering the political process, pacifists must adopt standards of judgment that are different from those they apply in personal life, since work in the political realm is based upon consequential calculations that finally render the pacifist commitments irrelevant.

The Quakers in Pennsylvania

In support of that position Lewy appeals once again to the tired example of the Quaker withdrawal from government of the province of Pennsylvania in 1756. The appeal to this example by Niebuhrian realists is simply question-begging. For just as they characterize pacifism from the perspective of their assumption that their own account of politics is normative, so the way they tell the story of the Quaker withdrawal from government in Pennsylvania presupposes the same kind of political history. As an antidote to that history, I refer Lewy—and all others in the future who would appeal to the Quaker experiment—to the account John Howard Yoder gives in his book *Christian Attitudes Toward War, Peace, and Revolution* (1983; distributed by the Co-op Bookstore, Goshen Biblical Seminary, Elkhart, Indiana; pp. 261–95).

Yoder points out that at least four facts must be taken into account. First, William Penn was not fully free to act according to his conscience at the beginning, since he had to administer a colony that was to be managed under the Crown and the British Parliament. As a result, he had to accept, at least in principle, the provision of the death penalty. Second, by the third generation some Quakers were not so strongly opposed to the death penalty as their forebears. However, they did try hard not to put anyone to death, and in eight years only three persons were executed. Third, by the fourth generation those Quakers in government were just that: fourth-generation Quakers. So in 1756 the Quakers did not have the same vision for a non-violent campaign with the Indians that the children of Penn and Fox had had. Finally, the Quakers had an exceptionally open immigration policy for Pennsylvania. With the passage of time they let German Reformed as well as Irish and British immigrants into the colony. Thus, as Yoder points out, by the 1750s the Quakers were in the minority in a colony they were running. The non-violent thing to do when you are in a minority is to let the majority run it.

Yoder then observes,

> It is a success of non-violence, not a failure, to let yourself be voted out of government. . . . The fact that the Quakers let that happen shows that you can, in a governmental situation, let your position on the sword be relativized at the most fundamental democratic level, namely, to let the majority rule. . . . They were moved by the success of their own ethics in letting people into their state who could vote them down. Nobody in New England let that happen. Nobody in the southern colonies let that happen. . . .
>
> The Quaker regime did work for eighty years. In global history that is a long time for any dynasty or any party to be in control of any government [pp. 271–72].

Lewy and all those like him who have been conditioned by the Niebuhrian framework will not be much convinced by this attempt to reread the Quaker experiment. They will not be convinced because they simply assume that Hobbes's account of politics—that it is no more than a contest of raw power—is correct. Moreover, I must agree with them that whether Hobbes, in principle, is correct or not, we increasingly live in a Hobbesian world. What I deny, however, is the necessity of that understanding of politics and our acquiescence to it. Again, as Yoder argues,

> The philosophical commitment that says that government by necessity is violence at the core, denies that there can be any significant historical change in the nature of social structure, and thereby denies that Christians can be obedient to Christ as Lord in the real

world. It denies this not on empirical grounds, but on philosophical grounds [p. 269].

The Quakers in Pennsylvania were successful in coming to a peaceful resolution with the Indians before others moved in who did not share their commitment. What pacifists wish to maintain is that we cannot let our political imaginations be stilled by the assumed necessities of those who would find the political in the language of violence.

Lewy hints at but does not develop a deeper issue. Quoting Sidney Hook he indicates that survival cannot be the be-all and end-all of a life worthy of men and women. Freedom is a more precious value than survival itself. Implicit in Lewy's appeal is the assumption that pacifists have a commitment to survival as the overriding moral good. That, of course, is simply not the case. As I argue and as Paul Ramsey argues in our book *Speak Up for Just War or Pacifism* (Pennsylvania State University Press, 1988), pacifists believe there is much worth dying for. In that sense pacifism is the most political of positions, since it refuses to accept the illusions of political order that promise security in place of the moral goods for which lives may at times have to be sacrificed. That is the real political issue at stake between pacifists and positions such as Lewy's. For the kind of politics that Lewy defends is a politics of deception, since it is based on the presumption that a polity can be built on the moral basis of self-interest. Such a polity cannot help being violent since it must hide the absence of any account of the good behind self-deceptive idealizations.

Lewy's Challenge to Pacifists

Having said all this, I must still admit that Lewy's book presents a deep challenge to pacifists. I suspect that the organizational history he relates is the result of an insufficient view of the kind of politics pacifists are called to embody in their lives. Certainly pacifists can join with other people of good will to protest actions of their governments that seem particularly reprehensible. I see no reason why Lewy should criticize pacifists for engaging in the kind of coalition politics that I suspect he would like to commend as a way of life for political realists. What is important is how we who are pacifists can make clear to those whom we join for concrete political purposes that our vision is captured by more determinative, or least different, loyalties than theirs.

For the issue is finally the relationship of truth and politics. It has often been pointed out that those who want to subject the political to the criterion of truth find it hard to avoid totalitarian or authoritarian modes of political life. However, truth is not a given but something that is discovered through our willingness to believe that the voice of the other might just be the voice of God. Therefore the commitment to non-violence requires the pacifist to respect those who think they must use coercion to protect the goods we hold in common. This does not mean that pacifists are called always to obey those in power; it does mean that we can be open to various political alternatives in the hope that we will discover ways of cooperating that make violence less necessary.

So pacifists cannot, in principle, be excluded from the political, once politics is understood as the ongoing discussion of peoples for the discovery of contingent truths. Of course that is exactly the understanding of politics that Lewy has disavowed in his way of construing the issue between pacifists and non-pacifists. So even though he has rendered a valuable service to us by revealing the selective humanism of pacifist movements in America over the past thirty years, I do not think it wise for us to underwrite the presuppositions of that analysis. For it can only continue to give us politics as usual in a way that is unfaithful to the cross of Christ as well as to the neighbor who has not yet accepted that cross.

In closing I want to raise an issue that is seldom discussed, one that I hope will help illumine the political question: how to understand the status of those who have participated honorably in war. One difficulty of the pacifist witness is that it seems to require the pacifist to ignore or dishonor those sacrifices—and I speak not just of the sacrifice of lives but also of the sacrifice many make in giving up their reluctance to kill. It seems that we must speak less than truthfully about what it means to participate in the common life of a people if it means we must lose the memory of those who have in the past fought in war.

For me to try to solve this would be foolish; I simply want to raise it up as a fundamental political issue for any good society. For I suspect that we are condemned to continue to fight wars exactly because we do not know how to honor people who have fought wars in the past while at the same time we work to avoid fighting further wars. It is my hope that pacifists will help us learn to tell the story of our lives in such a way that the valor and sacrifice of participants in past wars will be an honorable part of that story without entailing the repetition of war for our own lives.

8

The Commitment to Socialism

William McGurn

IN A SMALL jumble of steel and concrete in the midst of Asia's most dynamic city, Manh Chung Tu waits for a freedom that may never come. Mr. Manh is a Vietnamese in his mid-twenties, one of the thousands of boat people to wash up on Hong Kong's shores in recent years. He has been here six years—six years and one day on the sunny afternoon I met him. Over the walls, looped with barbed wire, the tops of the colony's blue-and-cream double-decker buses are just visible.

Mr. Manh has some 5,137 neighbors, close neighbors you might say, since at Sham Shui Po camp they live in two warehouses filled with row upon row of bunk beds, each bed three levels high, stacked three deep on either side of a center aisle as long as a football field. Makeshift curtains strung around the sides represent futile efforts at modesty; "a bloody stalag," says one British official visiting the site. Yet Mr. Manh and the others all say they'd sooner stay here than go back to Vietnam; they are willing to wait years in the hopes of that magic ticket to America. Back in Vietnam, there are reports of famine in the North, skirmishes with the Cambodian resistance (including the murderous Khmer Rouge), and an outflow of refugees now at its

William McGurn, former deputy editorial page editor of the *Asian Wall Street Journal*, was named Washington editor of *National Review* in May 1989. This essay is reprinted by permission from the *American Spectator* (October 1988).

largest level in years. Whatever you call this, it's not peace. So where are the peace workers today?

According to Guenter Lewy, they've long since moved on to other things, Central America and South Africa for example. The reason, says Lewy, is that the American peace movement was interested not so much in peace as in a unilateral American withdrawal that would "in effect make sure that the war would go on until the NLF and the North Vietnamese had achieved their objectives." In *Peace and Revolution*, Lewy charts how American pacifism moved from a principled repudiation of the use of arms to a whorish endorsement of armed struggle on behalf of some of the world's most brutal Communist insurgencies. It couldn't have been a more timely book. Coming as it did just after Congress quibbled over funding for the Nicaraguan *contras* and the Democratic party drafted a presidential platform labeling South Africa as a "terrorist state," *Peace and Revolution* makes bracing reading. We've seen it all before, says Lewy. The lessons his analysis contains are of import to pacifists interested in restoring integrity to their movement. More important, the book should be required reading for U.S. policymakers responding to similar pressure in trouble spots from El Salvador to South Korea today.

The Catalyst: Vietnam

Although Lewy takes time out to deal with the peace movement's flings with such countries as Nicaragua and Cuba, he amply demonstrates that the real catalyst for its sorry transformation was Vietnam. Prior to 1965, American pacifists had been careful to steer clear of any cooperation with Communists, and their principled refusal to distinguish between lawful and unlawful uses of force led them even to deny the legitimacy of the war against Hitler, as abhorrent as they held Nazism to be. With Vietnam, they became partisans and opened themselves to cooperation with Communists and their friends. "Unlike earlier conscientious objectors who had recognized the right of society to make decisions on war and peace but had claimed for themselves the right to refuse to abide by the command to bear arms," says Lewy, "the new 'resisters' engaged in acts of obstruction and even sabotage of the war effort.'' It wasn't long before NLF flags started flying at American peace rallies. In a way this was almost inevitable. Once the emphasis was shifted from non-violence to the establishment of a socialist order, the slope was slippery enough for advocates to slide easily into the propagandist role. In 1967, for example, A. J. Muste, a leader of the War Resisters League, argued that "politically sophisticated pacifists" had to distinguish "between the violence of liberation movements (of people who, in a situation where they have no real possibility of democratic means, resort to violence) and the violence imposed on these countries by imperialist powers, for example, the violence which the United States is carrying out in Vietnam at the present time.''

The head of the Indochina program for the American Friends Service Committee (AFSC), John McAuliff, likewise suggested in the aftermath of the fall of Saigon that America ought to rethink "the role of Marxist-Leninist ideology in Vietnam's success and consequently its application to our own and other struggles. . . . It is not in the interests of the American people to oppose socialist/communist revolutions in other countries. Moreover, if we try to understand what is in their best interests, we are likely often to support such revolutions in the Third World.''

Not surprisingly, these same groups were the last to criticize the newly installed Communist regimes in Indochina even after evidence of the reeducation camps and killing fields became overwhelming. Instead, they directed their energy at undermining the credibility of refugees bearing reports of persecution as well as those in their own movement with enough integrity to acknowledge that something had gone horribly wrong.

Betrayal of Pacifist Principles

Lewy's impressive documentation of these events has to convince even the thickest reader. Nevertheless, a little juggling of the arrangement, along with a tad more attention to the philosophical claims of pacifism, might have helped put the evidence in better perspective. True enough, the first few chapters discuss pacifism itself, and the book is dotted with criticisms by long-

time pacifists upset with the drift of their respective organizations. But a bit more development of this theme early on would
have underscored the author's main point, to wit: that the
American peace movement not only picked the wrong side in
Vietnam, but betrayed its own principles in the process.

In his very first sentence Lewy correctly defines pacifism as
"the doctrine of those who are morally opposed to bearing arms
and who refuse to sanction war for any purpose, defensive or
otherwise." The magnitude of this claim needs to be fully taken
in before the seriousness of what happened in Vietnam can be
appreciated. For whereas most people will under certain conditions sanction war as a means to an end, a sometimes necessary
evil, pacifists make non-violence an end in itself. In other words,
while others have various mechanisms to allow for certain (but
not unlimited) use of force in pursuit of a just cause, pacifists
rule out questions of goals altogether.

Time and again *Peace and Revolution* illustrates how old-
timers in the movement—genuinely committed to this difficult
principle and seasoned by bitter experience with Communist
groups during World War II and the fifties—were most prescient
about where their movement was heading and why it was going
there. A good example was Alfred Hassler, who in 1973, after
almost a decade of futile opposition to the change, put his finger
squarely on the issue:

> A good many people in the movement, seeing the origins of the
> Indochina war in "the system," and recognizing that the institution
> of war will not be eliminated until the system is changed, let their
> logic drift into the untenable conclusion that the killing in Indochina
> could not be ended until the system, especially in the United States,
> was changed. Consistently, then, they became more assiduous for
> the victory by their side, which would be a defeat for the system,
> than an end to the killing and a transfer of the conflict, which was
> not all that simple, to the diplomatic arena.
>
> It is a point we pacifists need to get straight in our thinking. The
> broadest possible alliances are not constructive if they rest on the
> abandonment of our central belief. War is our first enemy; when we
> justify it for any ends (which is different from understanding the
> reasons people go to war) we have lost.

Even the brothers Berrigan, whose thoughts and writings
confirm the legitimacy of the pejorative "jesuitical," chastised

the peace groups for looking at North Vietnam as "an angel of light in comparison with the slouching Western beast." By then, of course, it was too late.

Personal and Public Morality

A good part of the new pacifists' problem was their misunderstanding of pacifism itself, a blurring of the lines between personal and public morality. Pacifism is by definition a highly personal option, given the fact that most of us agree that to stand by while the strong bully the weak can itself be criminal. It was such reasoning that reconciled Augustine to the duties of Roman citizenship, the great saint seeing the end as a "just order" rather than the mere absence of conflict. In short, the pacifist cannot turn his neighbor's cheek.

Given the inevitable tension of such a challenge, pacifism is not likely to remain true to itself when it attempts to become a mass movement. Like religious communities, pacifism can opt for purity, a way of example without retreating into naïveté. As George Weigel has put it in *Tranquillitas Ordinis*, "By witnessing to the truth of how things ought to be, pacifism could become a standard for measuring the gap between that moral and political horizon and things as they are." In 1955, Weigel notes, the AFSC published a study called *Speak Truth to Power: A Quaker Search for an Alternative to Violence* that did not shy away from the dilemma of power, was resolutely anti-Communist, and recognized that a genuine pacifist movement could lead even non-adherents to pay more attention to non-violent options. As Weigel further notes and Lewy more than proves, pacifism never did pick up this thread, to the great loss of both American society and the movement itself. If ever it does so, it will have to acknowledge its debt to these more traditional ethicists.

Apart from these philosophical shifts, there may be an even simpler explanation for the dramatic change in the American peace movement, mirroring the shift in America's mainstream churches, universities, and unions: the change in the kind of people who led these groups. Lewy points out that in the aftermath of World War I, pacifism became inextricably linked with socialism, particularly because of the argument that "wars are based on the economic rivalries of imperialist nations and are encouraged by the traffic in armaments carried on by profit-hungry capitalists.'' This in turn set up a "conflict of loyalties between the pacifists' ideals of non-violence and their aspirations to liberate the exploited and oppressed.''

By the time Vietnam rolled around, it was painfully clear that the commitment to socialism outweighed the commitment to non-violence, much as church elites found that this same commitment outweighed their religious doctrine. So whereas old-timers were people who were pacifists first and fuzzy socialists second, the new breed were committed socialists who didn't seem to comprehend the radicalism of the genuine pacifist position. This disturbed not a few people. *Peace and Revolution* is peppered with complaints, for example, that the AFSC was being increasingly run by non-Quakers often hostile to Quaker principles. Perhaps there's another book in this that might also ask why, even more than the commitment to "national liberation," the driving force of the new movement was a hatred of American democracy.

The Ongoing Importance

Why is any of this important today? As Lewy points out, although it is relatively small in numbers, the peace movement is perhaps more influential than ever, one example being the rejection by America's Roman Catholic bishops of the idea of deterrence and, more recently, of President Reagan's Star Wars program. It was these groups and their offspring that defeated funding for the Nicaraguan *contras*. And in the Philippines, it is the peace movement's financial and moral support that helps keep the insurgency alive and, even within the Aquino government, fuels the resentment against the U.S. bases there—this despite the overwhelmingly pro-American stance of the Filipino people.

For the American people, *Peace and Revolution* is a sharp reminder that the public realm has its own special virtues, particularly with regard to the use of force. For the American peace movement, it warns that being pure of heart is not enough once the line is crossed into public advocacy.

Toward the end of the book Lewy quotes Camus's warning that some forms of sincerity "are worse than lies." To learn that lesson from a book may be hard, but it is easier than learning it from a bayonet. Just ask the folks at Sham Shui Po.

9

The Political Relevance
of Truth

Daniel A. Seeger

IN FOUNDING the American Friends Service Committee in
1917, Rufus Jones and his associates were exercising a prophetic office. All prophetic action and utterance marries eternal
truths to the conditions of a particular era or civilization. Proph-
ets, rooted in a particular time and culture, can speak its
language, perceive its problems, and address these with reme-
dies.

On the religious scene of the seventeenth century, Quakerism
was considered a radical invention. But George Fox, its founder,
was not at all concerned with newness. He spoke of finding a
Truth "which was before the world was." He sought simply to
revive the Christianity that was practiced by the Apostles. Yet,
steeped as he was in the idiom and the needs of his own time,
he was able to give these ancient truths a powerful contemporary
force.

As we become more removed from the particular culture,
time, and place of a prophetic leader, the message must be
translated into a contemporary idiom, and in this effort some of

Daniel A. Seeger is regional executive secretary for the New York office of the
American Friends Service Committee. He is also involved in the work of the
Friends World Committee for Consultation, whose headquarters are in London. His articles have been published in *Friends Journal, Quaker Life*, and
elsewhere.

the original Truth of the vision can easily be lost. This is the fundamental challenge that faces all people of faith: how to adapt revealed truths to the contemporary scene; how to distinguish a valid adaptation that retains the core of eternal Truth from something that merely dilutes the vision with the world's way of doing things.

The often horrific history of religion is a tale of human failure to make these vital distinctions. It is a tale of maladaptations. During his seventeenth-century ministry, George Fox dismissed the then established Christian Church as "seventeen centuries of apostasy." This judgment is perhaps too extreme and fails to give credit to many manifestations of great sanctity nourished in official church institutions. But it does remind us of the difficulty, and of the frequent failures, of spiritual enterprise.

In relatively static cultures, a prophet's spiritual heirs have a less difficult task than in fast-changing cultures. There is more occasion for pondering and for worshipful seeking and listening. In a time when cultural evolution proceeds at a dizzying pace, the successful realization of a vision rooted in eternal things demands prophetic gifts almost equal in stature to the gifts of those who were the vision's original channels.

Rufus Jones and the other founders of the American Friends Service Committee were indeed acting prophetically. But, given all that has transpired in society during the more than seventy years since then, given the awesome and traumatic events the human family has endured, it is scarcely surprising that in the AFSC there have been lapses in faithfulness.

Our task is not to engage in recriminations over this, or to doubt the relevance of the prophetic vision. The fact that Christians have rationalized slavery, burned witches, and now prepare for a nuclear Armageddon should not distract us from pondering the message of Jesus of Nazareth. Nor should our human failures as pacifists deter us from renewing our vision and from witnessing with joy to its powerful relevance to the problems of contemporary life.

An Opportunity for Renewal

The publication of Guenter Lewy's *Peace and Revolution* provides us with an opportunity to practice such a renewal. But the book is very definitely a mixed blessing, and sorting out its meaning for us will not be easy to do.

In his final chapter Professor Lewy reveals a theory about the role of pacifists in political life that very few people, pacifists or not, can be expected to take seriously: "When the pacifist's conscience does not allow him to support policies that utilize force or the threat of force, the proper course for him is to remain silent." What would our silence have gained for humanity during the long years of the Vietnam war? Lewy further claims that in the real world it is not possible for pacifists to be both morally pure (by which he means consistently faithful to their pacifist beliefs) and politically relevant. It is interesting that he can reach such a conclusion in a chapter about the political relevance of pacifism without ever mentioning the names of Mohandas Gandhi or Martin Luther King, Jr.!

This brief and simplistic chapter of philosophical conclusions is preceded by a lengthy historical narrative recounting the currents of thought within the peace movement in the 1960s through 1980s and their impact on the policies and programs of four notable peace organizations.

One might wish that the product of such massive research had been put to the service of pacifists for us to sort out its implications *en famille*, rather than having it presented in the context of a public attack on the philosophy of pacifism itself. Nevertheless, we must accept some responsibility for this turn of events, since we in the pacifist community have so often avoided the discipline of creative dialogue and of worshipful seeking in private. We must recognize that the sorts of "debates via memorandums" that Lewy so extensively exposes are not manifestations of the kind of patient waiting upon the Lord that must undergird a truly prophetic activism.

Recounting the history of the peace movement and of the currents of thought within it is an enormous task. Although he is seeking to advance a certain perspective (as any writer motivated to address a large and complex subject probably would want to do), one senses in Lewy's book an attempt to be accurate about the data he presents. There are occasional omissions and inaccuracies in detail. Nevertheless, he successfully captures the flavor and the tone, as well as the overall contours, of one of the significant streams of events, and he correctly identifies many of the key issues and currents of thought.

What Lewy Doesn't Mention

Simultaneously with the stream of events that Lewy narrates, many other things were taking place in the American Friends Service Committee that he does not mention. For instance, the AFSC carried on extensive and heroic programs directed at relieving suffering in many parts of the world. There were also intensive internal dialogues about issues not covered in Lewy's book. Some aspects of the story that were omitted might show some of what is included in a more favorable light. Lewy's failure to give an account of the AFSC's extensive relief work within South Vietnam seems a serious omission. But it is probably also true that a more extensive presentation of data would reveal a mix of strengths and weaknesses in the AFSC rather similar to that which Lewy demonstrates.

Furthermore, while most of an organization's energies are being devoted to traditional and unassailable work, a smaller proportion might be devoted to matters that account for much more of its impact on the body politic, and in connection with which it may be redefining itself in crucial ways.

Lewy has gathered a significant body of data that is worth serious pondering. That its presentation is flavored throughout with his antipathy for the peace movement does not, I think, absolve us from facing the fact that neither this prejudice nor the possibility of a distortion through selectivity can explain away so much that is regrettable in what he reveals. Clearly we are dealing with a period when, though we may not deserve all the reprobation Lewy heaps upon us, we are definitely not at our most insightful and centered best.

The very important question is: Have the lapses of this period been overcome, or are they waiting to recur under the pressures of some future crisis?

U.S. Betrayal of Values

Lewy does not seem to realize the extent of the crisis that overtook official American democratic institutions during the period about which he writes. He often seems to suggest that the doctrine of containing Communism and the prosecution of the Vietnam war were routine expressions of the American democratic will as registered by smoothly functioning institutions and processes, and that the pacifists' dissent from this was a kind of petulance by a minority.

The excesses that overtook the peace movement cannot be detached from their larger political context—from the profound betrayal of democratic and constitutional values perpetrated at the highest levels of government, and from the protracted cruelty an undeclared war represented for those sent to fight it from both sides and for their many, many civilian victims. Lewy fails to appreciate the extent to which peace-movement excess was stimulated by the excess and lawlessness of the establishment. This does not excuse the peace movement. Our steadfastness in Truth ought not to depend on the devotion of politicians to civil propriety. But awareness of this interactive dynamic between the peace movement and an official culture gone very far awry is necessary for a full understanding of what occurred. The response by the peace movement ought to have been characterized by unflagging efforts to strengthen and extend democratic practice and institutions, employing genuinely non-violent civil disobedience when truth demanded it.

It is probably true that during much of this period it was the general will of the American people that Communism be "contained." But did the American people have any way of knowing what the implementation of this policy goal meant for the daily life of people living under Somoza, Batista, Duvalier, the Shah of Iran, or Marcos, just to take some examples? People in such countries were expected to suffer political conditions for decades that Americans themselves would scarcely have tolerated at all. The United States may not have been guilty of establishing all these dictatorships, but that our policies extended their life to a very great extent is beyond doubt. As a result we were largely responsible for reinforcing situations that tended to inspire a desperate, at times ruthless quality in would-be liberationists. If the American people could have perceived what was going on during all those years of behind-the-scenes support for tyrants, they might still, perhaps, have wanted to contain Communism, but they most certainly would have insisted on a more humane strategy, which also would have been a more effective one in the long run.

The problem is that foreign-policy design and implementation is beyond the reach of the sort of democratic oversight that the American people can exercise, however fitfully and imperfectly, over the domestic conditions they experience every day. Public attention is focused on foreign-policy issues only after conflagrations have broken out and opportunities for constructive choices are lost. Till then, policy formulation is subject to the pressure of very limited constituencies with special axes to grind, usually of a commercial or ideological sort.

Consider the folly of the Reagan administration's policy in Central America, in both its conceptualization and its implementation. Consider the allegations that criminal acts were carried out within the White House by policymakers wishing to circumvent the will of Congress. Consider the failure of the tug of war between the Administration and those in Congress who wished to resist its errors to generate any policy expressive of the decency and greatness of the American people. This is indeed sobering.

The Declaration of Independence and the Constitution of the United States are in many ways prophetic documents. But they were written by people inhabiting a far different world. The need of the American people to find prophetic ways to live out the great principles enunciated in these eighteenth-century documents under contemporary conditions is no less urgent than the need for the peace movement to put its house in order.

The paradox of Lewy's critique of the peace movement is that he castigates us for tolerating in our ranks too many people who are very much like himself. His essential premise, made clear in his astonishing final chapter, is that philosophically rigorous and "pure" pacifism is politically irrelevant; political relevance, he argues, involves some accommodation with the processes of violence and war. This proposition, of course, is the same one preached to us from within the movement by those who design the compromises with violent revolution that Lewy finds so reprehensible. Granted, Lewy and the peaceniks he criticizes would choose different wars with which to sympathize. Yet in defending the use of violence in some circumstances, while apparently disallowing its use by the many millions who have needed liberation from U.S.-supported tyrannies, Lewy does not manage to define a moral position discernibly more lofty than that of the violent or quasi-violent peace-movement liberationists he criticizes.

Lingering Questions for Pacifists

Nevertheless, the many documents and the connecting narrative that Lewy has given us should prompt us to explore a series of questions:

1. How does a spiritually based pacifist organization prepare its committees and staff to deal with the wrenching questions that its activist life throws up before it? How much worshipful waiting in silence upon the Lord is done, when is it done, and by whom? How much energy goes into memorandum wars or verbal debate, as opposed to devotional readings and silent worship? How are the great underlying questions common to all the AFSC's diverse activities articulated and deliberated, so that an element of consciousness and intentionality, guided by divine leading, informs a corporate response to them?

In expending an annual budget of $20 million, how much time and energy should be given to the cultivation of the things of the Spirit? Is it reasonable to assume that the private, *individual* life-in-worship carried on by some committee members and staff is sufficient to undergird the spiritual basis of the *corporate* life of the AFSC, which can involve issues often unknown to faith communities at even a moderate distance from it?

2. From its inception the AFSC has generated unease among some Friends. Is the current degree of this unease simply a manifestation of "business as usual," or is there something uniquely significant about it? Can the AFSC retain its essential character if it is not linked in vital ways with the Religious Society of Friends, if members of the Society do not, in general, feel some sense of participation in and ownership of the AFSC? How are such vital relationships nourished?

3. The AFSC is appropriately "ecumenical" in the composition of its staff, committees, and constituents. Beyond a doubt, many people from faith traditions other than Friends are highly qualified to advance all spiritual and practical aspects of the AFSC's life. But is it not also true that maintaining an authentic Quaker character in the AFSC is scarcely possible if there are fewer and fewer Friends working on its staff and committees?

4. At times, the leadership group in the AFSC and the circle of influential or "weighty" people in the Religious Society of Friends overlap substantially. For such Friends, work in the AFSC is one expression of their allegiance to the life of the society, not a distraction from it. But how can we ensure that the pressures of AFSC work do not become so consuming to those Friends involved in it that their participation in the wider Society of Friends becomes marginalized? How can we ensure that the self-protective dynamic, common in all organizational life, does not cause the AFSC to hold at arm's length those experienced Friends who raise disquieting questions about its policies and programs?

5. How does the AFSC's "ecumenical" or universalist composition affect its Quaker character? The AFSC would be quite different if it were made up of Friends collaborating with active Jews, Buddhists, Christians, Hindus, and other people of faith who are pacifists and whose pacifism is rooted in their faith, than if it were made up of Friends collaborating with highly secularized colleagues who derive their worldview from the European Enlightenment or from Marxist sources, and who might regard the organization's pacifist tradition as a cultural quaintness to be tolerated.

The AFSC is at neither of these extremes. Moreover, I want to be clear that I do not use "Marxism" as a scare word; I would never want to see an AFSC devoid of people within its ranks qualified to advance the powerful analysis of the political economy that Marxism has to offer. But how do we decide what mix from among the possibilities will best ensure that the AFSC is both universalist and an authentic expression of Friends' testimonies? Which of the several available kinds of liberation theology do we incorporate into the AFSC, and why? When reaching beyond North Atlantic cultures to embrace some of the diversity of world views and insights in the First, Second, and Third Worlds, do we absorb Maoists or Buddhists, or both? These are just a few examples from a vast variety of possibilities. How are such balances attended to?

Some Ways of Approach

In the New York Regional Office of the American Friends Service Committee, where I work, we have tried several new practices that seek a way forward in these areas. We have co-sponsored with New York Yearly Meeting two offerings of the Quaker Studies Program, a twenty-four-week curriculum originally developed by Philadelphia Yearly Meeting, so that staff and committee members of every faith and background could join with local Friends to explore the values that animate the AFSC and the Religious Society of Friends. Aside from the obvious benefits to the persons enrolled in the program, this co-sponsorship of an activity by an AFSC regional office and its local Yearly Meeting—an activity focused on an exploration of Friends values—symbolically affirms an important community of interest.

As a regional executive secretary of the AFSC I spend substantial amounts of my personal, extracurricular time, plus up to 7 per cent of my AFSC staff time, in activities related to the Religious Society of Friends. My approach to these activities is not that of doing "public relations," seeking to sell the AFSC or to tell its story to an important constituency. I am simply to try to be of service to the Religious Society, and to absorb what I can of the spiritual currents I encounter there to enrich my AFSC work.

A third thing worth mentioning is the important role of youth for the renewal of a prophetic vision. The AFSC works with many constituencies of youth. Many of these young people come from religious and cultural backgrounds that make us rightfully wary of "proselytizing" them. But it is fair to observe that in recent years the AFSC has been weak in responding to those young people who turn to us specifically desiring an experience of Quaker activism and an exposure to Friends values. This

160   DANIEL A. SEEGER

seems particularly so if the young people happen to come from middle-class backgrounds. In the New York office we have inaugurated the Youth Service Opportunities Project, now an independent organization with Friends and people of other faiths on its board. The YSOP draws a diverse constituency of young people into service projects that provide a Quaker undergirding and interpretation.

The Political Relevance of Truth

In summary, the proposition that Professor Lewy shares with those in the peace movement whom he most criticizes—that a purely pacifist position is not particularly relevant—is, of course, untrue. Gandhi and Martin Luther King, to cite just two of the most conspicuous examples, were profoundly relevant politically, and their non-violence was always philosophically unassailable. Indeed, it is the attempt to achieve good ends by evil means that always is irrelevant, always compounds human suffering. True power and true effectiveness are achieved, not by those who seek them, but by those who serve the Truth alone for its own sake. This is the only genuine radicalism, and the only realistic program for a better future for humankind.

In his insightful book *Beyond Majority Rule: Voteless Decisions in the Religious Society of Friends*, Michael J. Sheeran correctly observes that among practicing Friends a cleavage tends to occur between those who experience the "gathered" or "covered" condition in reaching corporate decisions and those who do not. The practice of unity in the decision-making does not require that every last person feel comfortable with each decision taken; but clearly the amount and seriousness of earnest disquiet that was simply overridden within the AFSC during the 1960s and 1970s marked a substantial lapse from Friends practice.

Whether errors analogous to those will recur depends on the matter of decision-making practice more than any other. In the future, when faced with wrenching circumstances such as the Vietnam war presented, will the AFSC be able to wait to achieve a "gathered" or "covered" condition before proceeding? Will we have the faith to realize that hasty expedients adopted in the face of grave circumstances do not really lessen overall human suffering? Will we achieve the balance necessary to realize that not everything that proclaims itself anti-establishment and pro-liberation is an expression of Truth, and that history is as replete with untruthful revolutions as with untruthful established-states-of-affairs? Will we be able to resist the temptation to try to counter official untruth with an equal and opposite untruth? Neither violence nor untruth will dispel ignorance and evil. Only Truth will do this. This is the law of the universe, ancient and inexhaustible. And only our silent worship and our practice of unity can hold us in the power of that law and life that alone can enable us to render a truly prophetic service.

10

The Violent Pacifists

Rael Jean Isaac

THE SUBTITLE of Guenter Lewy's valuable book is *The Moral Crisis of American Pacifism.* A better one would be: "The Moral *Collapse* of American Pacifism," for the crisis is long past. The four major pacifist organizations he examines—American Friends Service Committee (AFSC), Fellowship of Reconciliation (FOR), War Resisters League (WRL), Women's International League for Peace and Freedom (WILPF)—now work cozily with Communist fronts and form part and parcel of the various radical "peace-and-justice" coalitions that advocate disarmament at home and the triumph of the Third World Marxist-Leninist insurgencies abroad.

The four organizations were born during or immediately after World War I, and from the beginning there were ideological stresses within them. Lewy shows, indeed, that the arguments that would undermine pacifism in the 1960s were raised as early as the 1920s, when the new organizations faced their first crisis, the temptation of Marxism.

First Crisis: Marxism

In a landmark 1928 essay entitled "Pacifism and Class War," A. J. Muste, for many years the most prominent American

---

Rael Jean Isaac is the author, with Erich Isaac, of *The Coercive Utopians.* Her articles have appeared in the *American Spectator,* the *New Republic, Commentary, Atlantic, Midstream,* and *Politique Internationale.* This essay is reprinted by permission from *Commentary* (September 1988; all rights reserved).

pacifist, expanded the definition of the sorts of violence that pacifists should oppose; they now included "the economic, social, political order in which we live." At the same time, Muste excused the violence perpetrated by those fighting against the American "order" by initiating what was later to become a favorite device of pacifist authors: a "calculus" of violence. Ninety per cent of the violence in the world, he wrote, was perpetrated by the forces of the status quo; it was therefore "ludicrous" for people to focus on the 10 per cent actively committed by those rebelling against the repressive system. Similarly, in 1933 Devere Allen argued that "all the violence that Communism in this country advocates and desires is as a drop in the creek as compared with the violence which we live under in the present economic system."

As Lewy shows, the pacifist organizations weathered this first crisis, aided by the strong consensus of the membership that violence of any kind must never be condoned. A 1933 poll of the membership of the Fellowship of Reconciliation produced a lopsided majority of 877 to 93 opposing class violence as well as international violence. Those insistent upon Marxist doctrine— which in the FOR at one point included the organization's executive secretary, J. B. Matthews—were forced to resign.

In fact, up to the early 1960s the pacifist organizations remained clear-headed in recognizing that Communists were not proper allies. Each of the organizations issued statements like the FOR's 1940 declaration that

> the Communist party rejects pacifism in principle. . . . For the FOR to be associated with the CP in "anti-war activities" could therefore only confuse multitudes of people as to our aim and function and thus stultify our efforts.

But all this was to crumble in the face of the second moral crisis of the pacifists, the Vietnam war.

Second Crisis: Vietnam

During the course of U.S. involvement in that war, the pacifist organizations became open partisans of a North Vietnamese victory and abandoned their opposition to participating in united fronts with Communists. The arguments rejected in the 1930s now became cornerstones of pacifist thought. In 1970, the national council of the FOR, invoking the increasingly familiar "calculus" of violence, adopted a statement exonerating the behavior of the radical New Left fringe: "Santa Barbara students who burned a branch of the Bank of America . . . committed a very mild act of violence in comparison with, for example, the dropping of 12,000 tons of bombs on South Vietnam by the American high command." Similarly, WILPF president Kay Camp insisted that the impetuous act of the students could not be equated "with the institutionalized violence of our government."

Like the distinction pointed to earlier by A. J. Muste, a distinction came to be drawn at this time between the violence of the oppressor and the violence of the oppressed, which had to be "understood" and judged in different terms. According to a 1968 statement by War Resisters International (the parent body of the American WRL), the violence of Americans was "criminal" while that of the oppressed, at home and abroad, was "tragic." WRL's Dave Dellinger declared that he did not repudiate or oppose "the violence of the victims."

Within each of the organizations, as Lewy documents, there were warnings that pacifism was being undermined by these stands, but the warnings were ignored. Albert Hassler, the longtime executive secretary of the FOR, wrote in 1968 that terms like "the violence of the status quo" were having a subversive effect, and that pacifists were becoming believers, if not in "just war," then in "just revolutions." Jim Forest, also of the FOR, wondered about "the collapse of our faith in the pacifist insight: that the means control the quality of the end." But the opponents of the new trend were fatally hobbled because they agreed with the majority about the war in Vietnam, where (in Hassler's words) the United States was doing "obscenely indecent things." This made them hesitant about pressing their case, either inside or outside the organizations. Once they saw that their views were repudiated by the majority, they remained quiet, or, at best, bowed out.

Apologists for Oppression

Since the end of the war, the pacifist organizations have gone on to become mere apologists for a series of "progressive" regimes and terrorist bands. Lewy details the depths to which they sank in the immediate post-Vietnam era. As reports of oppression in "liberated" Vietnam reached the West and the seas became filled with boat people, the pacifist organizations simply denied that any human-rights violations were taking place at all. When a number of former anti-war activists, led by Joan Baez, published an open letter to the government of Vietnam protesting its treatment of dissidents, leaders of the WILPF (including its president and vice president) signed a counter-statement in the *New York Times* declaring that Vietnam "now enjoys human rights as it has never known in history."

Even the massacres taking place in Cambodia under Pol Pot failed to stir a response. According to John McAuliff, head of the AFSC's Indochina program, accusations against the Cambodian regime were part of an American "misinformation" campaign aimed at discrediting "the example of an alternative model of development and social organization." Not until Vietnam invaded and seized Cambodia, and publicized the atrocities of the Pol Pot regime, did the AFSC admit to the horrors that had occurred, and even then it put the primary blame for the fate of Cambodia on the United States.

The policy of working in coalition with groups professedly dedicated to "peace and justice" has led to the preposterous spectacle of WRL participation in a 1984 Libyan-influenced "peace" conference in Malta. Many delegates came with Libyan financing, and Qaddafi's Green Book was distributed to participants. In his report on the conference, David McReynolds of the WRL argued: "Rather than being frightened by the Libyans, should we not welcome the fact that revolutionary movements, including the Libyans, are interested in dialogue with non-violence movements?" A similar disposition has informed the multifaceted activities of the pacifist organizations in Central America, where again they have made common cause with radical forces openly espousing and engaging in violence. In short, most leaders of pacifist organizations today seem to share the sentiments expressed by a leader of the WRL: "There is one crime worse than murder: to retire from the revolution."

Pacifists and Violence

In the last chapter of his book, Lewy examines the moral dilemmas of pacifist witness in a democratic order. Here he argues that pacifists have a legitimate role to play as bearers of the humanitarian conscience, reminding the rest of us of the link between means and ends. As Lewy writes: "The pacifist vision of a world free of the threat of war can help build support for the development of an ordered political community at the international level able to resolve conflicts peacefully and justly." But—he goes on—when pacifists enter the political arena to propose policies for their nation, they become subject to what Weber called the "ethic of responsibility," which involves taking into account the realities of power and the likely consequence of political decisions: the policies they advocate must be judged by their results. Finally, while pacifists may, for themselves, "seek individual salvation through ethical absolutism and purity," they have no right to sacrifice others to this vocation.

There can be no quarrel with any of this. But on the basis of his own evidence, Lewy could have gone much further in exploring the corrupting consequences that ensue when pacifists destroy the traditional meaning of violence in order to endorse the violence of those they favor. The reasoning goes like this: if, as David McReynolds maintains, the violence of unemployment is as real "as napalm falling on Vietnam," then it is no more reprehensible to work to bring down a government adjudged guilty of causing unemployment than to permit it to continue in existence; indeed, it may be less so, because a "small" amount of "just" violence can lead to the overall lessening of violence in the world. In this way do self-styled pacifists move from abhorring to advocating violence.

Increasingly, indeed, violence has become the touchstone by which pacifists identify those worthy of their support. The more violent a group, the more just its cause must be—always provided, of course, that the cause is "progressive." Thus all four pacifist organizations identify with the PLO, a movement whose declared goal is the destruction of a national state and the removal of most of its present inhabitants.

The logic of their position forces the pacifist organizations to encourage and support even higher levels of violence, for if peace depends on the elimination of the injustices they have identified, the more violence is directed toward this end, the closer we will come to peace. Meanwhile, of course, the pacifists themselves sit on the sidelines, applauding. "I advocate non-violence. I practice non-violence," says Dave Dellinger; but, he goes on, the traditional non-violent movement "has been much too passive and much too ineffective, and I am not interested in the purity of the movement. I am interested in social effectiveness." Given the new ground rules, pacifists can simultaneously pursue revolution and underground warfare while retaining their pacifist virtue—the ultimate moral luxury.

That the major pacifist organizations have continued to enjoy credibility with so many people—the AFSC raises millions of dollars annually on the strength of its humanitarian image—is one of the scandals of American political life. In helping to expose the true theory and practice of pacifist organizations today, Guenther Lewy has performed a vital public service.

11

Lewy's Double Standard

James Matlack

G UENTER LEWY has written an industrious, impassioned book on a serious topic that deserves full discussion—the interplay between pacifist principles and the organizational responses made by prominent peace groups in the 1960s and 1970s, especially under the impact of the Indochina war. For participants and analysts alike, there is much to ponder and assess in looking closely at those turbulent decades.

I wish that Professor Lewy's book were not only industrious and impassioned but carefully written, accurate, and balanced as well. Alas, I do not find it so. While *Peace and Revolution* may occasion fruitful inquiry and exchange, I find the book itself badly flawed. Instead of being a guide to the issues and events under review, it is an obstacle to understanding them better.

My comments will be in three sections: Lewy's method and overall approach, his treatment of the American Friends Service Committee (AFSC), and some perspectives on his basic thesis that in the 1960s leading U.S. pacifist organizations abandoned their traditional values and became apologists for totalitarian states and revolutionary violence.

LEWY'S METHOD AND APPROACH

Throughout *Peace and Revolution* Guenter Lewy positions himself as a defender of pacifist integrity, as he laments the alleged

---

James Matlack is director of the Washington office of the American Friends Service Committee. He previously held academic and administrative posts at several colleges and universities.

loss of spiritual moorings and forsaking of non-violence of the four groups he has studied as "one of the great moral tragedies of our age." I do not think he proves his case on the abandonment theme, but there is a deeper falseness to his stance. He himself is not a pacifist. Indeed, as his remarkable last chapter makes clear, he scorns pacifism in any form. His posture as a "defender" allows him to set up his own narrow definition of pacifism—a most curious and ahistorical one—and then to discredit *all* pacifists, whether bona fide or not in his eyes.

The book is full of rules and integrity tests for pacifists, and many individuals are labeled apostates. In the end, however, even Lewy's *true* pacifist is robbed of political voice and relevance. The best of the lot are purists—utopian perfectionists— who cannot enter the policy debate but are reduced to an injunction of silence. Society may tolerate such spiritual misfits as long as others are willing to die in defense of the general freedoms, but the pacifist credo must be utterly repudiated because "if allowed, [it] would indeed guarantee the triumph of tyranny." This is not a defense of pacifist ideals but a fundamental argument to discredit all pacifists and thereby remove an obstacle to the robust use of American power and military force in the world.

There is a second contradiction at the core of Lewy's conception. While he labels the work a study in pacifism, he cares much more intensely about anti-Communism. For all the detailed exegesis of organizational stances, the apostasy that energizes his criticism is not falling away from "pure" non-violence but failure to denounce Communists. Lewy insists that "the principled rejection of Communist theory and practice remains a litmus test of political and moral integrity." Anti-Communism—not renunciation of violence—is the bedrock upon which his analytic structure rests, with confusing and paradoxical effects upon his critique of the pacifists.

His inconsistent focus upon non-violence is further clouded by his mistaken notions about the history, theory, and practice of civil disobedience. He rejects it, calling it an effort to "circumvent and override the democratic process" and therefore an illegitimate, coercive, and ultimately violent form of advocacy.

Distinctions are not kept between disciplined and non-violent protesters who accept the penalty of the law and any unrelated "crazy" who may make a scene at a demonstration. Only rarely does Lewy mention the impressive efforts made by pacifists to train marshalls, control crowds, and curb violence at countless protests. Instead, he sees any resort to civil disobedience as a knowing invitation to violent confrontation.

There is a further distortion concerning civil disobedience and non-violence. Lewy asserts that pacifists made only individual decisions to refuse personal military service but rarely engaged in collective public action prior to the 1960s, when the turn toward violence beset them. He portrays that turning as a tactic of the past twenty years—not an expression of deep conviction—for expressing alienation from the U.S. government as well as solidarity with liberation struggles. This is false to the AFSC's record since 1917, and it is totally absurd with regard to Quakers, who went to jail under Cromwell and Charles II and were hanged in Boston Common by the Puritans for acts of public civil disobedience two centuries before the *Communist Manifesto* was written.

Purely a Paper Trail

Lewy's methodology is strangely partial and incomplete. He spent long hours in archives but apparently did little fact-checking or speaking with participants to gain an understanding of the context for the many documents he quotes. His critique seems purely a paper trail, bloodless and abstract, a chilly exercise in dissection. All the passion comes in Lewy's own assertion of a highly personalized and dogmatic context. How much better to have talked with those whom he quotes to ask for *their* recollection of the context, *their* passions and interpretations. Perhaps this would have yielded data too complex to fit into the paradigm he had in mind.

The failure to do simple fact-checking on old documents (if not to interview their authors) leads Lewy into gross error and repeated misrepresentations that undermine the reliability of his conclusions. It becomes evident that he did not learn some of the most basic facts about the AFSC before rendering a sweeping condemnation of the organization. Two examples (out of many) illustrate this point.

In regard to the AFSC's response to famine in Cambodia in 1979, Lewy notes that a "Cambodian Relief and Reconciliation Fund" was set up to solicit funds to be spent "on a 50/50 basis for food support and political interpretation."

> Presumably the effort to communicate to the American people the explanations developed by Russell Johnson and others in the AFSC about the deeper roots of the Cambodian tragedy was as important to the AFSC as the actual relief of starvation [p. 144].

What Lewy failed to find out before making this caustic comment is that the fund in question was a small-scale project of a peace-education staff in New England that may have garnered a few thousand dollars. The major Cambodian relief effort by the AFSC was carried on from the main office in Philadelphia, not by the Peace Education division but by the International Division, which Lewy never mentions in the book even though it has the largest staff and budget of all the units in the AFSC. In fact, the AFSC sent more than $2 million in food and agricultural aid to Cambodia and another $1 million in medical and school supplies.

Elsewhere Lewy quotes from *The Grenada Papers*, where Ian Jacobs, an assistant to Maurice Bishop, reports on a tour in the United States. Jacobs says that a donor offered up to $2,000 to pay for a word processor if a tax credit could be arranged for him, and that he (Jacobs) asked an AFSC contact to pass the contribution through the AFSC. Then Lewy says, "We do not know whether the plans for this money laundering operation were actually carried out" (p. 154). He apparently never checked on the tale before putting it in his book. Instead he immediately describes AFSC staff who "wax enthusiastic" about Grenada, leaving the impression that they would comply with the scheme. Had he checked, he would have found that the AFSC would not and did not approve such a transfer of funds. Better to leave the reference as hearsay and innuendo. This is not scholarship; it is casual slander.

Crediting Only the Critics

In the voluminous reading of files that Lewy undertook he seems to have had one steady goal: find the critics. The voices that come to us from the paper trail are almost exclusively accusing and complaining. In the way that Lewy presents them, the critics are always right. It is a one-sided dialogue. We rarely get the other half of the debate or considered responses to complaints. Too often it is an indictment with no defense allowed. Jim Forest condemns human-rights violations in Vietnam, but we never hear what Paul Quinn-Judge says in response. A major distortion is created by Lewy's tendency to credit all the critics and *only* the critics with true concern, moral sensitivity, and accurate analysis. The world is both more complex and more balanced than that.

There are more specific problems with the documentation in *Peace and Revolution*. Often quotations are used as ornaments for prior assumptions rather than as building blocks in an argument. The reader is not informed that juxtaposed quotes actually refer to different topics or come from different time periods. Important distinctions collapse in the strange logic of Lewy's indictment. Dave Elder summarizes reports from field staff and is labeled "a defender of Communist Vietnam," presumably because he did not preface the report with a stout denunciation of Communist abuses. David McReynolds attends a conference in Malta whose sponsor got some funds from Libya; thereafter it is several times alleged that the War Resisters League formed an "alliance" with Qaddafi. Many who attend conferences of, say, the Ethics and Public Policy Center would no doubt be surprised to learn that their employers were thereby forming an alliance with the sponsoring organization.

Because of the systematic faults in Lewy's overall approach and methodology, I have great difficulty giving credence to his conclusions. I wish that these defects did not loom so large, because the issues he raises deserve vigorous and thoughtful debate. That debate is hampered by the over-simple, partisan methodology of the book. As Jim Forest, one of the heroes of true pacifism as portrayed in *Peace and Revolution*, has said:

"Lewy's argument is not so much that of an historian as of a lawyer for the prosecution who uses only evidence that strengthens the indictment. His book is less a work of scholarship than a political tract."

AMERICAN FRIENDS SERVICE COMMITTEE

I am a birthright Quaker. I was associated with the AFSC as a member of the board and of various committees through the 1970s, and I became a staff member in 1983. Obviously my perspective on the book is rooted in this experience. As Thoreau said in *Walden,* "I should not talk so much about myself if there were anybody else whom I knew as well."

I cannot speak in detail about the other groups and personalities analyzed in the book, but I find Lewy's treatment of the AFSC often biased, misinformed, or pressed to a formula drawn from his own preconceptions rather than from the evidence provided.

The AFSC that I know is much larger, more complex, more diverse in its projects and concerns, more active in struggling to "see what love can do," than Lewy's rigid cross-sectional view suggests. AFSC staff in the field around the world work amid great pain, stress, anger, desperate need, and brave efforts to secure justice and self-empowerment. It is unfair and misleading to issue a sweeping condemnation of the AFSC from perusal of the archives without giving any weight to the staff engagement in the real world, to the totality of the enterprise.

Lewy either does not know or chooses to withhold basic facts about the AFSC, such as the existence of the whole International Division, whose non-appearance I noted previously. Since AFSC work and policy formation frequently combine the efforts of more than one division, Lewy's one-dimensional perspective is partial and inevitably skewed. At times it is wildly mistaken.

Misrepresenting the Board

As a dynamic, evolving, multi-faceted agency, the AFSC looks to its board for coherence and consistency rooted in Quaker values and in the ongoing search for Truth. The board meets in a spirit of worship and often falls into prayerful silence in the midst of a heated discussion. Quaker doctrine and policy are not set by an abstract blueprint but are actively sought in an ongoing process of clarification, of continually seeking more Light on even the most familiar problems.

When Lewy condemns the 1984 AFSC guidelines on engaging in civil disobedience for allowing "easy resort" to such actions on merely an "intuitive feeling of moral outrage," he leaves out the most crucial element in the decision-making process: the Board of Directors. Here as so often elsewhere, he equates a paper statement with an authentic action. Only the board can approve AFSC participation in civil disobedience. Board members are guided by the printed advice, to be sure, but they decide on specific cases under the leading of the Spirit and in a unified sense of rightness. Lewy has never sat in such a meeting when a request is under lengthy discussion or when the board denies approval after laboring over a proposal.

A similar oversimplification concerns the AFSC's participation in coalitions: Lewy mistakes printed guidance for the actual, dynamic process of decision-making. Here he compounds his error by asserting that the AFSC organized a protest in 1983 for which a number of Communist and New Left groups expressed support, when in fact the AFSC joined a long list of co-sponsors but in no sense "organized" the event.

When he does focus on the AFSC Board of Directors, he misunderstands the nomination process for board membership, which allows him to describe a cabal through which "control of the board by the Philadelphia national office is assured." In this way, he alleges, leftist and pro-Marxist viewpoints are protected and perpetuated in the AFSC.

Lewy is simply wrong on another charge. Each region (of which there are nine) appoints a representative to participate fully in the deliberations and decisions of the Board of Directors. These nine representatives are chosen independent of national office influence. Further, by definition, every member of the AFSC board is a Quaker and a member of a Yearly Meeting. Although in some years the number of board members chosen from the group of corporation members appointed by Yearly

Meetings has been a point of controversy, it is the full corporation that approves nominations to the board. Therefore Lewy's
statement that ''the Yearly Meeting members are all but unrepre-
sented on the board of directors'' is simply untrue. But he
apparently prefers a conspiratorial view.

The Conspiracy Mentality

This conspiratorial assumption is at work throughout *Peace
and Revolution*, marring Lewy's case. Many times a single
staffer is taken as expressing the official position of the whole
organization, even when writing or speaking apart from AFSC
tasks. Russell Johnson was not the whole AFSC; he was one of
ten regional peace secretaries. Would not some examination of
the others be relevant to judgments about the entire organization?

The conspiracy mentality gives extraordinary powers to specific and suspect participants. The AFSC board may sound
''reasonable,'' but the staff cabal are really ''in control'' and
pursue their leftist dreams as they please. When staff leaders
issue cautions on controversial actions, Lewy gives no credit for
AFSC self-discipline but assumes that runaway program staff
will flout such advice. When the AFSC forms a panel of eight
experts (five of them Quakers) to draft the booklet *Peace in
Vietnam*, Lewy cites a suspect association for two of them—
leaving six unnamed—and then assumes that the wayward views
of the two must have tainted the entire project. Any involvement
in a public event by one of his proscribed groups or leaders is
always enough for Lewy to turn the event into a worst-case
confirmation of his thesis.

The heart of Professor Lewy's argument lies in the alleged
transformation of the AFSC and other pacifist groups during the
ordeal of the Indochina war. The AFSC argued publicly against
U.S. intervention in Vietnam from 1954—*not* 1964—onward.
We did not come late to a position for total withdrawal of
American forces out of ''infatuation with'' or ''loyalty to'' the
NLF but out of longstanding analysis and conviction.

The AFSC expressed support for the Third Force in South
Vietnam from the late 1960s and did not, as Lewy asserts, turn

reluctantly to Third Force options in 1974. AFSC representatives met with leaders of the Buddhist School of Social Service as early as 1965. In 1968 an AFSC staffer made a plea directly to the U.S. ambassador that Buddhist and Third Force groups be respected and brought fully into the political process in South Vietnam, only to be summarily rebuffed.

I think that the AFSC stayed reasonably consistent in its policy stances on the Indochina war despite the turbulence and passions of the era. I do not agree that the organization sold out its principles, was "loyal to the NLF," or abandoned its central tenet of non-violence. Lewy's attempt to show the contrary is flawed by overstatement and mishandling of the evidence. *Peace and Revolution* shows an astonishing ignorance of actual AFSC programs within its framework of condemnation.

In one case Lewy mentions a dispute over a newsletter of the Buddhist Church that was denied access to AFSC facilities. From this scant base a preposterous allegation follows: the AFSC "[excluded] the Buddhists from its medical aid program and [limited] this aid to the NLF and North Vietnam." This seems to be a combination of Lewy's most florid fantasies and his failure to check facts. The actual aid programs of the AFSC's International Division were conducted in South Vietnam throughout the war on an emphatically non-exclusionary basis. A majority of patients treated over eight years were, broadly speaking, surely Buddhists. At least $2 million was spent on the AFSC medical and prosthetics center at Quang Ngai alone. Small token shipments of medical aid were also sent to the NLF and to North Vietnam at the time in question. How can Lewy's larger accusations remain credible when he allows such glaring errors, always to the detriment of the AFSC?

Professor Lewy castigates the AFSC for "wishful thinking and denial of painful realities" in its attitude toward Cambodia under Pol Pot—indeed, for issuing "an apologia for the unfolding horrors of revolutionary Cambodia." Whatever the errors of analysis and expectation—and there were culpable ones—facts about the bloody rule of the Khmer Rouge became more widely known *after* 1979. I was a member of the AFSC delegation that reached Phnom Penh in September of that year, the first representatives of a private Western voluntary agency to visit the city in four years. It was a scarring experience. Our reports afterward were unsparing on the genocidal conduct of the Khmer Rouge. Given Lewy's criticism of the AFSC for misjudging them up to 1979, what can be said for those who defended the Khmer Rouge after 1979? How would Lewy evaluate the position taken by the Reagan administration in the early 1980s when Jeane Kirkpatrick cast a series of votes at the United Nations to seat the Khmer Rouge as the lawful representatives of the Cambodian people?

Extending the Indictment

Professor Lewy carries over his indictment of the AFSC's policy stances on Vietnam—in brief, that we espoused violence and wanted the Communist side to win—to AFSC engagement with southern Africa, Central America, and the Middle East. Our refusal to denounce all Marxist influences and to lecture the oppressed against any recourse to violence converts readily, in Lewy's lexicon, to "making another region of the world safe for Marxist-Leninist revolution." I will not examine these cases in detail, but they are flawed, overdrawn, and simply wrong in many of the same ways as those I have drawn attention to previously (e.g., the assertion that AFSC field staff "vilify" Israel when not a single instance is cited).

In the midst of a rather fevered analysis of AFSC pronouncements on Central America, Lewy notes that a staff gathering in 1980 issued a "minute" (in Quaker parlance) on non-violence in Latin America. He finds that this statement exceeds previous AFSC positions in "openly [endorsing] violent struggle." Prompted by this staff memo, a far-reaching discussion ensued throughout the AFSC and resulted in a formal position paper entitled *AFSC Perspectives on Non-Violence in Relation to Groups Struggling for Social Justice.* Since I presided at one of several board sessions devoted to this concern and served as the principal drafter of the final statement, I take particular exception to Lewy's casual dismissal of its message. What he calls "certain rhetorical disclaimers" are, in fact, the most considered and unequivocal expression of the AFSC's continued adherence to non-violence. I cite some of its core sentences:

> Our most basic pledge is to forswear violence and to affirm the power of love in all settings. . . .
> Although we see the frequently gross disparity between violence of the powerful as against violence of those seeking to end their own oppression—although we yearn for and work for an end to all galling exploitation—we cannot endorse the use of violence. The AFSC stands firm on its Quaker heritage in denying the legitimacy of violence however extreme the provocation. We have not and will not formulate a theory of "acceptable" revolutionary violence. As George Fox [founder of Quakerism] said long ago: "The spirit of Christ, by which we are guided, is not changeable, so as once to command us from a thing of evil, and again to move us to it; and we certainly know . . . that the spirit of Christ . . . will never move us to fight and war against any man with outward weapons."

How can one say it more plainly? Yet Lewy persists in seeing encouragement of leftist guerrillas and loyalty to violent regimes as official AFSC policy.

Two more aspects of the treatment of the AFSC in *Peace and Revolution* must be mentioned. The first is Lewy's attempt at the close of chapter ten to drive off AFSC contributors because, he asserts, we hoodwink them about our real intentions, policies, and programs. Remarkably, the only programs he cites are the AFSC's support for "literacy courses and training programs" in the Third World and its backing of "local human rights organizations of the left." On this basis alone the AFSC is characterized as "a multimillion dollar international pressure group" that is undeserving of further public contributions. Is Lewy really opposed to literacy courses or is this just a part of a sustained effort to discredit the AFSC on any grounds, real or imagined?

More serious fault is found with the alleged constant AFSC lies to its supporters about AFSC "sympathies for Communism" and "support of revolutionary wars." Only this false premise about the AFSC's stance allows the charge of "deceit" to be lodged in the first place.

Given his mindset, it is not surprising that Lewy entitles a section "The AFSC Is Charged With Serving the Communists."

The FBI and the CIA give the AFSC a clean bill of health as sincere but misguided. Chuck Fager finds that the moral confusions and follies of the AFSC "are of its own making and not the KGB's." "And yet one cannot leave it at that," says Lewy. Here and elsewhere in the text, in discussing the three other pacifist organizations as well as the AFSC, he proceeds to entertain notions that traitors are at work, that KGB cadres may indeed be entrenched in leadership roles. These innuendoes are an exercise in paranoia and character assassination that, lacking concrete proofs, have no place in a book issued by a reputable publisher.

THE BROADER PICTURE

Let me close with a few reflections extending beyond the text. The first is to acknowledge that mistakes were made, judgments faltered, values were put in jeopardy over the period and on the issues under examination. I have been very critical of *Peace and Revolution*. This does not mean that I present myself or the AFSC as free from error or beyond the need for repentance and forgiveness. I resent the particular, systematic blaming in Professor Lewy's text, but I own to my frailty in navigating the turbulent waters of the 1960s.

Remember about the AFSC that, in contrast with the other groups in Lewy's book, the majority of our staff are in direct service work across the United States and especially overseas. They encounter firsthand and every day the conditions that many analysts and advocates of peace, freedom, justice, and security only theorize about. Our interpretation and advocacy emerge from this hands-on experience in the field. When staff form judgments about the role of U.S. policy in their local setting or the uses of U.S. tax dollars in situations of conflict or injustice, they and we feel compelled to speak out. Our first responsibility is to be concerned about the conduct of our own government and to speak truthfully as we are led.

Upholding Democratic Values?

Guenter Lewy is fiercely dedicated to upholding democratic values and practices. Unlike some protesters that he refers to, I did not see a complete breakdown of these worthy ideals in the United States during the 1960s, but we came closer to such a collapse than Lewy acknowledges. There were grave abuses at the highest levels of our government. The corruption of the democratic process was dismaying, with secret, illegal conduct and sustained deception in the pursuit of war and victory. It can fairly be asked who first despaired of democratic values, and whether radical protesters really did more to undermine democratic practices than did the cynical leaders who took us into and so deceitfully kept us in the Indochina war.

Lewy's dedication to democracy matches his forceful anti-Communism, but these two are not always synchronized. He evades the problem of giving assessment when according to his criteria a leader or government is only *half* right. The government of South Vietnam was, after all, a shallow pretense as a democracy, a corrupt and repressive regime. The military figures who ruled the land had previously fought at the side of the French and against their countrymen seeking an end to colonial rule. Benedict Arnold is the American counterpart, but at least he *started* on the better side of the independence struggle. How far can one go in pretending that going to battle for Khan or Minh or Ky or Thieu was somehow a defense of democracy rather than simply resistance to what was perceived as a Communist takeover?

The problem in Lewy's paradigm extends beyond Vietnam and produces one-sided results elsewhere in his justifications for the use of force. Lewy urges support for the Afghan rebels, the *contras* in Nicaragua, and UNITA in Angola as ''democratic'' factions. But the Afghan guerrillas are essentially feudal and deeply undemocratic in their political conceptions. The *contras* have been run from the top down with leaders, until quite recently, simply installed by the CIA. Many of UNITA's top lieutenants quit two years ago over Savimbi's high-handed cult of personality. Besides, Savimbi is only currently an anti-Communist, having spun through every point on the political compass including a stint as a devout Maoist. How are these movements reconciled with the required adherence to democratic values in Lewy's model for the acceptable use of force?

Double Standard for Violence

A pervasive paradigm in *Peace and Revolution* generates a one-sided approval for violence. Lewy is just as selective and doctrinaire in this regard as those he most condemns for leading pacifists astray. In his concluding chapter he argues that political relevance is gained only through an accommodation to war and violence. (His "true pacifist" is silent on the sidelines.) Yet Lewy will not endorse recourse to violence in all cases, only in those in defense of the security of the United States and in opposition to the Soviet Union or Communist surrogates. Pacifists are much blamed for falling into selective use of violence— they are barred in Lewy's scheme from having "favorite wars or revolutions"—but Lewy himself unabashedly denies to liberation struggles the same legitimacy in taking up arms that he freely grants to anti-Communist endeavors.

Professor Lewy's framework for consideration of violence leads to very disturbing conclusions. For example, no liberation struggle can be authentic or deserve our support if Communists are at all involved. Since the Communists are always the worst and most menacing option, they must be opposed in every case even if this involves defeating or deferring the liberation effort. Should we, after all, have adopted Admiral Radford's scheme for using nuclear weapons to help the French keep control over Vietnam? How does liberation *ever* come to an oppressed people if the United States is duty-bound to oppose their struggle unless they purge themselves of Communists and Marxist influences? Under this approach, if Moses had had a sufficiently left-wing assistant, the Children of Israel would still be in Egyptian bondage and Pharoah would be entitled to tactical nuclear weapons.

What is more disturbing about Lewy's paradigm is that any criticism of a U.S. role in support of a regime in turn opposed by a Communist-tainted liberation effort is promptly converted into positive sympathy for the Communists. Whatever the content of the critique, it is taken to be aid and comfort to the enemy. Similarly, Lewy takes any criticism of the human-rights record of an ally as *intended* to give advantage to the Communists. Pushing the issue even further, he denounces advocacy for lowered military expenditures in order to spend more on social needs as really intended to weaken the United States in the face of global peril from the Communist threat. His injunction of silence thus extends to all critics of U.S. foreign and military policy, not merely the pacifists.

Is there a "compulsive anti–anti-Communism," as Lewy suggests, and have pacifists engendered it? Let me offer one quotation from a 1988 AFSC publication:

> The view of the Soviet Union that prevails today in large portions of our governmental and journalistic establishments [is] so extreme, so subjective, so far removed from what any sober scrutiny of external reality would reveal, that it is not only ineffective but dangerous as a guide to political action. . . .
>
> This endless series of distortions and oversimplifications; this systematic dehumanization of the leadership of another great country; this routine exaggeration of Moscow's military capability and of the supposed iniquity of Soviet intentions; . . . this reckless application of the double standard to the judgment of Soviet conduct and our own . . . these are the marks of an intellectual primitivism and naïveté unpardonable in a great government [*What Are We Afraid Of? An Assessment of the "Communist Threat" in Central America*, a NARMIC-AFSC study by John Lamperti, South End Press, 1988].

When I say that the writer of these words is not an AFSC staffer but George Kennan, author of the containment policy after World War Two and probably the American scholar and diplomat most experienced in dealing with the Soviets, I trust that some ground is open for discussion of whether an excessive and distorting anti-Communism affects the formulation of U.S. policy.

Let me close with a few lines from W. B. Yeats's poem "Meditations in a Time of Civil War":

> *We had fed the heart on fantasies,*
> *The heart's grown brutal from the fare;*
> *More substance in our enmities*
> *Than in our Love.*

The challenge before all of us who care about the tradition and values of pacifism, whatever our theology or politics, is to become and remain persons who can put more substance into our *love* than into our enmities, who are not led into callousness by the pursuit of fantasies or obsessive abstractions. I must confess that I find the author's voice in *Peace and Revolution* too deeply engaged with obsessive abstractions, with a resulting callousness about accuracy and a stridency in making his case. In a symbolic sense, the energy of the book comes from "fantasies" about Communists and anti-Communism. To the extent that I, in turn, have fallen into a reactive mindset flawed by my own "fantasies," I ask the reader's and Guenter Lewy's pardon. Let us explore our differences honestly but tenderly, so that we build substance in our love as well as in our understanding of the historical record and the values of the pacifist tradition.

12

Modern Pacifism: Wrong From the Start

William R. Hawkins

W HILE AT one time pacifists were single-mindedly devoted to the principle of non-violence and reconciliation, today most pacifist groups defend the moral legitimacy of armed struggle and guerrilla warfare, and they praise and support the Communist regimes emerging from such conflicts.'' This is the thesis of Guenter Lewy's study of the most enduring and successful segment of the radical left, the so-called peace movement. Lewy concentrates on four organizations: the American Friends Service Committee (AFSC, founded 1917), the Fellowship of Reconciliation (FOR, founded 1914), the Women's International League for Peace and Freedom (WILPF, founded 1915), and the War Resisters League (WRL, founded 1923). By examining Old Left groups, Lewy chronicles how the New Left gained power during the 1960s and has held it ever since.

In Lewy's large cast of characters, one who stands out is Stewart Meacham, a onetime Presbyterian minister who joined the AFSC in the 1950s and headed its peace-education division during the Vietnam war. The AFSC had decided in the early

William R. Hawkins is director of the Foundation for American Ideals and a policy analyst for the U.S. Business and Industrial Council. He has written for *Chronicles*, *National Review*, *The National Interest*, and numerous other journals. This essay is reprinted by permission from *Chronicles* (December 1988).

1930s not to join Communist-front groups or allow its officers to lend their names to movements "whose ultimate objectives are short of the universal and religious ones" pursued by the AFSC. In 1962 Meacham signed a declaration to the World Peace Council that dissociated the American peace movement from the government-sponsored "peace groups" of the Soviet bloc.

However, by 1967 Meacham was calling on pacifists to "relate constructively" to revolutionary struggles, and to find ways to respond when the United States attempted "by violence to suppress a revolutionary struggle," as in Vietnam. A year later, Meacham went to North Vietnam and returned convinced that Hanoi "is in fact a decent government" that would respect South Vietnam's autonomy after reunification, would maintain "a mixed economy focused on the needs of the people," and would pose no threat to its neighbors. He believed the claim of Hanoi's prime minister, Pham Van Dong, that "we fight well because we believe in decency and humanity of all people."

Meacham was also on the steering committee of the National Antiwar Conference (July 1969), along with leaders of the U.S. Communist party and the Socialist Workers party, and was a co-chairman of the New Mobilization to End the War. The "New Mobe" was a group based on the "non-exclusion principle," the new term for a united front between pacifists and the hard left, including those affiliated with Soviet-front groups and those who openly worked not for peace but for the military victory of the Communists.

When in 1975 questions were raised about the establishment of concentration camps and the suppression of religion by the victorious Communists, Meacham denounced such concerns as "support of the imperialists in our land against whom we once joined hands in common struggle":

> Our Vietnamese friends have displayed both grace and courage in a prolonged, bitter, and successful struggle, and now they are seeking to heal the wounds of war, restore their ravaged land, and move ahead to a just and confident society. We ought to remember our debt to them and do what we can to help.

A trip to Vietnam in 1977 only confirmed Meacham's convictions about the Communist regime. One of his colleagues on the trip, Wallace Collett, a businessman who was chairman of the AFSC board, even compared the lives of those who were forcibly exiled to the jungle gulags (euphemistically called "new economic zones") to America's pioneer families building new communities on the frontier. The word "humane" could not be used often enough in the reports issued by the AFSC about Vietnamese "socialism."

The Other Three Groups

The same process was repeated by the other groups Lewy studied. As late as 1966, the WILPF executive committee could vote not to endorse the "International War Crimes Tribunal" set up by the Bertrand Russell Peace Foundation, because only allegations made against Washington and Saigon would be tried. But by 1968 the WILPF policy committee was stating, "We can never condone wrongdoing by any nation, but neither can we equate our military action in Vietnam with the actions of the North Vietnamese or the NLF." The Communist cause was just, the American cause was not. At the 1970 WILPF annual meeting, President Katherine Camp condemned the U.S. "military mentality" as the chief source of evil in the world:

> It is exploitation by uncontrolled economic enterprise and the planned-for deprivation of the unequal. It is the anti-human attitude which has forged a worldwide anti-Communist military alliance and which supplies most of the nations of the world with the machinery of death, in defiance of mankind's best hope for peace, the U.N. It encourages the growing number of military dictatorships throughout the world. Its logical conclusions are apartheid, genocide, and war.

At the WRL, David Dellinger was asking whether it was not possible "to look approvingly on the struggle of the National Liberation Front without endorsing or applauding its violence." Instead of adopting a "plague on both your houses" view, he argued, pacifists should "step up the tempo of our non-violent action here in the United States, to try to stop American aggression at its source rather than leave the whole burden on those who suffer its impact."

At the FOR, Executive Secretary Alfred Hassler was pushed out after the national council voted to make the People's Peace

Treaty the basis for ending the war. That treaty, drawn up in Hanoi, called for an unconditional U.S. withdrawal and the installation of the Provisional Revolutionary Government in Saigon.

The insistence on an immediate American withdrawal, followed by the demand that all aid to the South Vietnamese be ended, was the device for reconciling pacifists with pro-Communists. Everyone knew that a policy basing "peace" on the premise that only the anti-Communist side would be prevented from fighting was the same as a policy favoring a Communist victory. Its advantage was that it could be stated in traditional pacifist terms, as opposition to war-making. This is a time-tested formula being used today in the debate over Central American policy and the nuclear-arms race.

Continuing the Support

The large-scale exodus of boat people from Indochina, the deployment of Soviet bombers and warships to Vietnamese bases, and the genocide and continuing war in Cambodia have done nothing to disillusion the AFSC or the other groups on the righteousness of the "revolutionary struggle" in Southeast Asia and elsewhere in the Third World. Revolution, however, must always be defined in leftist terms. Anti-Communist guerrilla movements, as in Angola and Nicaragua, are obviously only bands of reactionaries and mercenaries in the employ of imperialists.

Even the Afghan resistance to foreign invasion is outside acceptable limits because it is part of the East-West struggle. Although the AFSC condemned Moscow for invading Afghanistan, it also attacked the Afghan resistance as a collection of landlords and tribal chiefs opposed to land reform and social change, and further tainted by the aid received from the CIA. The AFSC also sought to justify the Soviet invasion. One AFSC pamphlet cited by Lewy states: "From a Soviet perspective, it may have occurred to them that the United States might have been tempted to seize a destabilized Afghanistan and turn it into a new listening post on Russia's southern border." The WILPF only found the Soviet invasion "regrettable," and noted "the

Soviet interest in having close relations with a neighboring country.'' Aid to the Afghan guerrillas was to be opposed because it merely fueled the global U.S.-Soviet confrontation, for which the United States is primarily to blame.

In 1981, the AFSC disarmament program published a pamphlet falsely claiming that the USSR had ''virtually no power projection forces,'' whereas the United States was ''the only nation capable of projecting and sustaining its power by military force globally.'' This made the United States the real threat to peace in the world. The pamphlet *Questions and Answers on the Soviet Threat and National Security* also dismissed the Soviet occupation of Eastern Europe as being the natural result of ''two German invasions,'' while praising Moscow's support to help ''Third World nations throw off their yoke of colonialism and neo-colonialism.''

Wrong From the Start

Lewy's history is based on an extensive investigation of the official records and publications of the AFSC at its national headquarters in Philadelphia and of the FOR, WILPF, and WRL at the Swarthmore College Peace Collection. It is full of revealing quotations and the sordid details of the alliance between pacifism and America's enemies—what in a more frank and healthy period would be branded treason. However, his attempt to draw a clear line at the Vietnam war between an authentic pacifism and a new radical creed that merely uses pacifism as a device to seize the high moral ground in political struggles is too neat. Lewy also accords the old pacifism too much credit as a noble exercise in idealism:

> Pacifists, committed to the supreme value of non-violence, remind the rest of us who are not pacifists of the link between means and ends. Their personal ''No'' to killing carries an important ethical message. The pacifist vision of a world free of the threat of war can help build support for the development of an ordered political community at the international level able to resolve conflicts peacefully and justly.

This is an exercise in wishful thinking. None of Lewy's four groups deserves any praise for its ''idealism,'' even at its very beginnings. These groups were on the wrong side from the start. That is why the New Left found it so easy to gain control of them. All four groups were founded during or immediately after World War I. The war shattered both the liberal faith in natural progress and America's isolation from global power politics. The resulting intellectual turmoil provided an opening for radicals. The dominant world view of the founding generation was fashioned by the philosophy of socialism. As Lewy himself states in his first chapter:

> The pacifist organizations that were founded during and after World War I included a strong core of socialists, and all pacifists stressed the importance of opposing the imperialism of the capitalistic order, of ending the arms race and achieving economic and social justice in order to remove what they considered to be the ultimate causes of war.

A. J. Muste, a Protestant minister who was a leader of the FOR 1926–29 and again 1940–53 (during the period between he worked with the Trotskyist American Workers party), argued in a 1928 pamphlet that the capitalist status quo was by its nature violent and therefore pacifists had to be revolutionaries. Only if capitalism were ended could violence be ended. This line has become commonplace. For example, in an AFSC pamphlet written forty-four years later, James Bristol, a former Lutheran pastor, claimed: "While two wrongs never make a right, before we deplore terrorism it is essential for us to recognize fully and clearly whose terrorism came first, so that we can assess what is cause and what is effect."

Capitalism Causes War

At the core of the entire peace movement is the Leninist theorem that imperialism is the highest stage of capitalism, and thus capitalism is the principal cause of war. It is true, of course, that capitalist states have used military force to expand as well as to protect their territories and interests; but they are hardly unique in this respect. World history is largely military history, from the dawn of time until the present day. All societies of any scope or duration have made recourse to the sword. This is why pure pacifism has traditionally been dismissed as hopelessly naïve.

But the modern union of socialism and pacifism has had profound policy consequences. The evenhandedness of the old pacifism was based on the view that all wars were conflicts between rival camps of capitalist-imperialists, and therefore both sides were to be condemned. In 1939 all four of Lewy's groups could join with other anti-war organizations to issue *How to Keep America Out of the War*, a book arguing that the war against Hitler was "not a war between democracy and totalitarianism, but a death grapple between rival imperialists, with aggressors arrayed against oppressors." Britain and France were merely status quo empires attempting to defend their ill-gotten gains. Both sides were depicted as tools of financial barons.

However, now that America's enemies are no longer other "capitalist" members of Western civilization but avowed opponents of capitalism (the Soviet bloc) or anti-Western regimes (the Third World), evenhandedness no longer applies. The opposing camps are no longer moral equivalents. Capitalist America is seen as the moral inferior. Thus when Lewy concludes that "since pacifists do not want to use force in the defense of the society in which they live, they argue that American democracy is not worth defending," he has it backwards. The Left decided that America was not worth defending first. It is now using non-violence as a moral argument to undermine America's survival.

In the United States this line of attack against capitalism has proven much more effective than any straight presentation of socialist doctrine, particularly with the "children of affluence." The peace movement tells them that any system that links rights with duties, and that requires discipline and sacrifice to support the continued provision of material goods and personal advancement, must be oppressive. And when they violate traditional norms of conduct and shirk their patriotic responsibilities, the peace movement is there to soothe their consciences with false moralizing.

Lewy has given us a valuable study of the most notorious

actions of the modern peace movement and a grim warning of where that movement wants to lead America. But if the movement is to be stopped, it must be combated on an even deeper level. The old pacifism as well as the new radicalism must be exposed as a creed unworthy of respect.

13

Pacifist Ethics and Pacifist Politics

John Richard Burkholder

To UNDERSTAND the importance of Guenter Lewy's book and why so many of us find it troublesome, we must distinguish between the author's purpose and his product. He has in fact aroused the pacifist movement and thereby done us a service, but probably not in the way intended.

Lewy gives us a lot of information about pacifist organizations. Although the narrative is rather lifeless, we learn a great deal about problems, policies, personalities, and decisions.[1] And Lewy found what he was looking for: the four organizations he surveyed have in fact given a lot of attention to Third World revolutions and have been reluctant to criticize revolutionary violence. That's important. But the whole story is distorted because of Lewy's perspective. Is this new agenda really evidence of defiance and deviousness among the pacifists, as he claims, or is it something else?

Why Fear Pacifists?

Lewy seems to condemn pacifists on alleged moral grounds. Why? Are pacifists really such a threat to the American system

John Richard Burkholder is professor of ethics and director of the peace studies program at Associated Mennonite Biblical Seminaries in Elkhart, Indiana. He is the co-editor with Calvin Redekop of *Kingdom, Cross, and Community* and the co-author with John Bender of *Children of Peace*.

as he claims? Such an assertion seems almost laughable to those of us who identify with at least part of the movement. If Dave McReynolds or Russell Johnson or Ron Young were in the White House or anywhere near it, then Lewy might have reason to warn about what he sees as pacifists' political irresponsibility, disregard of consequences, consorting with the enemy, and so on. But we pacifists know ourselves to be weak, scattered, ineffective, unheard. Why should anyone be afraid of us?

Some persons from the four organizations Lewy discusses played important roles in the massive anti-war movement twenty years ago. But that is all history. We must distinguish those ad hoc anti-war coalitions from long-term pacifist commitments and organizations. (To be fair, Lewy does make that distinction most of the time.) And even that huge popular surge of anti-war activism did little to change the course of history. A series of recent studies concludes that the movement did not stop the war but at best helped make it stoppable.[2]

Do Lewy and others see the pacifist organizations as such a threat to their own interests and politics that the movement must be stopped? Many of the pacifist leaders have been held in high moral regard (even if seldom listened to). Must they now be discredited, lest they achieve new status and power in a critical time when America's role in the world is being reassessed?

MISPERCEPTIONS OF PACIFISTS

Lewy is straightforward about the purpose of his book: to expose the "remarkable transformation" in which American pacifism moved from occupying a high ground of moral rectitude to defending revolutionary violence and forming unholy alliances with Communist governments. His method is to analyze the activities and pronouncements over a twenty-year period of the four major pacifist organizations: the American Friends Service Committee (AFSC), the Fellowship of Reconciliation (FOR), the War Resisters League (WRL), and the Women's International League for Peace and Freedom (WILPF).

Lewy defines pacifism as "the doctrine of those who are morally opposed to bearing arms and who refuse to sanction war for any purpose" (p. 3). This seems clear enough. The confusion begins as soon as he seeks to relate his basically behavioral definition to the world of politics. In the next paragraph he writes: "The theory and practice of pacifism must be distinguished from the views and efforts of those who are engaged in organized endeavors to prevent war" (p. 3). What does this mean? That the only true pacifists are those who do not get involved in political efforts to prevent war, who are concerned only with preserving their own pure moral stance? Such a criterion would apply normally only to the classic sectarianism typified by the socially and politically withdrawn elements of the historic peace churches—those Mennonites, Brethren, and Quakers who for centuries have sought to teach and practice, however imperfectly, that kind of principled absolutism. Indeed, Lewy early on refers to the three historic peace churches as exemplars of the pacifist creed.

Does Lewy mean to draw so clear a line between the realms of morality and politics? That at least would be a useful criterion for further discussion. Yet that cannot be what he intends, because he sees no real problems in the activities of the four pacifist organizations prior to World War II. All four were heavily engaged in political activity in the early part of the twentieth century—making pronouncements on public policy, forming political coalitions, responding to political events. But not until they make *certain kinds* of public political moves in the 1960s do they draw Lewy's fire. It begins to appear that the question of the proper morality of pacifism is not *whether* to engage in politics but *which* politics, *how* to engage, and *why*.

Proper Pacifism According to Lewy

Near the end of his first chapter, Lewy proposes a further dimension of his emerging criterion: good pacifists will keep quiet when a war breaks out. He observes that the American pacifist movement, while denying the moral legitimacy of World War II, did not seek the defeat of the United States, or even try to stop the war.

Not until the final chapter, however, does he explicitly enlarge upon his concept of proper pacifism. Here his mentors are Max

Weber and Reinhold Niebuhr, whom he evokes to formulate anew what at first appears to be another version of that simple bi-polar ethic: either be a pure pacifist and avoid politics, or get involved and then be responsible for consequences. In short, choose to be either Amish or mainstream American. Yet Lewy doesn't really stay with that simple formulation. He seems willing to admit pacifists into the political process: in a democratic system "all political voices have a right to be heard" (p. 236). Pacifists are "entitled to participate . . . and to propose policies like any other citizen" (p. 242).

But not *quite* like any other citizen. For Lewy then repeats the claim that it is downright immoral for the pacifist to propose pacifist politics in the real world, since they clearly will not work. Following pacifist proposals would result in the sacrifice of many other people, and would therefore be immoral. We must "judge the role played by pacifists in our society not in terms of the intentions they proclaim . . . but in terms of results and consequences" (p. 247).

Let us accept that perspective for the moment. In real politics, it is indeed results that count. Still we need to examine more closely the relation between making particular policy judgments and assessing consequent ethical responsibility. Lewy's unstated assumption seems to be that it is more immoral for pacifists to propose policies that may turn out to be disastrous than for militarists, or neutralists, or anyone else, to do so. This sounds like a double standard.

My basic problem with Lewy's argument is that by beginning with an arbitrary and simplistic definition of pacifism, he has forced an alien framework on his material. Had he looked more carefully at what these organizations and their leaders claim to be and to be doing, he would have discovered, both in their charters and in their policies and activities, a worldview much broader and more complex than the simplistic one he tries to impose on them.

The standard histories of American pacifist movements in the twentieth century place the four organizations in a context of progressive and even radical social reform. As Charles DeBenedetti puts it, "the forms of their commitment have been diverse and changing. . . . American peace seekers have always been a mixed lot. But then they were not acting out of a need to fit the categories of latter-day historians."[3] DeBenedetti notes such elements as opposition to war, support for internationalism, non-violent resistance to injustice, anti-militarism, and the advance of other causes such as feminism, anarchism, socialism, and even capitalism.

Linking Justice and Peace

Lewy has ignored much of the spirit of pacifist ethics—the driving convictions that have inspired most of his key actors—because he has imposed an inadequate ethical-political grid on them. We see this early on, when he prefigures his argument by speaking of "a conflict of loyalties between the pacifists' ideals of non-violence and their aspiration to liberate the exploited and oppressed" (p. 4). This misses the internal logic of most of the activist pacifists. Liberation and non-violence are not in conflict for the integrated pacifist.

The linking of justice and peace has characterized much of the history of the individuals and movements that Lewy is bothered about. These pacifists have refused to accept Reinhold Niebuhr's forced choice of being either irrelevant or compromised. They have tried to change the public image of pacifists from that of escapists or even cowards to that of activists who take seriously the demands of justice. Not content with simply being pure and doing right, they have sought to do good—to change the world by removing the conditions that make for war and creating an environment conducive to liberty and justice for all.

This holistic worldview inspires the service projects of the AFSC and the international efforts of the FOR. Representatives of this vision include such figures as A. J. Muste and John Swomley of the FOR, Barbara Deming and Dave McReynolds of the WRL, Dorothy Detzer and Dorothy Hutchinson of the WRL, Elise Boulding and Clarence Pickett of the AFSC. Along with many others, they have projected a non-violent global strategy and a new paradigm for politics. Lewy pays attention to only a very narrow segment of this body of work. He ignores hundreds of pages of books and essays, looking only for the bits and pieces that fit his scheme.

"More-Than-Americanism"

Lewy also misunderstands the global orientation of his subjects. What he refers to as "anti-Americanism" could be better described as "more-than-Americanism." Pacifists identify with the entire human community and the long sweep of history. For the pacifist, citizenship in a particular nation-state is just not that important. He cares less about national interests than about the well-being of the people of all nations.

Since most pacifist leaders are not parochial in their worldview, they do not see the U.S. national interest as paramount. This does not mean, however, that they reject the ideals that the United States at its best represents. What Lewy criticizes is directed not against America but against particular policies of certain governing officials. Lewy appears to confuse U.S. national interest, which he seems to define as the position of the U.S. administration during the Vietnam era, with the obviously worthy goal of advancing liberal democracy. The pacifist critique—at least the version that I share—is compatible with an abiding concern for the American dream, the vision of what the United States could be and ought to be.

These are high ideals. Obviously, the attempt to actualize them will founder at times. In their efforts at political relevance, pacifists do not ignore consequences, but they do measure by different goals and norms. And who is competent to judge ultimate outcomes?

Another clue to the inadequacy of Lewy's grid is his almost complete neglect of the major icons of the pacifist movement: Mohandas Gandhi and Martin Luther King, Jr. Although the FOR actively supported much of King's work, Lewy's only reference to King lists his assassination as one of the violent events of 1968 (p. 37). Gandhi makes it into the index of the book only because his name appears in quotations from WILPF and AFSC statements.[4]

Why does Lewy essentially ignore King and Gandhi? Perhaps

because their activist political involvement does not fit into his framework.

ON DOING POLITICAL ETHICS

Lewy's book purports to deal with the moral crisis of American pacifism, and ethical language abounds. "Principles of non-violence and reconciliation," "moral legitimacy," "pacifist principles," "moral rectitude," "moral integrity," "intellectual honesty"—phrases of this kind are scattered throughout.

But though the language of ethics appears frequently, there is no attempt to define terms or to state an ethical standpoint until the last chapter.[5] Lewy never really defends or expands his ethical grounding; he provides no compelling reasons why pacifists must be judged by his standards.

Not until page 240 does he explain how he developed his ethical framework. His resources are Max Weber and Reinhold Niebuhr. According to Lewy:

> In the final analysis, then, there is no such thing as a political position that is truly pacifist. The pacifist is committed, in the words of Max Weber, to an "ethic of ultimate ends" that affirms the sanctity of human life. He feels responsible not so much for the political consequences of his actions but primarily for seeing that the flame of pure intentions is not squelched. This is the purpose of his exemplary acts, his protest against violence, his refusal to kill. The possibility that good intent may lead to bad results is essentially irrelevant [p. 241].

This is not a fair use of Weber's classic statement (which addressed a much different situation in which people in power were acting irresponsibly), and it does not adequately clarify the morality of pacifism. In this key statement and the accompanying text, Lewy makes three assertions:

1. Pacifists (and indeed all moral agents) must choose between an ethic of intention ("ultimate ends") and the ethic of responsibility, of results and consequences.

2. The practice of pacifism in the real world can lead only to disaster.

3. Therefore the true pacifist, who is committed to absolute non-violence, can operate only at the level of intentions.

In other words, the only form of pacifism with which Lewy finally feels comfortable is a lofty idealism, an uninvolved "plague on both your houses" view. Such pacifists "avoid the moral dilemmas posed by the world of statesmanship and state-craft and seek individual salvation through ethical absolutism and purity" (p. 242). Pacifists can make a personal witness and preach about this purist ideal, but they should not meddle in the messy realm of politics.

Passive Support for Government

At first glance, Lewy's model of pacifism seems objective and neutral, but its actual impact is passive support for the policies of one's own government. Lewy argues that pacifists must remain silent when their governments propose policies of force (p. 248). Denied an independent standard of judgment, pacifists end up in the same box as the German Christians who kept silent about Hitler's atrocities in the 1930s. But moral beings—and Lewy repeatedly calls for pacifists to be moral—can and must make judgments! Why must the pacifist be prevented from choosing between the tyrant and his victims?

Lewy is inconsistent about the proper role for pacifists in politics. Although he argues forcefully that the pacifist dare not make judgments about the relative good or evil of particular policies (p. 240), on the very next page he qualifies this by noting, in apparent approval, the position of the British pacifist C. J. Cadoux: a pacifist can approve of certain wars waged for good causes without contradicting his own refusal to participate in that war. Lewy appears to accept this "realistic pacifism," as long as it does not claim to set forth a program that will work in the world of power. In that world, the pacifist becomes subject to the "ethic of responsibility," which will negate any pacifist policy because of its likely disastrous consequences.

Although Lewy seems to recognize that this "either/or" cri-terion is inadequate for assessing the majority of the activist pacifists who figure prominently in his book, he never carefully analyzes a pacifism that seeks to be both politically relevant and subject, at least in some measure, to the ethic of consequences. Such a pacifism, while refusing to take up arms, nevertheless claims the right to make judgments about the political realm, to assess the relative justice of particular causes, to seek to discern the lesser evil in real conflicts. As John Howard Yoder has observed, "Not all causes are equally just, not all conflicts are at a point of last resort, not all weapons are equally discriminating, not all intentions are equally valid."[6]

The Just War

The language in the preceding paragraph is of course drawn from the classic criteria of the just war. In view of the long history and significant impact of the just-war tradition, it is surprising that Lewy all but ignores this framework for ethical discourse about war and peace. All but one of the four indexed references to the theme are embedded in quotations from others.

Lewy's one sustained reference to just-war thought again reveals the strictures of his ethical system:

> There is, of course, a moral case that can be made for armed rebellion and revolution. In some situations no peaceful recourse is available against tyranny and oppression, and resort to violent struggle, if successful, may actually save lives and reduce human suffering in the long run. But such a pragmatic calculus is forbidden to the true pacifist, who must uphold the principle of non-violence and oppose the use of force for any and all purposes.
>
> Still less can a real pacifist adhere to a "just revolution" philosophy and pick and choose the rebels he will support—Marxist guerrillas in Southeast Asia and Central America but not the Afghan mujaheddins or Angola's Unita, who fight against Communist rule over their countries. A pacifist's principles preclude his having favorite wars or revolutions [p. 240].

The criteria anyone—pacifist or non-pacifist—uses to make an ethical analysis of warfare will look very much like the classic just-war doctrine. It was the application of such a moral calculus that brought about the massive questioning and consequent negative judgments of U.S. intervention in Vietnam and Central America. Most participation in the anti-war movements in the last twenty years was not, as Lewy correctly observes, based on principled pacifism. But when such a protest *is* grounded in ethical reasoning, the language and logic have to be of the "just war" variety.

Indeed, it could be argued that the reason American pacifists criticized World War II comparatively little lay in their respect for the just-war logic. Lewy applauds their silence. But when aerial bombing became massive and indiscriminate (Dresden), even Reinhold Niebuhr protested. Surely the pacifist can join with other moral observers in the use of just-war thought.

The Public Forum

In a democratic society, people must have the opportunity to evaluate the likely consequences of a range of policy options. American political culture assumes that citizens have some moral responsibility for what government does in their name, and it provides the opportunity (some would call it a duty) to participate in the political process in a pluralistic setting. Pacifists, like everyone else, should be invited to join in efforts to influence government policies in a free exchange of ideas and convictions. Why should the system fear the voice of a tiny minority with very little political clout? Pacifists by definition do not engage in violence. They simply seek to "speak truth to power"—and power can choose not to listen.

Lewy holds that it is immoral for pacifists to propose or support policies that might cost the lives of others. But then the same criterion must also be applied to the other side. Surely the decisions for war also involve terrible risks of life and death. Who can predict and measure consequences? And who takes responsibility for the unintended ones?

What about the consequences of past wars? During World War II, pacifists generally opposed unconditional surrender, a policy that possibly lengthened the war. It wasn't pacifists who bargained with Stalin and gave Eastern Europe over to Soviet totalitarianism. Who takes responsibility for the outcome in Indochina: billions of dollars, thousands of tons of explosives, millions of human casualties—and no significant gains.

I suggest simply that both pacifists and just-war warriors should be more modest in their claims for the likely consequences of their proposals.

Confusing Moral and Political Judgments

Lewy's subtitle points to the "moral crisis" of American pacifism. But even if all his judgments were correct, there would be little if any evidence of actual moral misdeeds. Although he raises the question of "intellectual honesty" early on (p. viii), he presents no substantial evidence of deceit. Nor does he document any significant failure of pacifists to live up to their own creed of non-violence (though there may in fact be a lack of rigor and balance in their opinions of the violence of other parties).

Rather, the problem Lewy has with the pacifists is their *political* judgments—they consistently take what he considers the wrong side. But unless you consider wrong-headed politics (as determined by Guenter Lewy) inherently immoral, it is difficult to accept the claim that pacifism is suffering from a "moral crisis."

My point is that Lewy confuses moral and political judgments. He criticizes pacifists for taking the side of the oppressed and expressing their support (always non-violent) for a particular revolution. Truly moral pacifists, according to Lewy, should remain neutral. Yet at the same time he wants pacifists to be totally loyal to the American nation-state. That is not neutrality; that's taking sides! Unless one believes that unwavering patriotism is a moral duty, the real issue is *political* rather than moral.

OF LOYALTIES AND EXPERIENCES

Thus far I have argued not only that Lewy is confused in applying his purist pacifist principle to the moral and political judgments of the pacifists he deals with, but that from the beginning he has missed the essence of pacifist ethics—or at least the ethical motivation that inspires many of his key actors. He pretends to know that pacifists despise America, and he even claims to know how they pray (pp. 243, 248)! Yet in fact Lewy seldom probes beneath the skin to ask why these pacifists think and behave the way they do. He imputes the worst kind of motives without really taking time to listen to the heartbeat of his protagonists.

The formative period for many of Lewy's characters, the 1960s, was a time of much raw emotional energy. In contrast to the more ivory-tower-like setting of the 1930s when the pacifist pronouncements Lewy respects were made, in the 1960s everything was afire. Crucial decisions had to be made quickly, under pressure, on the muddled ground of earth-shaking events, often without adequate information about possible implications and consequences. Yes, there were excesses, and in retrospect some of the judgments seem naïve and ignorant. But the point is that major choices had to be made on the scene by persons passionately engaged in living out their own history.

For the AFSC in particular, Vietnam was much more than a political question. The Quakers had been there doing peace and development work for years, since long before Kennedy sent in military advisors. The Quaker project at Quang Ngai, where scores of volunteers learned a great deal about war and politics in Vietnam while providing significant humanitarian service, is not mentioned in Lewy's book. In fact, all the organizations maintained international ties across various divides, not just East-West. The peace movements have been trying to think and work globally for decades.

Lewy almost completely ignores the meaning of this internationalist orientation. For example, the alleged instances of support for revolutionary movements must be understood, not as simply perverse political judgments derived from some ideological bias, but as something much more complex. Organizations like the AFSC have for years been sending workers to Third World settings in which they are expected to identify with oppressed peoples in agonizing circumstances. When this occurs and the worker comes to see the oppressor as the enemy, he or she is faced with hard questions about conflicting loyalties, ethical principles, modes of action.

To illustrate from my own experience: I continue to receive letters from former students and friends who are volunteers in Third World settings. These are persons deeply committed to Christian non-violence; but new circumstances force them to ask what love means in their situation. None of my correspondents in such places as the Philippines and Central America has taken up arms, and I'm not aware of anyone who has counseled others to take that route. But I know that some have found themselves unable to criticize the choice for violence that their friends have made.

That kind of qualified loyalty, I suggest, is in principle no different from the experiences of the World War II conscientious objector whose public posture Lewy apparently approves. That kind of pacifist refused to bear arms but did nothing publicly to criticize the war effort. In fact, he may even have quietly hoped for an Allied victory, and he may well have maintained a personal friendship with his schoolmate who served in the military.

These subjective loyalties that lead to identification with revolutionary movements are of the same order as the emotional forces that keep most people tied to national tribal loyalties. They deserve more sustained study and critique than is possible here; I am simply making explicit the varied frames of reference that must be part of any discussion of the "whose side are you on?" controversy.

Again, the situation is defined quite differently when it is seen globally, with recognition of a North-South economic divide as well as the East-West ideological one. We have already noted that pacifists consciously adopt a more global worldview than most Americans. They wear tribal identifications lightly and see themselves as global citizens. Sorting out proximate and ultimate loyalties may put the nation-state further down the list than Lewy would like, but is that morally dishonest or wrong?

FREEDOM TO CHOOSE

The Mennonite tradition, to which I myself belong, has practiced deliberate social withdrawal for much of its history. But originally it did not. The Anabaptists of the sixteenth century were forced into isolation because the political authorities were not ready to deal openly with the challenge they represented.

All the more reason why today we are advocates for an open

pluralistic and participatory society. As Stanley Hauerwas has argued, Christian pacifism ought not to avoid the political arena; to argue for non-violence as central to the Christian social witness is not anti-political but profoundly political. "Once one disavows the use of violence, it means one has a high stake in developing political processes through which agreement is reached without the necessity of coercion." This entails working for societies as open as possible to the voice of dissent, for politics in essence is "the discussion of peoples necessary to discover the goods they have in common."[7]

Guenter Lewy seems frightened, even angry, at the prospect of absolute pacifists' gaining a large public following. But let us expand the discussion to the theological dimension. Let us suppose that in fact there is a God who wills that all people live non-violently—or, to remain at the level of public discourse, let us recognize that some persons among us firmly believe that truth.

Now to stand up in public and tell people that non-violence is God's way certainly appears to be arrogant. It also poses a danger, both for the teller and for the hearer who may become a believer, because there is no guarantee that doing God's will in this sense will lead to a long and happy life on earth. Indeed, it may entail martyrdom for many—at least until whole nations come to accept the way of non-violence.

But is this kind of appeal any more arrogant or dangerous than to tell people it is God's will for them to take up arms, to go out and kill other human beings, to be prepared to die by the thousands, in order to attempt to preserve a given political order?

Why can't Guenter Lewy simply have the democratic faith to let the audience be the judge? I find it sadly ironic that this vigorous advocate of freedom wants to foreshorten the scope of discussion. Let us agree, rather, from the perspective both of the free church and of the democratic society, that the hearers, the public, ought to be free to choose whether to take the way of the sword or the way of the cross. And we may even dare to hope that in such a moment of radical freedom, God will work a miracle.

14

Pacifism's Lack
of Moral Leadership

M. Holt Ruffin

FEW NATIONS of the world boast a tradition of citizen peace activity as old or as varied as that of the United States. Even before the founding of the American Peace Society in 1828, Americans associated in groups—first religious, later mostly secular—to propose alternatives to war or oppose U.S. participation in it. In each period of our history, such groups have had a particular character. During the late nineteenth century, according to one student of American peace organizations, they were "somnolent and inactive," surrounded by an "aroma of original benevolence" and based on a constituency of "respectable, rich, lazy, and conservative people."

World War I and its aftermath changed this, giving rise to organizations different in social composition and outlook from those of the pre-war period. If Elihu Root—Wall Street lawyer, Republican, principal organizer in 1909 of the Carnegie Endowment for International Peace, and Nobel Peace Prize winner in 1913—personified the American citizen peace effort in the pre-

M. Holt Ruffin is executive director of the Northwest Regional Office of the World Without War Council in Seattle, Washington. He is co-author, with Lucy Dougall, of *Raising the Curtain: A Guide to Independent Organizations and Contacts in Eastern Europe.* This essay is reprinted by permission from the September 1988 issue of *Crisis* magazine (Box 1006, Notre Dame, Indiana 46556).

war period, then Jane Addams—Chicago settlement house worker, organizer in 1919 of the U.S. chapter of the Women's International League for Peace and Freedom (WILPF), and also a Nobel Peace Prize winner—more closely personified it in the post-war period. Much less interested in legalistic issues of national policy and diplomacy, Addams emphasized the moral dimensions of peace activity, envisioning a "communal internationalism" based on a worldwide transformation of personal values, reaching even to issues of wealth and poverty and the institutions of a market economy.

Yet Addams was neither a doctrinaire socialist nor a revolutionary. More mild than militant in style of advocacy, a principled pacifist, a fan of Tolstoy, Jane Addams was fully committed to democratic values and non-violent processes of social change. As she wrote in 1922, "we are not obliged to choose between violence and passive acceptance of unjust conditions for ourselves and for others; [we] believe, on the contrary, that courage, determination, moral power, generous indignation, active good will, can achieve their ends without violence."

Within a few years of the founding of the U.S. chapter of the WILPF, three other pacifist groups were organized in the United States: the American Friends Service Committee (AFSC), established in 1917 as a Quaker organization; the Fellowship of Reconciliation (FOR), a Christian pacifist organization created in England in 1914, whose American branch was established in 1915; and the War Resisters League (WRL), U.S. branch of War Resisters International, founded in 1923 as a vehicle for non-religious opposition to war.

For about seventy years, these four organizations have been the main cylinders of the engine of American pacifism. Through the statements and speeches of their representatives, their lobbying activities, the literature they publish and promote, and the conferences, demonstrations, and other events they sponsor, they have epitomized pacifist thinking and action. Little known or understood by most Americans, they have nevertheless had a substantial influence. Their growth and development parallel the emergence of the United States as a great power on the international stage, and they have benefited from the tendency of

American politics to move in ever more populist and participatory directions. In the post–World War II period, the nuclear war threat has also boosted the audience these groups naturally reach.

The Non-Violence Question

As Guenter Lewy notes in the introductory chapter to *Peace and Revolution*, although the thirties and forties posed difficult challenges for pacifist organizations, they succeeded in remaining bound to the mast of non-violence. They did not abandon pacifist principle for just-war theory of any kind. Leaders such as the FOR's A. J. Muste hopped in and out of bed with bad company, but the organization as a whole (despite the fact that many pacifists leaned toward socialism) rejected coalitions with class-war-oriented or anti-democratic forces on the left. When J. B. Matthews, a Protestant minister on the leadership staff of the FOR, told a crowd of 22,000 people in Madison Square Garden in April 1933 that "the dictatorship of the proletariat is the only answer to Fascism" and five months later became chairman of the Communist-dominated American League Against War and Fascism, he initiated a crisis that led the organization's national council to poll its members on the question: "Should the FOR hold on to non-violence in the class war as well as international war?" Eight hundred and seventy-seven respondents answered yes; 97 said no.

The FOR subsequently decided not to renew Matthews's contract and, in so doing, precipitated the resignations of both Reinhold Niebuhr, who then described himself as a Marxist and a Christian, and Roger Baldwin, founder of the American Civil Liberties Union, who had stated at the 1933 FOR conference that "the ethics of Jesus are identical with those of communism."

Today such integrity in the face of powerful moral and social currents outside the organization would be unthinkable in either the FOR, the AFSC, the WRL, or the WILPF. Guenter Lewy argues, with devastating documentation, that in the mid-sixties these four organizations abandoned positions of principled pacifism and their declared commitment to "speak truth to power," becoming instead apologists for Third World Marxist-Leninist revolutionary forces and defenders of the revolutionaries' use of violence. Indeed, it is no longer correct, strictly speaking, to describe any of them as "peace" or "pacifist" organizations. Characteristic of the new AFSC are the views of John Mc-Auliff, head of the Indochina program, who concluded an analysis of the lessons of the Vietnam war for the peace-education staff of thirty-three AFSC regional offices in 1975 with these words:

> It is not in the interests of the American people (though it does benefit our political/economic leadership class) to oppose socialist/communist revolutions in other countries. Moreover, if we try to understand what is in their best interests, we are likely to support such revolutions in the Third World.

Four months earlier McAuliff had responded to press stories about the unfolding horrors of Cambodia by describing Khmer Rouge rule as an "example of an alternative model of development and social organization" and had stated that the bloodshed did not differ greatly from the experiences of our own American Revolution and Civil War, or those of other Third World countries.

Such obstinance in the face of unpleasant facts about Communist practice was by no means limited to one person, one organization, or one issue. As Lewy shows with example after example, a clear pattern developed on the part of all four pacifist organizations during the mid-sixties: always condemn acts of war, violence, or other inhumanity when committed by the United States or its allies; never condemn such acts when committed by Marxist-Leninist forces.

Open Letter to Vietnam

On May 30, 1979, an "Open Letter to the Socialist Republic of Vietnam," organized by Joan Baez and other anti-war activists and published in the *New York Times*, gave representatives of the four leading peace organizations a chance to recapture a portion of their lost honor. If the evidence was not all in at the time of the fall of Saigon and Phnom Penh in the mid-seventies, it was certainly in by 1979. The bloodbath ''myth'' had proven true, the independence-of-the-NLF myth had proven false, the North Vietnamese had shown they were not all gentle poets and artists, and on a limited scale the domino theory had been vindicated.

The Baez letter condemned the mistreatment and torture of prisoners in Vietnam, stating that ''for many, life is hell and death is prayed for.'' Signers included peace activist Daniel Berrigan and Staughton Lynd and Bradford Lyttle of the WRL. But WRL staffers David Dellinger and David McReynolds refused to sign, the former arguing that the letter contained ''wildly inflated charges from discredited sources.''

The WILPF went a step further. One month after the letter appeared, the U.S. Peace Council (U.S. affiliate of the Soviet-controlled World Peace Council) published a rebuttal entitled ''The Truth About Vietnam,'' signed by, among others, the president, vice-president, U.N. representative, and two other prominent officers of the WILPF. Among its assertions was that the re-education program of the Vietnamese was ''absolutely necessary'' and showed a ''remarkable spirit of moderation, restraint, and clemency.''

A handful of true pacifists fought the revolutionary drift of their organizations, but they failed. In the main there was little dissent, and of that, little was publicly aired. In 1975 Al Hassler, ousted as executive secretary of the FOR four years earlier, concluded that pacifism itself had become ''one of the casualties of Vietnam.''

Why did this occur? The Vietnam war was, properly speaking, the occasion for the casualty but not its cause. Closer to the explanation, Lewy suggests, was the explosive growth in the mid-sixties of New Left organizations such as Students for a Democratic Society and the allure these groups held for coalition politics, especially when so many key figures in the pacifist world already were predisposed to New Left political philosophy. Most American pacifist organizations resolved the contradictions between the spirit and doctrine of non-violence and the revolutionary radicalism of the New Left by ignoring the former. As Lewy notes, this was facilitated by the fact that the staff of all these organizations were often not consistent or committed pacifists themselves. Among the AFSC staff, for example, Quakers were a slight majority in the early sixties, but their number had declined to only 19 per cent by 1985.

Influence of Pacifism

Pacifism has played an important role in twentieth-century American society and indirectly has significantly influenced American foreign policy and international politics. Those who ignore this relationship do so at their peril. Those aware of it will recognize the great importance of *Peace and Revolution*.

In 1988 Henry Kissinger admitted to a group of Vietnamese assembled in Paris to mark (to mourn?) the fifteenth anniversary of the treaty he had signed with Le Duc Tho in 1973 that he had made a serious misjudgment at that time. While he had correctly appreciated the intensity of America's desire to withdraw its forces from Vietnam, he had not fully appreciated the peace movement's desire for a victory by the Hanoi government. While he had focused his efforts on "Vietnamizing" the fighting and negotiating a treaty that anticipated and defined violations by the North Vietnamese, he had overlooked changes that had occurred within his own society, such that the Congress in 1975 was unwilling to enforce that treaty even through continued provision of the means of self-defense to South Vietnam and Cambodia. This change was in good measure the achievement of the American peace movement.

The word "tragedy" will probably be used by some to describe the story contained in Lewy's book. *Peace and Revolution* can be interpreted as the story of the death of American pacifism in the mid-sixties; one cannot read it without a deep sense of regret. Yet tragedy requires a feeling of real greatness lost, so that whatever constitutes the tragic event, there is a sense of good possibilities forsaken or high hopes abandoned. This element is missing in Lewy's book, largely because it was absent in the organizations themselves.

Lack of Moral Leadership

The fact is that the major deficiency in American pacifist organizations as they entered the Vietnam war era was in leadership. In a certain sense the decades of the thirties and forties had not truly tested the principles or the leaders of the AFSC, FOR, WRL, and WILPF. The thirties was a period of strong isolationism, which poses no threat to pacifism. The forties was dominated by war, but war against fascism. Pacifists, being generally on the political left, were largely sympathetic to the ends of the war once it was declared. If they condemned resort to war by the United States, they also condemned Germany, Japan, and Italy. Their position tended to be a narrow one, involving a personal refusal to kill, on moral or religious grounds. Separation of means and ends was relatively easy.

But in Vietnam, the enemy was a revolutionary government of the left, not of the right, and in a Third World country to boot. It employed violence in a cause to which many American pacifists were sympathetic. Here feelings about ends and means seemed to run at cross-purposes. It was a constant refrain of the New Left that to condemn Hanoi's violence at the same time as Washington's—or to call for a ceasefire, elections, and negotiations instead of withdrawal and an aid cutoff—strengthened the cause of "imperialism." In such a situation, only pacifist leadership at least equal in intellectual and moral strength to that in the New Left would have been capable of avoiding the swamp into which pacifism wandered. This did not exist.

Few leaders possess the character and depth of insight to be able to interpret the dictates of the ethic of non-violence in radically differing historical circumstances. One who seems to have this gift today is Poland's Lech Walesa. It is a pessimistic conclusion, but after reading Lewy's book, one is inclined to believe that only a person of these dimensions could now restore the principle of true non-violence to American pacifism.

15

The Logic of Pacifism

David Little

WHATEVER ELSE *Peace and Revolution* may be, it is a book about moral argument in a political context. In that respect, it undertakes to do two things. First, it lays out at length and in interesting detail the fundamental moral debate within the American pacifist community over the application of the principle of non-violence in political disputes. According to the author, this debate was brought to a head by U.S. Indochina policy in the sixties and early seventies, though it has broader implications. Second, the book evaluates that debate. Lewy contends that the faction currently dominating the pacifist community has made serious mistakes in grasping both the logic of pacifism and the source of real danger in the world today. Because of these mistakes, there is a "moral crisis" among American pacifists.

The book makes its greatest contribution in performing the first of its tasks. I am not competent to say whether Lewy's description of the personalities and positions of the disputants is accurate in every particular. But the general outlines of the conflict, substantiated by the evidence he presents, ring true, especially for those of us who were on the scene during the Vietnam debates.

David Little is professor of religious studies at the University of Virginia and resident scholar at the United States Institute of Peace in Washington, D.C. He is the co-author, with John Kelsay and Abdulaziz Sachedina, of *Human Rights and the Conflict of Cultures: Western and Islamic Perspectives on Religious Liberty*.

During the Vietnam era, pacifists struggled among themselves over the status of non-violence. Was it an absolute principle that could never be compromised? Or might the principle require adjustment in the interest of justice under some circumstances, particularly when desperate oppression made the resort to violence understandable? Were all forms of active violence to be uniformly condemned as immoral no matter who perpetrated them, or should such acts be tolerated and even condoned when they were committed by "passive victims of repression," as the Vietnamese who fought against the United States were frequently described?

Lewy is at his best in laying out the various twists and turns of that debate over several decades. To reexamine the arguments that were characteristic of that period is a valuable way of reassessing the "Vietnam experience," and of thinking conscientiously about the connection between morality and politics today.

Although Lewy is clearly correct in identifying the dispute over non-violence as the underlying source of contention among pacifists, his analysis of the "logic of pacifism," as well as his appraisal of pacifist arguments, is not, overall, as illuminating as his history of the dispute. Here the book suffers from a failure to apply the very standards of careful thinking that Lewy rightly demands from the pacifists themselves (*Peace and Revolution*, p. 247; subsequent references are to this book unless otherwise noted). In his zeal to unmask what he believes are the excesses and the intellectual carelessness of many contemporary pacifists, Lewy himself is, on occasion, excessive and careless.

Two Kinds of Pacifism

In Lewy's view, there are essentially two kinds of pacifism. One is apolitical, committed to non-violence as an end in itself and indifferent to consequences. The other strives to be politically responsible; it calculates the effects of non-violence under varying circumstances, and balances non-violence with other principles of political action, such as justice.

In differentiating these two types, Lewy uses Max Weber's

classic distinction between two kinds of ethic. The first, an "ethic of ultimate ends," takes responsibility only for purity of intentions and for faithfulness to the ultimate goal (in the case of pacifism, a world without war), not for intermediate consequences. The second type, an "ethic of responsibility," takes account, as Weber understood it, "of the realities of power and the likely consequences of political decisions" (pp. 241–42).

In Lewy's view, traditional American pacifists—the heroes of his story, such as Alfred Hassler of the Fellowship of Reconciliation, Charles Bloomstein of the War Resisters League, and Jo Graham of the Women's International League for Peace and Freedom—embraced the ethic of ultimate ends. Pacifists of this sort commit themselves absolutely to the principle of non-violence. They forswear any attempt to compromise it by considering the relative effectiveness of non-violence in various situations.

Pacifists of the first type occupy, for Lewy, the moral high ground. They consistently communicate "an important ethical message" (p. 241), namely, an admirable testimony against violence and killing wherever and by whosever hands it may occur, and the importance of the peaceful resolution of conflicts. That message remains pure because traditional pacifists know that "at the moment [they] enter the political arena to seek to influence the policies of their nation, they cease to speak as pacifists and become subject to . . . the 'ethic of responsibility' " (p. 241).

It is precisely this point, according to Lewy, that escapes the second type of pacifist. Under the influence of New Left thinking in the sixties and early seventies, these pacifists disregarded the conceptual divide between an ethic of ultimate ends and an ethic of political responsibility. They thereby subverted the legitimate message of pacifism by subjecting it to political manipulation.

Reducing Violence and Death

Despite the apparent tidiness of all this, the situation is a bit more complicated, as Lewy's own evidence and argument show to some extent. To begin with, even Max Weber did not always stand by his rigid distinction:

However, it is immensely moving when a mature man . . . is aware of a responsibility with heart and soul. . . . In so far as this is true, an ethic of ultimate ends and an ethic of responsibility are not absolute contrasts but rather supplements, which only in unison constitute a genuine man—a man who can have the "calling for politics" ["Politics as a Vocation," in *From Max Weber*, Gerth and Mills, eds., p. 127].

While Weber does not elaborate on this line of thinking, he properly suggests by these remarks that proponents of an ethic of ultimate ends, such as traditional pacifists, are not quite so preemptorily disqualified from the "calling for politics" and from a concern with the consequences of their actions as Lewy postulates.

It is not at all clear why a pacifist who is devoted unconditionally to the principle of non-violence is automatically ineligible to present arguments within the political arena for non-violent solutions to armed conflicts, thereby trying to persuade others of the value of such solutions. As Lewy reports it, that is exactly what Alfred Hassler tried to do in 1971 in the debate within the executive council of the FOR over how to end the war in Vietnam. While David McReynolds and other opponents of Hassler within the council called for immediate unilateral withdrawal of all U.S. forces, Hassler offered an alternative strategy that involved a worldwide campaign for a general ceasefire followed by free elections (p. 71). The debate, it appears, was over which policy would most effectively minimize violence, and thereby best serve the principle of non-violence, to which both sides of the argument were presumably committed.

Each side in the dispute is, admittedly, responsible for trying to make an *empirical* case that its proposed policy will in the end involve less violence and killing than the other. The point is, though, that Hassler no less than McReynolds is responsible for arguing the consequences in that way. Moreover, in doing so, *neither side* necessarily commits any logical sins by disregarding or compromising the principle of non-violence. There is nothing in the record to indicate that both parties were not arguing from that principle, whichever side might have had the stronger empirical case.

Contending that one policy rather than another would minimize violence is an enormously difficult task, but nevertheless one that is both morally and politically important. In my view, Lewy's reasons for summarily preferring Hassler's position are unconvincing. He says, "By putting the emphasis on a unilateral American ceasefire and withdrawal, the council [siding with McReynolds] in effect made sure that the war would go on until the NLF and the North Vietnamese had achieved their objectives" (p. 71).

But why is that so clear? It seems highly unlikely that the Communist forces in Vietnam would have accepted Hassler's policy of a general ceasefire and free elections, instead of continuing to achieve their objectives anyway. Moreover, U.S. policy eventually amounted to unilateral withdrawal permitting the achievement of Communist objectives. Why shouldn't the U.S. government have undertaken that policy in 1971, as McReynolds and his confreres advocated, rather than waiting until 1975 to do the same thing? What exactly was gained in terms of reducing violence and death (or anything else, for that matter) by continuing to prosecute the war for four more years?

Permissible Political Participation

My objections to Lewy's interpretation in no way rest, be it noted, on an acceptance of the pervasive belief among New Left pacifists, such as McReynolds, that the United States is the dominant cause of violence in the world and that Communist regimes in places like Vietnam invariably represent a golden prospect of peace with justice. Lewy substantiates the prevalence of this questionable belief among the "anti–anti-Communist" pacifists, a belief that undoubtedly increased the confidence of McReynolds and his associates that unilateral U.S. withdrawal from Indochina would dramatically improve the chances for peaceful and humane reconciliation. In the light of subsequent evidence in Indochina and elsewhere, that particular belief appears patently mistaken.

The point is, however, that leaving aside all naïveté and romanticism about Communism, the McReynolds proposal might still have been a *defensible political policy* in 1971, based simply on a realistic comparison of the amounts of violence and death that would be probable consequences of this and other policies. In any case, here is an example of pacifist participation in political discourse that may be understood on both sides of the debate as thoroughly consistent with devotion to non-violence. Therefore this example undermines Lewy's attempt to classify pacifists as "purists" and "consequentialists" in order to favor the one over the other. As I have said, things are much more complicated.

By providing what I hope is a more nuanced understanding of the logic of pacifism, I do not intend to rule out other forms of pacifist argument that might indeed resist political involvement, and thereby conform more strictly to Weber's dichotomy. I only suggest that a fully consistent version of pacifism need not do so.

Attitudes Toward Communism

In a neoconservative spirit, Lewy of course makes a great deal of the conflicting attitudes toward Communism within the pacifist community. According to him, it is an additional virtue of the purist or traditional pacifists that they are committed to democratic values as represented in part by the United States, and are opposed to Communism. By contrast, the basic error of the New Left pacifists is that they reverse things. The idea that Communism is in general a more promising proponent of demo-cratic values than the "capitalist free world" is for Lewy the hallmark of intellectual and moral bankruptcy. Even more than consequentialist thinking itself, the advocacy of "politics that are couched in the language of peace and justice but that in fact support and promote some of the most brutal and ruthless forces in the world" (p. 242) is what makes the new pacifists not only mistaken but reprehensible.

The problem with this, as with much neoconservative thinking about the "Free World–Communist" polarity, is that it is no less excessive and indiscriminate than the positions it criticizes. Even prior to the remarkable developments in the Communist world in the late 1980s, it has always seemed painfully obvious that in formulating policies toward both Communist and non-

Communist nations, it is both prudent and wise to *look carefully and in depth at individual cases*, and not to trust much in grand claims about "authoritarian" versus "totalitarian" regimes. This goes, of course, for both New Leftists and New Conservatives.

It is wrong to equate Marxist revolution with peace and justice; it is also wrong to equate the formal trappings of democracy with peace and justice. What may be true about "brutality" and "ruthlessness" under Communism in Indochina is not necessarily true about conditions under Communism in Nicaragua. That is particularly the case when the record in Nicaragua is compared with that in neighboring "democracies" like Guatemala and Honduras, as well as with the prospects there might be for democracy and respect for human rights under a government controlled by the Nicaraguan resistance. These are complicated matters. But that is just the point. They may not be disposed of with the wave of a slogan, either of the New Left or of the New Conservative variety.

If in the process of arguing a political case, pacifists oversimplify or make biased assumptions, as Lewy shows they have done on occasion, they must of course be held accountable. But then the case against them must be made with care and precision. Lewy does not always do that. In my judgment, for example, he does not make a strong case against certain pacifist sympathies in his onesided discussion of U.S. policy in Central America. Moreover, pacifists are not alone in being bound by the requirements of responsible argument; those apply equally to everyone. In the last analysis, the only way to test for oversimplification or bias is to examine the details of an argument in all their complexity. Saluting to ideological generalities of any sort is not likely to help.

Revolutionary or Counter-Revolutionary

But what of Lewy's charge that New Left pacifists have actually contradicted their commitment to non-violence when, on the model of Liberation thinking, they have explicitly favored "revolutionary violence" over "counter-revolutionary violence''? Is that not, by any account, a clear violation of pacifism?

Two things may be said about that. First, if a pacifist gives direct aid and support to acts of violence or to a movement that advocates the use of violence, such an action does indeed contradict the principle of non-violence, and the person who did it could hardly be considered a consistent pacifist. In fact, it is not clear why such people would want to go on claiming the label. Lewy is correct to call their credentials into question.

Second, however, I see nothing logically inconsistent if a pacifist decides that one of two parties in an armed conflict is more just than the other, and more likely, if victorious, to create conditions of justice and lasting peace, and then undertakes *non-violently* to weaken the fighting capacity of the unjust party, or to cause the unjust party to withdraw from the conflict. That is, I would suppose, essentially what the McReynolds position in the FOR dispute reviewed above came to. Such an argument, like any other, is naturally accountable for its claims of the fact and its predictions of outcome. If such a pacifist policy proved to be mistaken, the problem would be, not that the policy considered consequences, but that its calculations of consequence were awry.

The Pacifist's "Right"

Finally, Lewy makes a most peculiar claim toward the end of the book about what a pacifist ''has a right'' to do or not to do. He says that pacifists have a right to decide, to opt out of the political process and, like proponents of an ethic of ultimate ends, to stand witness on the sidelines to the purity and goodness of non-violence. But, he says, ''they have no right to sacrifice others for the attainment of this vocation'' (p. 242). Lewy then goes on to blame modern American pacifist organizations for doing just that. By advocating pro-Communist policies that produce ruthlessness and brutality, present-day pacifists wind up sacrificing others to their cause.

What Lewy means by ''no right to sacrifice others'' in pursuit of a non-violent cause is not at all clear. Precisely what sort of right is it that the pacifist does not have? Could it be that Lewy thinks the pacifist has no *right of reason* to do such a thing, that if pacifists "sacrificed others" in the name of non-violence they would be inconsistent?

But that cannot be correct. Consider an absolute non-political pacifist suddenly called upon to protect an innocent victim against a violent assault. As a rule, pacifists argue that non-violence precludes the use of physical force in that situation, even though the assault may result in the death of the victim. What if, following Lewy's prescription, we said to the pacifist in this case that he or she had no right to sacrifice another in the service of witnessing to the principle of non-violence? Refraining from using force in this context, even though a life is "sacrificed," is exactly what it means to witness to non-violence! Presumably, this implication would apply in the same way to any pacifist, even of the more "consequentialist" type, who was endeavoring to apply the principle of non-violence. If lives are "sacrificed" in the process, the pacifist is not being inconsistent by permitting that to happen.

If Lewy means that the pacifist has no *moral right* to act in this way, then he must show that pacifism as such is morally unacceptable. That is true because, as we have shown, pacifism as such is premised on the "right" to sacrifice others in the cause of non-violence, if need be. Without this right there is no pacifism. However, since Lewy ascribes "moral high ground" to at least some kinds of pacifism, the lack of moral right cannot be what he has in mind.

Perhaps, in the last place, Lewy means that the pacifist has no *civil right* to sacrifice others in a non-violent cause. That might mean that if pacifist policies have not been democratically adopted, then a pacifist has no right to try to act on them, particularly when lives are sacrificed as a result. That might further mean, as Lewy himself indicates, that there is no right to civil disobedience in the face of electoral defeat: "Minorities must respect the legitimate decision-making processes of a democratic system even if the outcome seriously displeases or even disturbs them" (p. 180). Such capitulation was called for during the Vietnam war, when "at no time did a majority of the American people support the kind of unconditional, unilateral withdrawal from Vietnam'' demanded by groups like the American Friends Service Committee. Rather than proceeding to call for acts of civil disobedience against the war, the AFSC and others, according to Lewy, should have simply continued to operate within the democratic process to try to change laws and policies.

Lewy's position here is untenable, I believe. In fact, he himself opens the door to a different and more defensible stand. "An individual," he says, "should accept the moral legitimacy of the law *unless he has succeeded in winning his way to a clear moral decision establishing that the law is truly unjust*" (p. 180, my italics). Clearly, many pacifists and others during the Vietnam war period had made what they believed were conscientious determinations of just that sort. Accordingly, the course of civil disobedience appeared to be the only one open to them. Lewy of course cautions against the frivolous use of this appeal to conscience. However, to admit resort to conscience at all in such matters is to leave it up finally to each person to decide, on pain of taking the consequences of disobedience, when the way has been won "to a clear moral decision establishing that the law is truly unjust."

Strictly speaking, it would not be proper to call a right to civil disobedience a "civil right," for such action is by definition outside the law. Perhaps it is better described as a moral right (of conscience) that is closely relevant to civil life. But in any case, we have shown that, contrary to Lewy's denial, such a right does exist. Whether that right has been exercised correctly in a given case is a subject for conscientious disagreement.

PART THREE

Lewy Replies

Pacifists in a
Democratic Society

Guenter Lewy

THE RESPONSES to *Peace and Revolution* assembled in this
volume run the full range from harsh denunciation to hearty
approval. The majority of the critics appear to agree that I
described developments correctly, though many disagree with
my assessment of their broader implications. Some say that my
not being a pacifist impaired my analysis. I am said to have
followed merely a paper trail in my research: I should have
turned my findings over to the organizations involved for internal
use instead of going public, or should at least have talked to
persons involved in making the statements I quote to learn of
their context.

I welcome this opportunity to continue the dialogue begun at
the colloquium on *Peace and Revolution* sponsored by the
Ethics and Public Policy Center in the fall of 1988. This discussion is important because whatever non-pacifists like myself
may think of the contribution pacifists have made to world
peace, this philosophy is in fact politically significant. As the
Ethics and Public Policy Center has correctly emphasized in all
of its work, ideas and values have consequences.

Furthermore, as I wrote in the last chapter of *Peace and
Revolution*, "pacifists, committed to the supreme value of non-
violence, remind the rest of us who are not pacifists of the link
between means and ends. Their personal 'No' to killing carries

227

an important ethical message.'' As I see it, during the last two decades the four major pacifist organizations have abandoned their unequivocal commitment to this valuable moral principle. Those who at one time were among the keepers of the humanitarian conscience have become apologists for movements and regimes that are anything but humanitarian. I took no pleasure in recounting this sad story; I regard it as a moral tragedy of major proportions. My hope is that further discussion of these events and their significance will draw attention to the tragedy and will encourage a process of reform that even some pacifists regard as long overdue.

What Is Pacifism?

I do not think we can develop ''correct'' definitions of abstract concepts; all such definitions are arbitrary. I used a definition of pacifism that seemed appropriate for the four organizations I dealt with—opposition to bearing arms, and a refusal to sanction war for any purpose, defensive or otherwise. Until the 1960s, this was indeed the position of the major pacifist groups in this country. For some of them, this stance had roots in the Quaker declaration of 1660: ''We utterly deny *all* outward wars and strife, and fighting with outward weapons, *for any end, or under any pretense whatever*; this is our testimony to the whole world'' (my italics). For others, the refusal to bear arms and the opposition to war were derived from non-religious moral principles. Common to all was the conviction that the commitment to non-violence was absolute and should not be abridged for any reason whatsoever. In the introductory chapter of *Peace and Revolution*, excerpted in this volume, I recount some of the debates over this issue and how, until the upheavals of the 1960s, they all ended with a reaffirmation of the binding quality of non-violence.

As James Turner Johnson points out, my definition of pacifism does not cover all groups in history that have considered themselves pacifist. It does have the advantage of capturing the original major thrust of the four organizations with which I was concerned. My conclusion that these groups have compromised their pacifist convictions is based not on a rhetorical trick, related to my definition of pacifism, but on a detailed exposition of events and activities. The quoted testimony of important figures in the pacifist community like Alfred Hassler and Charles Bloomstein also attests to this far-reaching process of change. The long-term faithful service of these men to the pacifist cause should endow their judgments with a considerable measure of credibility.

Just War and Just Revolution

It was the veteran FOR leader Alfred Hassler who in 1968 charged that important segments of the movement against the war in Vietnam had become supporters of the National Liberation Front (NLF) and the revolutionary violence it practiced. Published in *Fellowship*, the official organ of the Fellowship of Reconciliation, Hassler's harsh critique clearly was addressed to the pacifist component of the anti-war movement, including many leading members of his own organization. Many in the peace movement, Hassler argued, had become so horrified by U.S. actions in Vietnam that they had moved to the opposite pole and supported anything the NLF and North Vietnam did. The NLF practiced terror, assassination, and the shelling of non-combatants. Its American supporters "justify and defend all the means used by the NLF and, in religious terms, substitute for the theology of the just war a theology of the just revolution. This is not a pacifist position" (quoted in *Peace and Revolution*, p. 65; subsequent page references are to this book unless otherwise noted).

Hassler's pleading fell on deaf ears. The major pacifist organizations increasingly came to favor an NLF victory. In the spring of 1975, *WIN* magazine, the organ of the War Resisters League, published a series of articles celebrating "the imminent victory of liberation forces in both Cambodia and Vietnam." One of the few pacifists to take exception to this glorification of military force was Ed Lazar, peace-education secretary of the New England regional office of the American Friends Service Committee. In an article entitled "Military Victories Are Not Cause for Celebration," Lazar expressed his amazement that people supposedly committed to peace and reconciliation would welcome the results of slaughter. It was easy, he wrote, to be opposed to war when the military advantage was with the bad guys, "but it is just as important to be opposed to war when the military advantage is seemingly with the more sympathetic side. To do otherwise is to support the concept of the just war" (quoted on p. 111). Tanks and guns, Lazar went on to say, could never be instruments of liberation; any armed victory represented "a setback to the ending of war." In December 1975, when it was all over, Hassler noted with deep regret that as a result of the newly prevailing tendency of pacifists to justify the killing violence of liberation movements, pacifism itself had become "one of the casualties of Vietnam" (quoted on p. 239).

Against the position of Hassler and Lazar, who stressed the incompatibility of pacifism and just-war thinking, several of my critics defend the right of pacifists to make judgments about the relative justice of parties in armed conflicts, or even to take sides. According to John Richard Burkholder, pacifists may, and indeed must, employ the language and logic of the just-war tradition in order to judge the moral justification of the resort to force by rival belligerents. A pacifist who wants to remain a pacifist, argues David Little, cannot give direct aid to acts of violence. However, he writes, "I see nothing logically inconsistent if a pacifist decides that one of two parties in an armed conflict is more just than the other . . . and then undertakes *nonviolently* to weaken the fighting capacity of the unjust party, or to cause the unjust party to withdraw from the conflict."

Leaving aside the question whether it is "logically inconsistent" for a pacifist to support one party in an armed conflict, I would argue that, historically, the major American pacifist organizations did not view their role in this way. Their position was that *all* resort to war was unacceptable, regardless of the degree of violence present or the goals of the competing belligerents.

This position can be faulted, as I have argued in my book and will re-argue here shortly, for failing to take into account the consequences of the resort or non-resort to armed force. However, the uniqueness of the pacifist message was precisely that it stressed the irrelevance of consequences and of rival claims of justice. "Nothing, but nothing, comes before peace," argued Charles Bloomstein in 1971 in criticism of what he regarded as the AFSC's support of the NLF. "Otherwise we certainly should have supported the Loyalists in Spain, the Allies over Hitler, and today the revolutionaries in South Africa." It was the inescapable obligation of a pacifist "to insist on peace first, and to seek justice under that aegis. We are convinced that justice cannot be achieved through violence, that to use that means results in neither justice nor peace." The task of the pacifist was to oppose all killing, not "to sift the various claims of the competing parties" (quoted on pp. 110–11).

The Pro-NLF Bias

A related issue of fact also requires comment. According to Charles Chatfield, the great majority of American pacifists opposed the U.S. war in Vietnam because they regarded it as "politically unjustified and immoral" and "not (as Lewy insinuates) in order to make possible a Communist victory." James Matlack and John Swomley make the same point. Now, there can be little doubt that many pacifists (and non-pacifists, for that matter) did indeed oppose the U.S. involvement in Southeast Asia because they considered it inimical to American interests and morally flawed. It is also clear, however, that the four major pacifist organizations gradually came to favor the Vietnamese Communists and, once committed, did everything possible to facilitate their victory. This was the conclusion of prestigious pacifist leaders like Hassler, Bloomstein, and Robert Pickus who were well acquainted with the thinking of their colleagues.

The pro-NLF bias of these groups is demonstrated by the fact that they sought as their primary objective, not a ceasefire to end the killing, but the speedy removal of U.S. forces. After the Paris peace agreement of 1973, not content with having achieved a U.S. withdrawal, they worked hard to prevent U.S. support for the government of Saigon, which faced a powerful and well-supplied opponent in the north. Given the fragility of the South Vietnamese armed forces and their dependence on American aid, no one could have had any doubt that the absence of aid would lead to a Communist victory.

Finally, on the NLF question, there is the record of pronouncements of leading figures in the groups under discussion. Two examples will have to suffice here.

In an article published in March 1967 entitled "Justice and Social Revolution," Stewart Meacham, head of the AFSC's peace-education division, argued that while pacifists condemned all resort to violence, this did not mean that they "should be aloof and unconcerned with judgments regarding the justice or the injustice of one side against the other." For pacifists supportive of the National Liberation Front, Meacham maintained, it was incumbent to establish "the relevance of non-violence to revolutionary struggle." They had to learn how to respond when the United States attempted "by violence to suppress a revolutionary struggle" (quoted on p. 29). The formula that would enable pacifists to assist the revolutionary cause in Vietnam without themselves engaging in overt violence, it was soon discovered, was to work for the withdrawal of U.S. forces. In this way, they could affirm their commitment to peace and non-violence and at the same time help their revolutionary friends in Vietnam.

The same position was enunciated in 1972 by James E. Bristol, director of the AFSC's program on non-violence. Pacifists, Bristol argued, should recognize the violence of the status quo in the Third World—the suffering created by lack of a decent standard of living and the brutal practices of the police and penal system. The thrust of their effort should be to remove injustice, not to urge non-violence. Pacifists should identify with the cause of the oppressed; "we urge all who are able in good conscience to do so to unite with them and support them in their revolution" (quoted on p. 48).

How could people committed to non-violence aid the revolution of the oppressed? "It will make it easier for the disadvantaged to succeed in their revolutionary struggle," argued Bristol, "if we remove both direct American domination and/or American support for their oppressors, and this, in turn, will serve to minimize the violence which they feel compelled to use to reach their goal" (quoted on p. 49). This, indeed, was the strategy that the major pacifist organizations followed in the Vietnam conflict and have since used in regard to Central America. Clearly a lot more is going on here than an effort to achieve peace and reconciliation.

Support for Liberation Movements

James Matlack denies that the AFSC supports revolutionary violence, and he quotes several passages from a 1981 AFSC statement "Perspectives on Non-Violence in Relation to Groups Struggling for Social Justice" to prove the organization's disavowal of violence. But the AFSC's record during the last twenty years contradicts these rhetorical disclaimers. They are empty words belied by practice.

While it is true that the AFSC has never sent arms to guerrilla groups, the organization along with the rest of the organized pacifist community has found other ways to support such "oppressed people" driven to a resort to violence. The AFSC pleads the cause of these violent movements before the American people and works to prevent U.S. aid to the governments under attack.

That was the strategy the AFSC used in Vietnam. And since pacifists had no leverage on the massive support provided for the Viet Cong by North Vietnam or on North Vietnam's military strategy itself, the inevitable result of this one-sided cut in aid was to help hand South Vietnam over to the Communists. The AFSC now employs the same game plan regarding El Salvador. As Daniel Seeger argued in a perceptive article published in *Friends Journal* in 1979, pacifists undermine their moral and political credibility when they sympathize with violent revolutionaries and simultaneously urge governments to respond nonviolently to revolutionary violence.

The identification with the "oppressed," it should be noted, is highly selective. None of the organizations dealt with in *Peace and Revolution* showed any sympathy for the Afghan *mujaheddin* fighting Soviet occupation of their country, or for Angola's UNITA struggling against Cuban-aided Communist rule. Matlack's dismissal of the Afghan resistance and Savimibi's UNITA as undemocratic is typical of the way the AFSC has reacted to these movements. Almost by definition, no anti-Communist rebellion can be a "liberation movement," and there are no truly oppressed people in the so-called socialist countries. The adjective "socialist" suffices to legitimate any revolutionary cause or regime, no matter how brutal and repressive.

The AFSC statement quoted by Matlack alleges that when "some of the oppressed resort to violence, they usually do so out of protracted distress, victimization, and despair at bringing change any other way." This view demonstrates a profound misunderstanding of the causes and consequences of revolutionary violence. As both the historical and the sociological literature clearly demonstrate, it is not the most victimized and desperate people who rise up in arms against their oppressors. Whether in Asia, Africa, or the Americas, it is not the poorest countries that experience guerrilla violence but those that have revolutionary leadership able to galvanize latent discontent.

The Catholic pacifist Gordon Zahn, quoted at length in my book, has pointed out that it is an easy play on words that helps excuse the violence of the guerrillas as a forced response to the violence perpetrated by the status quo. Moreover, many of the regimes that take over after the victory of Communist-led "liberation movements" are far more repressive than the brutal but inefficient dictators they replace. During the last ten years alone, several hundred thousand Vietnamese and Cubans have risked their lives to escape their self-proclaimed liberators. The exodus from Sandinista-ruled Nicaragua is no less massive—250,000 refugees in Honduras alone. Pacifists show little interest in these unfortunates.

Civil Disobedience

While American pacifists, with varying degrees of frankness, have embraced leftist-led national liberation movements, many of them have at the same time expressed their disdain for the "formal democracy" of capitalist America. A symptom of their contempt for the democratic process is their easy and frequent resort to civil disobedience whenever they find they cannot achieve their results through ordinary political action.

David Little disagrees with my criticism of pacifists and others who during the time of the Vietnam war resorted to civil disobedience. I argue that, as a rule, the citizen of a democratic society should abide by the law of the land or seek to change or repeal it. I see no justification for civil disobedience simply because one has failed to achieve a change in the law. Such a failure could be due simply to lack of the majority support needed for the change.

During the late 1960s and early 1970s, many opponents of the war in Vietnam had convinced themselves that a majority of the American people shared their opposition to the war and that, since their position did not prevail, democracy had failed. Both of these assumptions were incorrect. At no time did a majority of the American people support the kind of unconditional, unilateral withdrawal from Vietnam demanded by the radical anti-war movement. It was a minority view, and minorities must respect the legitimate decision-making processes of a democratic system even if the outcome seriously disturbs them. Civil disobedience is not justified by a failure to achieve votes. To think otherwise is to subvert democracy.

There are exceptions to these rules. Even in democratic societies, some individuals or groups may be prevented from fully participating in the electoral process. Blacks in the American South not so long ago lacked effective channels to redress, and therefore the civil-rights movement was fully justified in resorting to civil disobedience. Furthermore, in some extreme situations individuals may conclude after searching moral deliberation that they cannot in good conscience obey a law they consider unjust. The refusal of a doctor to give a lethal injection or to perform an abortion would be an example of such a situation.

In my view, anti-war activists during the Vietnam years who blocked ammunition trains or engaged in various other disruptive tactics did not fall within these exceptions. Not only did they follow coercive tactics of resistance, but they were attempting to undermine a national policy, an action I see as different from disobeying a law that commands me as an individual to do or not to do something. An individual's ability to judge the *moral* justification of his nation's going to war is limited. The difficulty of separating moral and political criteria in such cases is one reason why the courts have refused to allow the right of conscientious objection to a particular war.

Judgments on the degree of violence employed and on violations of the law of war while the war is still in progress are also notoriously difficult. As I sought to show in my book *America in Vietnam*, most of the allegations of a *deliberate* resort to war crimes on the part of the U.S. military turned out on close examination to be spurious. Many pacifists during these years may have *believed*, as David Little maintains, that the American war effort was unjust on both *ius ad bellum* and *ius in bello* grounds. However, I would not consider this belief, sincere as it may have been, an adequate moral justification for civil disobedience, especially since other means of redress were available.

The appeal to conscience is not a sufficient justification for civil disobedience. Those who enact the laws or formulate national policies also have moral reasons for their choices. An individual should not assume that his judgment is necessarily superior to that of the community. As we saw all too clearly during the Vietnam war years, the easy resort to civil disobedience can have a highly disruptive effect on society. Moreover, what is sauce for the goose is sauce for the gander. Once the appeal to the supremacy of conscience is conceded, what is to prevent defenders of the separation of races from interfering with social practices that offend their sense of morality? How can we criticize (as I think we should, regardless of our view of abortion) the opponents of abortion on demand who block access to abortion clinics? The way the law resolves the disputed moral issues of a pluralistic society may not always be ideal, but a better alternative does not present itself.

Pacifists in a Democratic Society

None of my positions has given rise to more objections and misunderstandings than my view that pacifism is a personal philosophy of non-violence rather than a prescription for public policy. Drawing upon Max Weber and Reinhold Niebuhr, I argued that the pacifist is as entitled as the next person to participate in the political process and to propose policies. He should recognize, however, that when entering the policy arena he must adopt standards of judgment distinct from those he applies in his personal life. National policies proposed by the pacifist should, like all policies, be judged not according to good intent but in terms of foreseeable results. As the Catholic theologian George Weigel has pointed out, "the morality of political judgment must include a consequential criterion. To argue, for example, that unilateral disarmament is the sole moral option, even if its results would be to make war more likely, is not an act of prophetic witness but a moral absurdity."

This does not mean that pacifist ideas like Gandhi's and Martin Luther King's advocacy of non-violent resistance are politically irrelevant. When the government in power has some respect for public opinion and the rule of law, non-violent resistance can achieve results; the campaign against the British in India and the American civil-rights movement are cases in point. However, the decision to adopt this tactic should be made in the light of likely consequences. Pacifists may choose non-violence as an absolute moral imperative, but they should not mislead others into thinking that non-violence will stop all acts of aggression and evil. To do otherwise leads to follies like Gandhi's urging the Jews of Europe to use *Satyagraha* ("truth-force") to prevent the Nazis from carrying out their plan to destroy the Jewish people.

Nobody will expect pacifists to be active supporters of nuclear deterrence, of the use of force against terrorists, or even of military aid to weak regimes facing the threat of foreign-sponsored subversion. But neither should pacifists reflexively oppose all such policies. The pacifist can argue that a particular policy is ill advised or counterproductive, but he should not seek to maneuver his country into a position that prevents all reliance upon power—a sure prescription for disaster, given the world in which we live. When the pacifist encounters what he sees as an insoluble conflict between desirable ends and unacceptable means—that is, when he agrees that certain policies are necessary to prevent worse ones but these necessary policies utilize force or the threat of force—in these situations, *and only in these situations*, the proper course for him is to remain silent, to refrain from taking a position. A historical precedent is the withdrawal of Quaker politicians from the government of the province of Pennsylvania in 1756 because they wanted to be neither a party to nor an obstacle to the waging of war against the Indians.The fact that, as Stanley Hauerwas points out, the Quakers by that time were a minority in the colony does not change the significance of this decision.

The Test of Consequences

To prevent misunderstandings, I want to repeat this central point of my argument.

I am *not* suggesting that pacifists stop being citizens. *Pace* James Matlack, I do *not* wish to reduce pacifists "to an injunction of silence." Still less do I want to prevent pacifists from developing independent standards of judgment, so that, as John Richard Burkholder charges, they would "end up in the same box as the German Christians who kept silent about Hitler's atrocities in the 1930s." I am suggesting that when pacifists act as citizens, they should accept the test of consequences to which all public policies must be subject.

Pacifists in World War II accepted this verity. They recognized not only that it would have been undemocratic to try to stop a war that their nation had democratically decided to wage, but that to do so would have helped bring about the triumph of a political system of unparalleled evil. I am arguing that pacifists should return to this view of their role in a democratic society. They should look at the foreseeable consequences of their actions.

Applying the test of consequences might have induced some pacifists to adopt different policies during the Vietnam war. To be sure, some pacifist leaders quite deliberately demanded an unconditional U.S. withdrawal in order to help their revolutionary friends win the war. But there were also many well-meaning rank-and-file pacifists who supported this policy because they genuinely wanted peace. If they had taken into account the likely consequences of their actions, they might have realized that a unilateral U.S. withdrawal would bring not peace but more killing. Many more innocent people have died in Southeast Asia since the American disengagement than died during the course of the war.

The recognition that this would be likely to happen made FOR leader Alfred Hassler oppose the demand for an unconditional U.S. withdrawal. There are situations, he pointed out in September 1970, "in which the heaped-up evil of the past . . . is simply more than love and non-violence can deal with—or at any rate, the amount of love and non-violence capable of being mobilized. In such periods the pacifist must reconcile himself to being irrelevant, standing aside unable to affect the course of the struggle though watching always for a means of ending [the killing]." In other words, Hassler, like the Quakers of Pennsylvania in 1756, felt he could neither support the war nor be a party to policies that would lead to the victory of America's opponent and a vast increase in human suffering.

Chuck Fager agrees with my basic point that public policies must be judged in terms of foreseeable consequences, but he denies that the anti-war movement should be held responsible for the disasters that have overtaken Southeast Asia since the end of the U.S. involvement. Without the efforts of the anti-war movement, Fager argues, the war might well have continued for many more years and have led to millions of additional deaths. We are dealing here with "might have beens," and the discussion must be somewhat speculative. Nevertheless, several established facts have a bearing on whether an alternative outcome was possible.

I nowhere assert that pacifists "were pivotal in undermining America's national will to win in Vietnam." Nevertheless, it is clear that the harsh rhetoric and confrontational tactics of the anti-war movement contributed decisively to the political polarization of the country and gradually created a sense among lawmakers, the media, and other elite groups that the country was coming apart. The anti-war movement did not end the war all by itself, but it managed to convince an ever-widening circle of influential and articulate Americans that, if only for the sake of civil peace, the war in Vietnam had to stop. Even many of those who for a long time had agreed with the basic rationale of the U.S. involvement eventually came to feel that, however just its goals, the social and political costs of the war were too high and the United States should cut its losses and get out. Coupled with a growing war-weariness, the fear of social disintegration eventually led American lawmakers to call it quits. Congress enacted increasingly restrictive military and financial constraints upon the conduct of the war and eventually forced President Nixon to sign a less than promising peace accord in 1973.

Other Consequential Criteria

This leads to a second important point. We know that the North Vietnamese did not decide on their final offensive until they were sure that Nixon was decisively weakened by the Watergate scandal and therefore would not dare to take on Congress over the reintroduction of U.S. air power. There is every reason to think that the Paris accord of 1973 could have been enforced through the use, or even just the threat, of air power. Furthermore, as General Van Tien Dung, the North Vietnamese chief of staff, put it in his retrospective on the final days of the war, the sharp reductions in U.S. aid to the Saigon government had forced President Thieu "to fight a poor man's war," suffering from serious shortages in spare parts, ammunition, and fuel.

The anti-war movement had labored tenaciously for these cuts and thus must bear part of the responsibility for their consequences. Had the South Vietnamese been adequately supplied and supported by U.S air power as during the North Vietnamese Easter offensive of 1972, they probably could have held their own. What is even more likely is that the North Vietnamese would not have launched an all-out offensive. In short, responsibility for the abandonment of Vietnam and the consequent horrors of the Vietnamese gulag and the tragedy of the boat people should not be attributed to the anti-war movement alone, but neither should its supporters be allowed to disclaim all blame. Although I take exception to some of Chuck Fager's observations on my book *America in Vietnam*, I agree with him that this is not the place to settle the debate over that war. Suppose we use some other examples to illustrate the moral dilemma I am talking about. Might the application of the test of consequences make American pacifists refrain from opposing military aid to the elected government of El Salvador, under attack from both the extreme left and the extreme right, so as not to leave it, like Vietnam, defenseless in the face of a well-supplied Communist insurgency? The issue here is not whether El Salvador is a full-fledged democracy. It is not. The issue is whether an FMLN victory will improve or worsen the chances for democratic development, escape from chronic poverty, and improved human rights. Given the explicit Marxist-Leninist commitment of the guerrillas, the answer should be clear.

Let us look at World War II. Should the application of consequential criteria—then or at least now with the benefit of hindsight—not lead us to conclude that indeed there are situations in which pacifists, in Hassler's language, should reconcile themselves to being irrelevant and stand aside (in my language, remain silent)? I for one am glad that during World War II the great majority of American pacifists did not mobilize an anti-war movement. Had there been such a movement as successful as the anti-war movement during the Vietnam conflict, I would not be writing these lines today. Like millions of others saved by the Allied victory over the Nazis, I would have ended up in one of Hitler's gas chambers.

Some Points of Personal Privilege

This rejoinder to my critics has deliberately focused on important issues of principle. These are the questions that both pacifists and non-pacifists must seek to clarify. Yet I feel entitled to respond to at least a few of the more personal attacks on my scholarship.

James Matlack charges me with "systematic faults in overall approach and methodology," including "overstatement and mishandling of the evidence" drawn from the archives I consulted. As a case in point, Matlack quotes part of a sentence from my book that allegedly charges the AFSC with withholding medical aid to the South Vietnamese Buddhists. In fact, this charge was made by an AFSC volunteer, not by me. Here, in context, is what I did say, with the few words Matlack chose to quote in italics: "In 1971 a former AFSC volunteer worker in Vietnam had expressed her concern about the AFSC's obvious bias in favor of the NLF [National Liberation Front] and its complete neglect of the Buddhists, who were avowed pacifists. *Not only did the AFSC exclude the Buddhists from its medical aid program and limit this aid to the NLF and North Vietnam,* but she had not even been permitted to use AFSC facilities in order to duplicate and mail to the United States a newsletter of the Unified Buddhist Church'' (p. 53). I assume that the AFSC worker writing this letter had in mind institutional grants rather than clinics operated by the AFSC such as the medical center at Quang Ngai, undoubtedly well known to her (as to me). The letter itself is in the Swarthmore College Peace Collection; my endnote gives details on how it can be located. I leave it to readers to decide who is guilty of selective and distorted use of archival materials.

In another place, Matlack accuses me of using innuendos and engaging in ''an exercise in paranoia and character assassination that, lacking concrete proofs, have no place in a book issued by a reputable publisher.'' As an example, Matlack refers to my discussion of the charge, sometimes made by right-wing elements, that the AFSC is a dupe of the Communists. In this discussion I pointed out that several FBI and CIA investigations had found this allegation to be without substance and had confirmed that the AFSC was ''a sincere pacifist organization.''A little further on I wrote:

> Given the Communist party's proclivity toward secrecy and manipulation and its frequently stated intention to work closely with the peace movement, one cannot, of course, be absolutely certain that there are no Communists in the AFSC. However, so far no evidence of Communist infiltration has surfaced, and one can probably agree with the appraisal of Chuck Fager, a Quaker, that the AFSC's mistakes and shortcomings are of its own making and not the KGB's. ''Serious as some of the AFSC's problems are,'' Fager has concluded, ''I for one am grateful that they so clearly do *not* include being run by Moscow or CIA manipulators'' [quoted on p. 193].

I went on to say that in my view ''the AFSC is neither a Communist front nor an organization controlled by the KGB.'' According to Matlack, I ''entertain notions that traitors are at work, or that KGB cadres may indeed be entrenched in leadership roles." Yet readers will find no such assertions or innuendoes in my book. They are Matlack's inventions. There are a few other such unfounded attacks upon the scholarship of *Peace and Revolution*. John Swomley charges that I omit important material that does not support my thesis, quote out of context, and in general use a " 'smear' technique unworthy of a person with academic credentials." Charles Chatfield calls me "a man of deep sincerity and a competent scholar," but in the same breath alleges that I make "selective use of evidence within the sources" utilized. This, he says, "is aggravated by the use of extended quotations that explain the positions of partisans with whom the author agrees, in contrast to limited quotations from others that serve mainly to document their deviance from allegedly authentic pacifism." I have not undertaken a count of who was quoted and at what length, but I am rather sure that such a count would not substantiate Chatfield's allegation of selectivity.

Daniel Seeger, not hesitant to state his criticism of me in matters of substance, says in his essay, "One senses in Lewy's book an attempt to be accurate about the data he presents. There are occasional omissions and inaccuracies in detail. Nevertheless, he successfully captures the flavor and the tone, as well as the overall contours, of one of the significant streams of events." Seeger goes on to say that "it is probably also true that a more extensive presentation of data would reveal a mix of strengths and weaknesses in the AFSC rather similar to that which Lewy demonstrates." And Chuck Fager writes that although I "may have misidentified an occasional tree of fact in the recent landscape, there seems little doubt that he has pretty accurately portrayed the forest of organizational evolution into which the trees fit." Coming from Friends with an intimate knowledge of the events I described and analyzed, these comments assure me that, within the limits of human fallibility, I have done a responsible job.

The restoration of the intellectual and moral integrity of the pacifist witness will have to come from within the pacifist community itself. Men and women willing to take on this tough assignment are few in number, but their courage and dedication may yet compensate for their weakness in size. Whatever the outcome in the short run, history will remember them for trying to do what honor and moral principle required.

Notes

PART I: GUENTER LEWY

Abbreviations in references to archival sources: AFSC, Archive of the American Friends Service Committee, Philadelphia; DG, Document Group; SCPC, Swarthmore College Peace Collection, Swarthmore, Pennsylvania.

1. On the origins of American pacifism generally, see Merle Curti, *Peace or War: The American Struggle, 1636–1936* (New York, 1936).
2. Devere Allen, *The Fight for Peace* (New York, 1930), p. 665.
3. Peter Brock, *Twentieth-Century Pacifism* (New York, 1970), p. 143; Lawrence S. Wittner, *Rebels Against War: The American Peace Movement, 1933–1983* (Philadelphia, 1984), pp. 8–9.
4. Muste, "Pacifism and Class War," *The World Tomorrow,* Sept. 1938; reprinted in *The Essays of A. J. Muste,* ed. Nat Hentoff (Indianapolis, 1967), p. 181.
5. Niebuhr, "The Religion of Communism," *Atlantic,* April 1931, p. 466.
6. Niebuhr, "Is Peace or Justice the Goal?," *The World Tomorrow,* 21 Sept. 1932, p. 277.
7. Matthews, "The Cross and the Sword," *Christian Century,* 6 Dec. 1933, p. 1541.
8. Matthews, quoted in the *Daily Worker,* 7 April 1933, p. 4; cited by Harvey Klehr, *The Heyday of American Communism: The Depression Decade* (New York, 1984), p. 101.
9. Charles Chatfield, *For Peace and Justice: Pacifism in America, 1914–1941* (Knoxville, 1971), p. 259.
10. Quoted in Charles Daniel Brodhead, "F.O.R. Holds Tense Session," *Christian Century,* 1 Nov. 1933, p. 1383–84.
11. The questionnaire text can be found in John Bennett, "That Fellowship Questionnaire," *The World Tomorrow,* 21 Dec. 1933, pp. 690–91.
12. Niebuhr, "Why I Leave the F.O.R.," *Christian Century,* 3 Jan. 1934, pp. 17–19.
13. "Communists and the United Front," *The World Tomorrow,* 1 March 1934, p. 100.
14. Page, "A Christian Revolution," *Christian Century,* 20 Feb. 1935, p. 236.
15. Chatfield, *For Peace and Justice,* pp. 258–59.

16. "Fellowship and United Front," *Fellowship*, April 1940, p. 59.
17. "The Way to Peace With Russia," *Fellowship*, April 1946, p. 60.
18. FOR national council statement, May 1948, published in *Fellowship*, Sept. 1948, p. 11.
19. Milgram, "Beware the Common Front!," *Fellowship*, Sept. 1948, pp. 9–10, 12.
20. Letter to the editor and editorial statement, *Fellowship*, Feb. 1949, p. 31.
21. Cited by Wittner, *Rebels Against War*, p. 205.
22. The full text of the declaration and its background can be found in a memo of Alfred Hassler, SCPC, DG 125, Acc. 81A-93, Box 9.
23. Hassler, "The World's Newest Peace Group," *Fellowship*, 1 March 1963, p. 26.
24. Cited in Gertrude Bussey and Margaret Tims, *Women's International League for Peace and Freedom, 1915–1965: A Record of Fifty Years' Work* (London, 1965), p. 39.
25. Cited ibid., p. 122.
26. Cited from *Peace and Bread in Time of War*, in *Beyond Nationalism: The Social Thought of Emily Greene Balch*, ed. Mercedes M. Randall (New York, 1972), p. xvi.
27. Detzer, *Appointment on the Hill* (New York, 1948), pp. 192–93.
28. SCPC, DG 43, Reference Material, Folder 45.
29. Hutchinson, "Living Within a Plan," unpublished autobiographical manuscript, SCPC, D. Hutchinson, Acc. 81A-96, Box 17.
30. Rough draft of minutes of the Peace Section Rancocas retreat, 21–22 Oct. 1933, in AFSC, Peace Section 1933, General Files, AFSC Peace Retreat (Rancocas), 1933.
31. AFSC, Peace Section, Emergency Peace Campaign, Correspondence and Programs and Reactions, 1936–41.
32. Clarence Pickett to Willard Uphaus, 23 Oct. 1951, quoted in Ralph Lord Roy, *Communism and the Churches* (New York, 1960), p. 217.
33. Muste, "Thawing but Unsettled: Report on What's Happened to the Cold War," *Fellowship*, July 1949, p. 23.
34. Muste, "Communism and Civil Liberties," *Fellowship*, Oct. 1949, p. 10.
35. Muste, quoted in Nat Hentoff, *Peace Agitator: The Story of A. J. Muste* (New York, 1963), p. 162.
36. Thomas, quoted in Hentoff, *Peace Agitator*, p. 166.
37. Finch, "An Observer Reports on the Communist Convention," *Liberation*, March 1957, p. 5.
38. Mygatt, quoted in Jo Ann Ooiman Robinson, *Abraham Went Out: A Biography of A. J. Muste* (Philadelphia, 1981), p. 104.
39. Page, *How to Keep America Out of War* (Philadelphia, 1939), pp. 3–4, 56.
40. Muste, *Non-Violence in an Aggressive World* (New York, 1940), pp. 45, 139.
41. Muste, *The World Task of Pacifism*, Pendle Hill Pamphlet no. 13 (Wallingford, Pa., 1941), p. 27.
42. FOR executive board, "Our Way in the Midst of War," cited by Glen

Zeitzer, "The Fellowship of Reconciliation on the Eve of the Second World War: A Peace Organization Prepares," *Peace and Challenge,* Summer–Fall 1975, p. 50.

43. Detzer, *Appointment on the Hill,* p. 239.

44. Hutchinson, *A Call to Peace Now: Message to the Society of Friends* (Philadelphia, 1943), p. 33.

45. Lens, "China's Leap: The Human Cost," *Fellowship,* March 1959, p. 10.

46. Lens, "Cuba: A Second Look," *Fellowship,* 1 Nov. 1961, pp. 6, 16.

47. Halstead, *Out Now! A Participant's Account of the American Movement Against the Vietnam War* (New York, 1978), p. 80.

48. Hassler, "60 Years," *Fellowship,* Dec. 1975, p. 17.

49. Pickard, *Peacemaker's Dilemma: Plea for a Modus Vivendi in the Peace Movement* (Wallingford, Pa., 1942), p. 36.

50. Cadoux, *Christian Pacifism Re-examined* (Oxford, 1940), p. 141.

51. Trueblood, *The People Called Quakers* (New York, 1966), p. 206.

52. Weigel, *Tranquillitas Ordinis: The Present Failure and Future Promise of American Catholic Thought on War and Peace* (New York, 1987), p. 247.

53. Niebuhr, "The Christian Faith and the World Crisis," *Christianity and Crisis,* 10 Feb. 1941, p. 4; reprinted in *Reinhold Niebuhr on Politics,* ed. Harry R. Davis and Robert C. Good (New York, 1960), p. 151.

54. Niebuhr, *Christianity and Power Politics* (New York, 1969), pp. x, 28.

55. Ibid., pp. 25, 175.

56. Hartill, "The Philosophy of Christian Pacifism," in *The Church, the Gospel and War,* ed. Rufus M. Jones (New York, 1971), p. 53.

CHAPTER 2: GEORGE WEIGEL

1. Cf. my discussion of this point in *Tranquillitas Ordinis: The Present Failure and Future Promise of American Catholic Thought on War and Peace* (New York: Oxford, 1987), pp. 275–80.

2. Hauerwas's chief contributions include *The Peaceable Kingdom* (Notre Dame: University of Notre Dame Press, 1983), *Against the Nations: War and Survival in a Liberal Society* (Minneapolis: Winston Press, 1985), and his commentary on the Methodist bishops' letter "In Defense of Creation," in Paul Ramsey, *Speak Up for Just War or Pacifism* (University Park: Pennsylvania State University Press, 1988). Among Yoder's many works may be cited *The Politics of Jesus* (Grand Rapids: Eerdmans, 1972), *Nevertheless* (Scottsdale: Herald Press, 1971), and *The Original Revolution* (Scottsdale: Herald Press, 1972).

3. To take the most obvious example, the decision by pacifist agencies to enter coalitions with Communist organizations and others favoring the military victory of Hanoi and the NLF during the Vietnam era was a sharp change in both pacifist self-understanding and pacifist politics. It engendered vigorous, even strident debates within pacifist agencies. One may agree or disagree with Lewy's judgment that this decision represented an abandonment of pacifist principles, but one cannot deny that it represented a significant change.

4. Cf. Charles Chatfield, *For Peace and Justice: Pacifism in America,*

1914–1941 (Boston: Beacon Press, 1973), and Peter Brock, *Twentieth Century Pacifism* (New York: Van Nostrand Reinhold, 1970).

5. The research of Gene Sharp on the theory and practice of non-violence remains seminally important here. Cf. Gene Sharp, *The Politics of Nonviolent Action,* three volumes (Boston: Porter Sargent, 1973); Gene Sharp, *Social Power and Political Freedom* (Boston: Porter Sargent, 1980); and Gene Sharp, *Gandhi as a Political Strategist* (Boston: Porter Sargent, 1979). Cf. also my review of Sharp's more recent study, *Making Europe Unconquerable,* in *Crisis* (September 1986).

6. See Richard Wightman Fox, *Reinhold Niebuhr: A Biography* (New York: Pantheon Books, 1985), for an overview of Niebuhr's development. Cf. also the selection of Niebuhr's essays on the topic "Love and Justice and the Pacifist Issue" in *Love and Justice: Selections from the Shorter Writings of Reinhold Niebuhr,* reprint edition (Gloucester: Peter Smith, 1976), pp. 241ff.

7. For a critique of Niebuhr's critique of pacifism, see James F. Childress, "Reinhold Niebuhr's Critique of Pacifism," *The Review of Politics* 36:4 (October 1974), pp. 467–91. My own first cut at defining the necessity and the limits of Niebuhr's Christian realism may be found in two essays: "The Sensibility of Reinhold Niebuhr," *The National Interest* 5 (Fall 1986), pp. 80–89; and "The National Interest and the National Purpose: From Policy Debate to Moral Argument," *This World* 19 (Fall 1987), pp. 79–100.

8. By "eschatology" I mean that set of beliefs, shared by all orthodox Christians, that we live in expectation of the coming in glory of the Lord and his Kingdom in that consummation of history and creation that has been prefigured (indeed ratified and guaranteed) in the paschal mystery of Christ's death and resurrection.

"Apocalyptic" refers to the literary style and world-historical view of numerous Old and New Testament texts that explicitly address the nature of the "endtime." "Apocalyptic" is thus a subset of "eschatology," the broader theological category.

9. Again, see Hauerwas's epilogue to Paul Ramsey's *Speak Up for Just War or Pacifism.*

10. Cf. my essay "Intellectual Currents in the American Public Effort for Peace, 1930–1980," in *The Nuclear Freeze Debate: Arms Control Issues for the 1980s,* Paul M. Cole and William J. Taylor, Jr., eds. (Boulder: Westview Press, 1983), pp. 107–39.

11. Pacifists often point to pre-Constantinian Christianity as a time of pacifist ascendancy. The historical picture is in fact considerably more complex, as James Turner Johnson demonstrates in *The Quest for Peace: Three Moral Traditions in Western Cultural History* (Princeton: Princeton University Press, 1987), pp. 15–42.

12. Cf. Duane Friesen, *Christian Peacemaking and International Conflict* (Scottsdale: Herald Press, 1986).

13. Cf., for example, my argument that, in its intellectual trajectory, the just-war tradition is in fact precisely ordered to the pursuit of peace understood as dynamic and rightly ordered political community, in *Tranquillitas Ordinis,* pp. 330, 346, 357, 383. Here I argue that, in addition to the classic *ius ad bellum* and *ius in bello,* just-war reasoning contains a *ius ad pacem.*

14. Cited in *Crisis,* July–August 1987, p. 1.

15. Cited in *Thomas Merton on Peace* (New York: McCall, 1971), p. xxix.

CHAPTER 4: JAMES FINN

1. *Nevertheless: The Varieties of Religious Pacifism,* by John Howard Yoder (Scottsdale, Pa: Herald Press, 1971), sets forth a typology of about eighteen different kinds of pacifism, some of which would fit Lewy's definition and some of which would not. While other pacifists might not offer as generous a typology as Yoder's, they would be unlikely to offer as restrained a one as Lewy's.

2. *Fellowship,* July/August 1988, p. 3.

3. "USSR: A Time of Change and Hope," ibid., pp. 4–8.

4. John Lamperti, "Where the Thinking Stops," ibid., pp. 9–10.

CHAPTER 6: JAMES TURNER JOHNSON

1. John Howard Yoder, *Nevertheless: The Varieties and Shortcomings of Religious Pacifism* (Scottsdale, Pa.: Herald Press, 1971, 1976).

2. Ibid., p. 10.

3. *Peace and Revolution* (Grand Rapids, Mich.: Eerdmans, 1988), p. 3.

4. While this same position characterized the pacifist Anabaptists of this period in general, the case is complicated by the fact that some of them were willing to stand watch, a military duty, if they could do so without bearing a sword or spear (some would carry a staff, a non-lethal weapon). Similar distinctions between an individual's personal moral duty and the practice of war, an activity of the state, are found elsewhere as well. For a general discussion of this topic see James M. Stayer, *Anabaptists and the Sword* (Lawrence, Kans.: Colorado Press, 1972).

5. On the use of Origen as such an example, see C. John Cadoux, *The Early Christian Attitude to War* (New York: Seabury Press, 1982), pp. 79–81. Cf. Origen, *Contra Celsum,* VIII.lxxiii.

6. There are two issues, not one, at stake in the definition of pacifism around non-violence. For non-violence, in its normative contemporary form derived from the examples and teaching of Gandhi and King, is a set of techniques for individual and collective behavior designed for social protest and to enable persons involved in such protest to resist and survive the use of violence against them. This is not identical to the renunciation of violence as practiced by, say, the early Quakers or as enunciated by a contemporary Christian pacifist like Stanley Hauerwas. One of the difficulties in defining and analyzing contemporary pacifism in America is the pervasive elision of these two rather different meanings of non-violence into each other.

Another problem with Christian pacifism is that it is not at all clear that the renunciation of violence by the Christian individual or community on the grounds of fidelity to Jesus' teaching and example implies the rejection of war by the state. The case of the Swiss Brethren cited earlier provides a powerful example to the contrary; so do early Christian attitudes, where opposition to military service seems to have centered around opposition to idolatry (the Roman "military religion"), the desire to avoid ritual uncleanliness brought about by the shedding of blood, and the personal immorality Christians associated with soldiers. On the reasons in general see Cadoux, *The Early*

Christian Attitude, Part II; on the argument from idolatry see John Helgeland, Robert J. Daly, and J. Patou Burns, *Christians and the Military: The Early Experience* (Philadelphia: Fortress Press, 1985).

7. See Gene Sharp, *National Security Through Civilian-Based Defense* (Omaha, Neb.: Association for Transarmament Studies, 1985).

8. See Reinhold Niebuhr, *Moral Man and Immoral Society* (New York: Scribner, 1932), chap. 9.

9. See James Turner Johnson, *The Quest for Peace: Three Moral Traditions in Western Cultural History* (Princeton, N.J., and Guildford, Surrey: Princeton University Press, 1987).

10. This is not a peculiarity of recent American pacifism. Close reading of Peter Brock's histories of pacifism reveals its variegated character, and British historian Martin Ceadel has found four major sorts of pacifists in the anti-war movement in England prior to World War I (a movement that split apart once the war had begun). See Peter Brock, *Pacifism in the United States* (Princeton: Princeton University Press, 1968) and *Pacifism in Europe to 1914* (Princeton University Press, 1972); Martin Ceadel, *Pacifism in Britain, 1914–45* (Oxford: Clarendon Press; New York: Oxford University Press, 1980).

11. This parallels the situation in England; cf. Brock, *Pacifism in Europe,* and Ceadel, *Pacifism in Britain.*

12. For definition of this myth and analysis of its expression after World War I see Paul Fussell, *The Great War and Modern Memory* (New York and London: Oxford University Press, 1975); for a critique cf. James Turner Johnson, *Just War Tradition and the Restraint of War* (Princeton, N.J., and Guildford, Surrey: Princeton University Press, 1981), pp. 33–40. The utopian tradition also has ancient roots, but modern expressions may be said to begin with Erasmus. Persons in this tradition hold that the world is good but has been perverted by the machinations of self-interested princes and the states they control. These princes squander resources on armies and lead their states into war for trivial and venal reasons, with the result that the innocent suffer, morality is undermined, and material progress is radically impeded. War is the worst of evils because it is the father and mother of all other evils. While in theory there might be just wars, in practice there are none, because all wars flow from corrupt, venal politics.

The answer to all this—and the end to war—is social transformation. For Erasmus it was the uniting of Christendom under a single, virtuous, genuinely Christian prince—an updating of Plato's idea of the philosopher-king. For the "perpetual peace" theorists of the seventeenth and eighteenth centuries, it was the creation of a parliament or congress of European monarchs who would give up their private right to settle disputes by force of arms and would depend on the parliamentary body to end quarrels by arbitration and judgment—in effect, the blueprint for the League of Nations and, in modified form, the United Nations. For Jeremy Bentham and William Penn, who contributed books to the early Enlightenment phase of this movement, economic linkages among countries would provide an additional disincentive to war. In the nineteenth century the idea of material, social, and moral progress was added to the concept. Marx's utopia, the dictatorship of the proletariat, was one theoretical expression, and internationalist socialist movements sought to bring a state-transcending, warless, materially plentiful world into being. The link to American Protestant Christianity was made through "Christian social-ism" and through a transformed eschatology that sought to create a "Kingdom of God on earth." For fuller analysis of this tradition see Johnson, *The Quest for Peace,* chaps. 3–5.

13. It has been said that just-war theory and pacifism have a common beginning point: a presumption against violence or killing. (Cf. James F. Childress, "Just War Theories: The Bases, Interrelations, Priorities, and Functions of Their Criteria," in *Theological Studies,* vol. 39 [September 1978], pp. 427–45.) This is incorrect on two points. First, not all forms of pacifism, as the above analysis shows, share a presumption against violence or killing. Second, for just-war tradition (the term "tradition" is better than "theory," since there are many theories within the overall tradition) the presumption is not against violence or killing as such, but rather against *unjustified* violence or killing. The distinction, on both counts, is critical.

14. See Desiderius Erasmus, *Dulce bellum inexpertis,* in Margaret Mann Phillips, *The "Adages" of Erasmus* (Cambridge: Cambridge University Press, 1964), and his letter to Antoon van Bergin, Abbot of St. Bertin, no. 288 in *The Correspondence of Erasmus, Letters 142 to 297* (Toronto: University of Toronto Press, 1975).

15. See Stanley Hauerwas, *Against the Nations: War and Survival in a Liberal Society* (Minneapolis: Winston Press, 1985), and "Epilogue: A Pacifist Response to the Bishops" in Paul Ramsey, *Speak Up for Just War or Pacifism* (University Park, Pa.: Pennsylvania State University Press, 1988), pp. 149–82.

CHAPTER 13: JOHN RICHARD BURKHOLDER

1. It is regrettable that Lewy was so dependent on documents when most of the characters are still around. He claims to have "talked with many individuals in the pacifist community," but there is very little evidence of that. I found only one footnote that cites an oral communication (note 11, p. 270).

2. See *Peace and Change,* vol. IX, no. 2/3 (Summer 1983); the whole issue deals with perspectives on the Vietnam era.

3. Charles DeBenedetti, *The Peace Reform in American History* (Bloomington, Ind.: Indiana University Press, 1980), p. xi.

4. A quotation from the 1970 WILPF annual meeting on world revolution: "Even Gandhi, master of non-violence, insisted that it was better to oppose evil by any means than supinely to accept it and cooperate with it" (p. 86). Lewy has no comment on this oft-noted opinion of the master. In his critique of the AFSC 1984 statement on civil disobedience, Lewy challenges the appeal to Gandhi's campaigns as inappropriate justification because unlike Gandhi, U.S. citizens have other legal options (p. 180).

5. Some confusion between ethical and political judgments is evident; in normal usage, "principle" is ethical language while "policy" is political language, but Lewy seems to intermix them (e.g., see the index references to "nonexclusion, policy of").

6. John H. Yoder, review of Guenter Lewy's *Peace and Revolution,* in *Review of Politics,* vol. 50, no. 4 (Fall 1988).

7. Stanley Hauerwas, "Will the Real Sectarian Please Stand Up?," *Theology Today* 44, 1 (April 1987), pp. 87–94. Hauerwas goes on to commend Yoder's *The Christian Witness to the State* (1964) as an important statement of an authentic Anabaptist vision for political activity.

Index of Names